Transnational Constitution Making

This book examines the largely neglected but crucial role of transnational actors in democratic constitution-making.

The writing or rewriting of constitutions is usually a key moment in democratic transitions. But how exactly does this take place? Most contemporary comparative constitutional literature draws on the concept of constituent power – the power of the people – to address this moment. But what this overlooks, this book argues, is the important role of external, transnational actors who tend to play a crucial role in the process. Drawing on sociolegal methodologies but informed by new legal realism, this book develops a new theoretical framework for examining the involvement of such actors in constitution-making. Empirically grounded, the book uncovers a more comprehensive picture of how constitution-making unfolds on the ground. Illuminating the power dynamics at play during the legal process, it reveals not only the wide range of external actors involved but also the continuity between decolonisation and post-Cold War constitution-making.

This book, the first to provide an in-depth examination of external actor involvement in constitution-making, will appeal to scholars of constitutional law, sociolegal studies, law and development, and transitional justice.

Alicia Pastor y Camarasa is a researcher at the Swiss Graduate School of Public Administration at the Faculty of Law, Criminal Justice, and Public Administration of the University of Lausanne, Switzerland.

Part of the Law, Development and Globalization series

For information about the series and details of previous and forthcoming titles, see https://www.routledge.com/Law-Development-and-Globalization/book-series/CAV30

A GlassHouse book

Transnational Constitution Making

External Actors, Expertise, and Democratic Transition

Alicia Pastor y Camarasa

Routledge
Taylor & Francis Group
a GlassHouse Book

First published 2024
by Routledge
4 Park Square, Milton Park, Abingdon, Oxon OX14 4RN

and by Routledge
605 Third Avenue, New York, NY 10158

Routledge is an imprint of the Taylor & Francis Group, an informa business

A GlassHouse book

British Library Cataloguing-in-Publication Data
A catalogue record for this book is available from the British Library

Library of Congress Cataloging-in-Publication Data
Names: Pastor y Camarasa, Alicia, 1991– author.
Title: Transnational constitution making : external actors, expertise, and democratic transition / Alicia Pastor y Camarasa.
Description: Abingdon, Oxon [UK] ; New York, NY : Routledge, 2024. | Series: Law, development and globalization | Includes bibliographical references and index.
Identifiers: LCCN 2023057673 (print) | LCCN 2023057674 (ebook) | ISBN 9781032474014 (hardback) | ISBN 9781032478401 (paperback) | ISBN 9781003386186 (ebook)
Subjects: LCSH: Constitutional history. | Constitutional law. | Constituent power. | Transitional justice.
Classification: LCC K3161 .P37 2024 (print) | LCC K3161 (ebook) | DDC 342—dc23/eng/20240129
LC record available at https://lccn.loc.gov/2023057673
LC ebook record available at https://lccn.loc.gov/2023057674

ISBN: 978-1-032-47401-4 (hbk)
ISBN: 978-1-032-47840-1 (pbk)
ISBN: 978-1-003-38618-6 (ebk)

DOI: 10.4324/9781003386186

Typeset in Sabon
by Apex CoVantage, LLC

To Théodore and Lukas, who remind me every day,
in every way, what truly matters.

Contents

About the author

Alicia Pastor y Camarasa is a researcher at the Swiss Graduate School of Public Administration of the University of Lausanne. She received her doctorate from the University of Louvain and a Master of Laws from King's College London. Her research lies at the intersection of comparative constitutional law, legal theory, and socio-legal approaches to public law. Her latest research project centres on how legal norms are made examining the use artificial intelligence in law-making.

Acknowledgements

This book would never have been completed without the direct and indirect contribution of a great number of people. The project started as doctoral research undertaken at the University of Louvain (2016–2021). I wish to thank my supervisor, Professor Marc Verdussen. I am grateful for his trust throughout the years, which allowed me to keep exploring this topic over the course of my circuitous – yet deeply rewarding – intellectual journey. I also want to extend my gratitude to Professor Xavier Philippe, for sharing his practical experience in constitution-making processes, as well as for his open-mindedness when discussing my work.

I would like to express my deep gratitude to Professor Sophie Weerts, who has been a true mentor throughout this whole process: from completing the PhD to adapting the manuscript. The intellectual journey of completing this book has challenged me to consider how I wanted to engage in my discipline, what kind of research I wanted to pursue, and what kind of researcher I aspired to be. Sophie Weerts helped shape my understanding of public law, and her intellectual guidance, scientific rigor, and academic integrity have been an invaluable contribution to the completion of this book. I want to thank her for the in-depth discussions on constitution-making, which have impacted my thinking in unquantifiable ways. It is not an overstatement to say that I would not have finished this book without her intellectual and professional support.

I am also very grateful to Professor Jamie Rowen for hosting me during my research stay at the University of Massachusetts Amherst, a year that opened new academic horizons. Her insight led me to the literature that shaped my analytical framework and gave me the confidence and resources to engage in a socio-legal research.

To my friends and colleagues at the *Centre de recherche sur l'Etat et la Constitution* at the University of Louvain, who witnessed the origin of this manuscript, thank you for your spirit of camaraderie, support, and kindness, mixed with a necessary dose of humour and positive energy. Much of the work in revising this book for publication took place during a postdoctoral fellowship at the University of Lausanne, and I would like to thank my colleagues at the Swiss Graduate School of Public Administration for helping me cross the finish line.

I want to thank my entire family for their support. My sister Inès, for her presence in all circumstances and her sense of humour. My brother Pablo, for his heterodox views in his own discipline, which gave me strength to keep believing in my own project. I thank my parents for instilling in me the resilience needed to withstand the many storms of my academic journey. My mother, for being a model of determination and tenacity. My father, who fought for democracy in Spain and always insisted in asking the hard questions and always trying because *el no ya lo tienes*. I want to thank my aunt, Thérèse Geels, who provided crucial support at key moments of this project. In particular, I want to recognise my grandmothers – Mamy y la Yaya – who despite coming from different walks of life, were both deprived of the education they deserved; whether due to a civil war or a thick glass ceiling, their resilience is a constant reminder of the privilege I have to pursue my studies and a motivation to seek new heights.

To my friends and family, scattered around the world, who always lifted my spirits and brought joy to my days. Thank you Anaïs Mattez for sharing the ups and down of (academic) life with me; Anne-Sophie Bouvy for inspiring me with your own research and our long conversations about everything and nothing; Evelyn Lobão for showing me that you can parent with respect and grace, as well as enjoying a fruitful career; Fernanda Prates for expanding my horizons more than ten years ago in Porto and Belo Horizonte and being the first friend to provincialise Europe with patience and joy; Ona Tura, whose kindness and intelligence is a gift I am grateful for every day, thank you for the thrilling conversations always enjoyed with delicious food. I want to thank my dear Pastor cousins – Teresa, Julia and Isabel – for our shared roots and friendship that keeps blossoming in wonderful new ways. Finally, to Marine Sprimont, my oldest friend, whose steady, witty, brilliant presence I have been lucky to enjoy since that fateful day our French teacher sat me next to her in the hopes that I would stop talking (it didn't work).

My deepest gratitude goes to my husband, Lukas Clark-Memler, for his unwavering support over all these years; from big-picture philosophical discussions to the minutiae of proofreading. I am grateful for his sharp, critical mind and his intellectual companionship that has helped to shape how I see the world. I also want to thank him for the logistical and emotional help that was key in producing the first version of this manuscript during a global pandemic and the final version while coparenting an infant in a new country. As a woman and mother navigating the academic world, I would not have made it this far without a true ally and co-pilot by my side.

Finally, I thank my son, Théodore Pastor Clark, who was born during the preparation of this manuscript, for sparking joy and light wherever he goes, and transforming me into a better woman, mother, and citizen.

This project was made possible thanks to funding provided by the *Fondation Louvain*, through the creation of the *Democracy, Cultures, and Action Fund* (2016–2021), and also benefited from the generous support of the *Belgian American Education Foundation*, which funded a research stay at the University of Massachusetts Amherst (2018–2019).

Acronyms and abbreviations

2009 Guidance Note	Guidance Note of the Secretary-General regarding United Nations Assistance to Constitution-Making Processes
2020 Guidance Note	Guidance Note of the Secretary-General on United Nations Constitutional Assistance
Arusha Agreement	Arusha Peace and Reconciliation Agreement for Burundi
BCPR	Bureau for Crisis Prevention and Recovery
DGTTF	Democratic Governance Thematic Trust Fund
DRI	Democracy Reporting International
ICCPR	International Covenant on Civil and Political Rights
IGOs	International Governmental Organisations
INGOs	International Non-Governmental Organisations
International IDEA	International Institute for Democracy and Electoral Assistance
Max Planck Foundation	Max Planck Foundation for International Peace and the Rule of Law
OIF	International Organisation of la Francophonie [*Organisation Internationale de la Francophonie*]
OHCHR	UN Office of the United Nations High Commissioner for Human Rights
TWAIL	Third World Approaches to International Law
UN	United Nations
UNDP	United Nations Development Programme
UNDPPA	UN Department for Political and Peacebuilding Affairs
UNGA	UN General Assembly
UNSC	United Nations Security Council
UNSG	United Nations Secretary-General
Venice Commission	European Commission for Democracy through Law

Introduction

Demystifying 'We the People'

The British lawyer Sir Ivor Jennings is rarely mentioned in scholarly discussions of constitution-making, and yet, as the first Vice-Chancellor of the University of Ceylon, he was instrumental in the drafting of many constitutions throughout Asia in the mid-twentieth century. In his memoirs, Jennings recalls a late night in 1948, in a hotel room in Bandarawela, discussing the text of the future Constitution of Ceylon with the Governor-General of Ceylon, Sir Oliver Goonetilleke, and D.S. Senanayake, the first Prime Minister of Ceylon:

> Next door was a European, probably a planter. He soon came in to complain, very politely, that we were keeping him awake. We tried to moderate our voices, but he was in again after 15 minutes, and this time he was more vehement. When he came in a third time he was quite angry. We apologised, but we could not tell him that the first Prime Minister was settling the lines of the Constitution.[1]

Over six decades later, in another hotel room, this time in Tunis, a legal advisor working for the United Nations Development Programme (UNDP) discusses how he participated, informally, in the drafting of the new Tunisian constitution: 'The President [of the National Constituent Assembly] comes in the morning, he brings me work. . . . For instance, today it is the chapter on the judiciary'.[2] The advisor would spend the day commenting and annotating the chapters of the constitution before handing it back to the constitutional drafters: 'I give him [NCA President] his text and he gives me a new topic. And we work like that, in confidentiality'.[3]

This book explores how constitutions get made and who is actually involved in their drafting. The constitution is a legal phenomenon that is symbolically imbued with a variety of normative ideals: transparency, representation, legitimacy, democracy. This is particularly the case in the context of democratic transition. Indeed, when a constitution fails to deliver on its expansive set of promises, it can threaten the democratic project as a whole. Creating a new constitution, a prerogative of the constituent power, is generally seen as

DOI: 10.4324/9781003386186-1

the epitome of popular sovereignty, as the first three words of the Preamble to the United States Constitution make explicit: 'We the People'. Set against this shared imaginary that underpins how we typically think about constitutions, the reality of constitution-making is more complex and multifaceted. Far removed from the romantic idealisation of the exercise of popular sovereignty, which is immune to external interference, the process of writing a new constitution has, in fact, always been marked by a transnational dimension.

While the emergence of the transnational dimension of constitution-making is often associated with the post-Cold War period, a brief survey of historical cases reveals that the creation of a new constitution has overwhelmingly been pervaded by transnational elements, particularly in the initial drafting stage. Indeed, external assistance in constitutional drafting was a core marker of pre-modern constitutions. In ancient constitutions, the arrival of a foreign, sometimes legendary figure that arrived to draft fundamental laws was common: Solon in Athens, Lycurgus in Sparta, Plato in Syracuse.[4] In early monarchical constitutions, the figure of the foreign drafter was also not unusual. In 1772, Geneva-born Jean-Jacques Rousseau was commissioned by Michał Wielhorski, a Polish noble, to confidentially draft the Constitution of Poland.[5]

External influence is equally common in modern constitution-making processes. To take an obvious case, constitutions adopted during decolonisation were not drafted by 'the people' but by metropolitan authorities. Today, the transnational dimension of constitution-making is less obvious but no less persistent. New constitutions are often developed and/or adopted by a body that represents the people, in the form of a national constituent assembly. However, in the most recent cases of constitution-making – Kenya (2010), Tunisia (2014), Nepal (2015), and Chile (2020–) many external actors were present during the drafting stage, providing comparative legal and political expertise to constitution-makers. International organisations providing such advice include the UNDP, the International Institute for Democracy and Electoral Assistance (International IDEA), and the European Commission for Democracy through Law, commonly known as the Venice Commission.[6]

This introduction first lays out the empirical and theoretical puzzle of the transnational dimension of constitution-making, before moving on to describe the gaps and limitations of current studies in the field of comparative constitutional law and international relations. The third section details the epistemological and methodological choices made in this study, while the fourth section offers a summary of the contribution of this work for scholars and practitioners. The final section provides a chapter overview.

Understanding constitutional drafting as a transnational site

The phenomenon of constitution-making, particularly in the context of democratic transition, remains a black box to legal scholars. In 2009, a symposium held at the University of Texas School of Law bore the ominous title, 'What, If Anything, Do We Know about Constitutional Design?'.[7] Over a decade later, the answer to this question remains the same: very little.[8] While constitution-making *tout court* has been the focus of significant scholarly attention, there are few empirical studies on *how* this process actually unfolds.[9] Indeed, much of the literature dedicated to this topic fails to engage with fundamental questions related to who exercises political authority and where legitimacy is derived from.[10] As Angelica Bernal has recently commented, 'a strict focus on constitutional engineering in reigning approaches [has] resulted in a short-sightedness to critical foundational problems'.[11] Studies of constitution-making also tend to have a normative focus with less engagement in descriptive work, thus providing limited explanation of the actual creation of constitutional norms and their transnational dimension.[12] And yet the lack of knowledge regarding the concrete *how* of constitution-making has significant normative implications. András Jakab, Arthur Dyevre, and Giulio Itzcovich note: 'By sharpening our understanding of how constitutional law operates in its global diversity, studies based on empirical social science methods promise to foster a more informed . . . normative debate'.[13] Empirical knowledge of how constitutions are made can help them to achieve their normative goals.

This book contends that a theoretical cornerstone of constitutional legal scholarship, the notion of 'constituent power', is particularly ill-suited to study the transnational dimension of constitution-making. Philippe Dann and Zaid Al-Ali's seminal paper, 'The Internationalized *Pouvoir Constituant* – Constitution-Making Under External Influence in Iraq, Sudan and East Timor',[14] treats the notion of constituent power as central to constitution-making, which has consequently set the analytical tone for most studies of external actor involvement in the process.[15] The fact that constitution-making is understood through the lens of constituent power is not surprising, as the concept remains the theoretical backbone of comparative law and constitutional legal theory.[16] The challenge, however, is that the concept of constituent power limits the scope of inquiry for scholars to grasp the transnational element of constitution-making. Considering the fact that Cheryl Saunders recently argued that foreign advising is *the* defining marker of constitution-making in the twenty-first century, this is a problem for the literature.[17]

With that in mind, this book takes as a starting point the necessity of demystifying *We the People*, which looms large in the background of how the creation of constitutional norms is generally conceived – where the 'people' exercise their constituent power to make the constitution. The transnational dimension of constitution-making challenges this idealised vision shared by scholars and practitioners alike. In order to provide a more accurate and comprehensive account of the transnational dimension of constitution-making, this book provides an alternative theoretical lens to the constituent power. By paying close attention to the transnational dimension – and taking the presence of external actors in constitutional drafting seriously – this study broadens the scope of actors involved in constitution-making, beyond the idealised entity of 'the people'.

The goal of this book is to provide an empirically grounded account to inform theory building. Through a law and society approach, it aims to complement existing scholarly debates and deepen the understanding of the transnational dimension of constitution-making. The following research questions animate this inquiry: *what is the implication of the transnational dimension of constitution-making for the concept of constituent power? What is the role of external actors in constitution-making processes?*

The argument at the core of this study is that a new theoretical lens is needed to understand the transnational dimension of constitution-making, drawing on Bernal's 'founding beyond origins' framework to analyse how constitutional norms are created.[18] The current understanding of constitution-making and the theory of constituent power conceives constitution-making ex nihilo and in an idealised way. This book takes the opposite approach and unpacks how fundamental norms are created in situ in order to unfreeze this suspended moment in time to allow for an expanded look at how the new constitutional order is founded and, crucially, who participates in the founding. One of the original contributions of this study is to provide a new lens to study constitution-making; I have labelled this lens the 'development enterprise'. The 'development enterprise' refers to the broader legal reform endeavour, often of a legislative nature, undertaken in the context of structural economic and political reforms in Third World territories. The term 'Third World' emerged in the Cold War context to refer to non-aligned countries (it was later rebranded as 'developing states' or 'emerging markets').[19]

This research is fundamentally interdisciplinary, integrating insights from different disciplines to examine a legal phenomenon. The analytical lens draws from scholarship spread across the social sciences (development studies, international relations, sociology of international organisations), which addresses diverse facets of legal reforms, often of a legislative nature, undertaken in the context of structural economic and political reforms in Third World territories. These studies have examined the creation of legal norms, which are not constitutional in nature but are similarly characterised by a transnational dimension.[20] While the authors are often interested in different, non-legal questions, they provide useful cues to grasp the full picture of transnational involvement during constitution-making. Because these authors are outside the legal discipline, they provide an external perspective on law, which is inherent to the law and society approach developed in this book. These discussions help to elucidate the creation of constitutional norms, unveiling the foundational logic that underpins the constitution-making process and highlighting the often tacit 'background of common sense'.[21]

Indeed, a key pillar of the development enterprise is the particular 'background of common sense' that is shared among external actors, from decolonisation to today. This book argues that external actors conceive of liberal constitutions as a legal tool to accelerate social change, based on the 'modernisation rationale'. Third World countries should replicate the political systems of the West, in order to enjoy similar political and economic development.[22] Legal reforms are treated as a catalyst to reach liberal democracy. The lens of the development enterprise reveals the extent of expert involvement, a dynamic that tends to be side-lined in comparative constitutional scholarship but that is, in fact, central to constitution-making.

Transnational constitution-making in current debates

The transnational dimension of constitution-making is a timely topic for legal scholars. Until recently, this aspect was treated as an anomaly, in the context of 'imposed constitutionalism', where a constitution was not drafted by a representative body of the state but by foreign occupying forces. While there are such cases of direct imposition – including Japan, Germany, Italy, and more recently Afghanistan and Iraq[23] – most constitution-making processes include transnational elements. In the past decade, the comparative constitutional law literature has begun to address a variety of topics related to transnational constitution-making: from general considerations of external actor involvement,[24] to detailed discussions of particular external actors, such as the Venice Commission,[25] the United Nations (UN),[26] and INGOs;[27] as well as specific case studies of external actor involvement.[28] A volume published in 2019, *Comparative Constitution Making*, includes several chapters on the transnational dimension of constitution-making, indicating that this topic is no longer a niche field of study and is growing in popularity.[29] Despite this burgeoning interest, the work is largely produced by practitioners involved within these processes, which could explain the lack of critical examination of this phenomenon.

International legal scholars, in particular those interested in peace-building, have also addressed the involvement of international organisations in constitution-making.[30] Anna Saunders recently explored constitution-making as a technique to deliver peace and security,[31] Gaurav Mukherjee has discussed the role of international financial institutions in constitution-making processes.[32] The most comprehensive study of external actor involvement from the perspective of international law comes from Vijayashri Sripati, who provides an in-depth analysis of UN involvement in constitutional assistance from an international law perspective.[33] These studies offer useful insights and share a critical understanding of the political dimension of law. However, their focus centres on how external involvement in public law shapes the international realm. In contrast, this book is interested in how transnational actors influence constitutional norms.

The phenomenon of constitution-making and its transnational dimension has attracted interest from a wide range of scholarship in social sciences.

Scholars across disciplinary boundaries have noted the transnational dimension inherent in the creation of constitutional norms. The peace-building literature focuses on constitution-making peripherally, as constitutions are one of the tools used to translate peace agreements.[34] Recent work from sociologists and political scientists has emphasised that international (governmental and non-governmental) organisations are heavily involved in constitution-making.[35] Quentin Deforge examined the role of international organisations, such as International IDEA, during 'governance-related activities', which includes constitution-making.[36] Scholars of international relations have identified the rebranding of certain discourses in current debates. Amelia Odida's research on UN involvement in Eritrea and Libya argues that 'the colonial discourses which were exercised by UN officials and the Western allies during decolonisation are still at work in the UN's present-day policy of constitution-making, albeit in contextually specific forms'.[37] She shows how 'both subjects – former colonial territories and societies described as post-conflict – are problematised in ways which render them vulnerable and inferior, incapable of producing their own tools and ideas about how to govern'.[38]

While all of the aforementioned studies are valuable contributions to our understanding of transnational constitution-making, the present work is primarily interested in legal questions, which have received little attention in the literature. This section summarises how legal scholars, constitutional scholars in particular, have grasped the transnational dimension of constitution-making in current debates.

The porosity of constitutional legal orders

Transnational involvement in constitution-making is the manifestation of a broader phenomenon that has affected constitutional law as a whole. Constitutional legal orders, as a result of globalisation, have become more porous and increasingly situated within a transnational web of soft law instruments.

Globalisation, understood as the 'spread of transplanetary – and in recent times also more particularly supraterritorial – connections between people',[39] with all of its associated economic, social and political implications, has had a profound impact on the constitutional legal order.[40] Regardless of the label used – whether internationalisation, globalisation, or transnationalisation – scholars have recognised the increasing porosity that characterises the contemporary constitutional legal order.[41] Mark Tushnet goes so far as to suggest that globalisation, characterised as the 'convergence among national constitutional systems in their structures and in their protections of fundamental human rights', has become inevitable.[42]

The porosity of the constitutional legal order can been identified in two ways: vertically and horizontally. Scholars have noticed that constitutional legal orders can be affected in a top-down manner through international law, which is integrated directly within constitutional legal frameworks with varying levels of penetration.[43] International human rights obligations, for instance, can be incorporated into constitutions without directly referencing international human rights law; constitutions can grant a hierarchically superior status to certain international human rights instruments or require courts to ensure the respect of particular elements of international law. For instance, the Constitution of South Africa states in its Article 233: 'When interpreting any legislation, every court must prefer any reasonable interpretation of the legislation that is consistent with international law over any alternative interpretation that is inconsistent with international law'.[44] Scholars have also noticed that the porosity between different constitutional legal orders can operate horizontally, via informal non-binding mechanisms.[45] The body of norms is, in this case, the law of another jurisdiction – or more generally, comparative constitutional law. A substantive body of scholarship has focused on this phenomenon among judges when, for instance, a constitutional judge points to a foreign decision in order to reach a judgment.[46]

With regard to constitution-making, scholars have similarly recognised the porosity of the constitutional legal order. On one side, studies have examined international norms directly applicable to the process itself; these are largely normative.[47] As shown by Thomas Franck and Arun Thiruvengadam, following a 'survey of the practice of the international system in the application of treaty law and custom', there is 'no firm evidence of rules applicable to the process of constitution-making'.[48] On the other side, constitutional scholars have also pointed to the 'migration' of constitutional legal ideas through legal transplants during the drafting of a new constitution.[49] For instance, when a constitution-maker creates a constitutional norm, they may transplant a constitutional norm from a different legal order.[50] More specifically, Chaihark Hahm and Sung Ho Kim observe that there are different forms of external influence: 'from "constitutional borrowing" and "inducement" to "intervention" and outright "imposition"'.[51]

The transnational regulatory web

Creating a new constitution does not occur in a legal vacuum: it happens within an existing transnational regulatory web. As Ngoc Son Bui notes, 'due to the forces of globalization, constitution-making processes are inevitably influenced by global sources and norms'.[52] These norms constitute a web of what can be conceived of as disparate transnational legal norms. International lawyer Philip Jessup coined the notion of 'transnational law' during his Storrs Lectures at Yale Law School in 1955, where he argued that the term includes 'all law which regulates actions or events that transcend national frontiers. Both public and private international law are included, as are other rules which do not wholly fit into such standard categories'.[53] Transnational law thus covers a broad scope, including both international and national law, affecting both public and private actors.[54]

When a new constitution is written, it is inserted within an existing regulatory environment that is constituted of international legal norms and soft law instruments. The corpus of international law that frames constitution-making processes remains remarkably thin.[55] Cheryl Saunders argues that 'beyond the bare bones of the international legal system, there is no normative framework for international involvement in constitution making'.[56] Similarly, Hannah Lerner and David Landau point out that 'the actual number of international legal norms governing constitution making still appear to be quite slight'.[57] A brief survey of the different sources of international law that touch upon constitution-making, in both procedural and substantive terms, confirms this assessment. Regarding the involvement of external actors, the 1907 Hague Convention forbids occupants in cases of belligerent occupation to become involved with constitutional matters.[58] The UN Charter specifically prohibits in its Article 2(7) 'the United Nations to intervene in matters which are essentially within the domestic jurisdiction of any state',[59] except under the conditions of Chapter VII of the UN Charter which authorises it in contexts of 'threat to the peace, breach of the peace, or act of aggression'.[60] The International Court of Justice underlined this principle in *Nicaragua vs. United States*, asserting that 'State's domestic policy falls within its exclusive jurisdiction, provided of course that it does not violate any obligation of international law. Every State possesses a fundamental right to choose and implement its own political, economic and social systems'.[61]

Regarding the constitution-making process itself, there are very few obligations that stem from international law. This is still an important question to consider as states undergoing a constitution-making process may have already contracted obligations to an international human rights treaty. In the international human rights framework, Article 25 of the International Covenant on Civil and Political Rights (ICCPR), which enshrines the right to participate in public affairs, is a potential provision. Indeed, many countries undergoing a transition to democracy are signatories of the ICCPR, which raises questions whether specific obligations could apply to the process of making a new constitution. On the content of specific obligations contained within Article 25, the Human Rights Council merely notes that, 'it is for the legal and constitutional system of the State party to provide for the modalities of such participation'.[62] To date, there has not been a single new decision that sheds light on specific obligations by which a government in transition should abide. In its General Comment on Article 25, the Human Rights Council included the drafting and amendment of constitutions yet did not give any guidance except to remind states of the prohibition of discrimination.[63]

In terms of the actual content of a new constitution, international law once again leaves it to states to decide how to structure their government and revise their constitution.[64] To date, there are no specific obligations that have emerged from customary law either. While rules of *jus cogens* apply to the government in transition, their indeterminacy makes their influence marginal with regard to constitutional transitions.[65] International law may prohibit interference in a sovereign constitution-making process, but the process itself is certainly affected by global norms. Given that the existing norms that frame the constitution-making are soft law instruments, the transnational dimension is not prohibited by international law.

The regulatory web within which constitution-making is inserted includes soft law instruments.[66] Recently, several soft law instruments that are relevant to constitution-making have emerged, including international soft law and comparative constitutional law (i.e., the domestic law of foreign countries).[67] There are a variety of guidebooks by external actors that discuss the standards that should frame constitution-making from a procedural and substantial standpoint.[68] These standards are at an early stage of development and rely on observing the convergence among different constitutional legal orders of a diffuse set of principles.[69]

Concerning the involvement of external actors during constitution-making, the two guidance notes of the UN Secretary-General on constitutional assistance are noteworthy soft law instruments. The 2009 *Guidance Note of the Secretary-General regarding United Nations Assistance to Constitution-Making Processes* (2009 Guidance Note) has been widely addressed in the literature, as it is one of the few existing soft law instruments framing the involvement of external actors.[70] It is an eight-page document that lays out a policy framework containing guiding principles that ought to be followed by UN agencies when involved in constitution-making.[71] Its six guiding principles, derived from 'lessons learnt' of past involvement, cover the entire constitution-making process as well as the content of constitutions.[72] The 2009 Guidance Note enumerates the different components of a constitution-making process, focusing on procedure.[73] It outlines the need to '[establish] a representative body to prepare a draft of the constitution', to set up a 'public consultation process led by the drafting body to gather views and ensure input of the public on the draft constitution', and finally to submit the draft constitution to a representative forum.[74] Regarding the content of constitutions, the 2009 Guidance Note encourages compliance with international norms and standards[75] and also supports inclusivity, participation, and transparency.[76]

In September 2020, the *Guidance Note of the Secretary-General on United Nations Constitutional Assistance* (2020 Guidance Note) was adopted.[77] While it contains similar guiding principles, the 2020 Guidance Note distinguishes itself by tying constitution-making to peace-building and sustainable development, including a new section that fleshes out different types of assistance offered by the UN, including 'technical advice on constitutions and constitutional reforms process'.[78]

Studying external actor involvement is important to understand how constitutions are made today, especially considering the general trend of an increased reliance on soft law over hard law at the transnational level.[79] International scholars have noticed this move from hard to soft law,[80] with Charles Rogers observing that there has been a decrease in the signature of international law treaties along with the emergence of informal international organisations, which are created through non-binding legal instruments that have come to 'dominate global governance'.[81] In the domestic realm, a similar trend has been noted. Alexandre Flückiger, in his study on legislative drafting [*légistique*], shows that 'legislation', a hard law norm that was once that dominant object of study, has become embedded among an array of non-binding norms (guidelines and strategic plans).[82] In order to address a certain social problem, lawmakers now have a choice between using legislation or a variety of non-binding soft law instruments.[83]

This move towards soft law has resulted in the emergence of a new constellation of legal actors that must be studied in order to understand the creation of constitutional norms.[84] Alongside the actors that traditionally take centre stage in legal scholarship, which is largely still preoccupied with hard law, there are other actors involved in the making of soft law instruments, including private actors.[85] Transnational NGOs and private authorities, such as rating agencies or even civil society organisations, have been pointed out by scholars as a new breed of legal actors that are active in the making of international and domestic norms.[86] Roger Cotterrell highlights the expansion of the role of legal experts in crafting transnational legal norms:

> In a transnational context . . . the scope for both expert and non-expert elaboration of legal ideas seems greatly expanded. Much transnational regulation and policy formation now develops through the work of innumerable associations, organizations, or corporate bodies engaged in setting and developing standards.[87]

Legal experts, regardless of their label, are not only norm-creators but also act as vessels through which such norms travel. Gregory Shaffer's approach to this topic with a socio-legal understanding of transnational law as 'transnational legal ordering' is particularly useful. Shaffer focuses on the 'transnational production of legal norms and institutional forms in particular fields and their migration across borders, regardless of whether they address transnational activities or purely national ones'.[88]

Scholars have addressed the emerging transnational web of norms framing certain activities as a means of examining the gradual 'uniformisation' of norms.[89] Within the realm of constitution-making, Sripati argues that the UN, through its involvement in constitutional assistance, 'makes a new addition to the Civilized Standards: "Transparent, inclusive and participatory" constitution-making'.[90] Tom Ginsburg explains that constitution-making is 'becoming increasingly institutionalized as transnational'; however, he argues that 'the process is not itself governed by transnational law', and as a 'field is highly fragmented, with different organizations and individuals competing to provide advice and to influence the process'.[91]

Epistemological and methodological considerations

Law and society approach to constitution-making

As constitution-making straddles the border between law and politics, this study builds upon the tradition of law and society scholarship, qualitative research in social sciences, and constitutional scholarship. The research questions have led to the choice of undertaking a law and society approach, enshrined within empirical approaches to law using social sciences methods. Adopting a law and society approach to better understand the legal object 'constitution' is one of the contributions of this book.

A law and society approach understands that law is not autonomous or separated from the social and political world but instead is deeply embedded within it.[92] More specifically, the law and society approach adopted in this book lies within a broader and eclectic body of research, often referred to as New Legal Realism, which can be described as 'theory-driven empirical research about law in action that values qualitative as well as quantitative and experimental methods'.[93] New Legal Realism stresses the importance of an empirical study of law, motivated by informing different legal actors (e.g. policymakers, litigants, judges) about how the legal system actually operates in the world.[94] Scholars within this tradition aim to develop a dialogue with the social sciences in order to create a 'genuinely interdisciplinary form of legal knowledge'.[95] This book aims to follow a similar approach, using social science methodologies to develop a theory-driven, empirically grounded account of a complex legal phenomenon.

This approach is justified because the goal of this book is to describe how constitutional norms emerge within a particular political environment: democratic transitions. Constitution-making processes are embedded within broader political and historical dynamics.[96] Jon Elster argued in one of the first studies on the topic in 1995 that constitutions 'almost always are written in the wake of a crisis or exceptional circumstance of some sort'.[97] Twenty years later, Yash Ghai pointed out the broader political situation in which constitution-making unfolds: 'These are internal pressures but they are not unconnected with that series of economic, political, technological and social changes, often externally driven, that pass under the rubric of globalization'.[98]

Following a law and society approach requires adopting an external perspective on law. This variety of analysis seeks to observe how legal actors *actually* behave[99] – or as Véronique Champeil-Desplats explains, 'unpack[ing] legal actors' reasoning to shed light on their theoretical and ideological assumptions'.[100] Legal actors often have implicit motivations, and only an external point of view can shed light on these presuppositions. An external perspective is particularly useful for a descriptive analysis, as it helps to uncover how constitutional norms are *actually* made, especially when examining transnational dimension of constitution-making.[101]

In order to study the involvement of external actors an external perspective is not only more useful but necessary. Zinaida Miller's remark regarding the field of transitional justice rings true with regard to constitution-making:

> The role of international actors in the process of spreading the ideas and ideals of the 'movement' of transitional justice has not yet been fully explored in the literature, perhaps because of [. . .] the tendency of scholars or ex-commissioners to become consultants to, rather than fully external critics of, the enterprise. Thus, rather than offering a critical exploration of the influence of one area on another or of resulting patterns of invisibility, the literature tends to discuss the possible 'toolbox' or the 'lessons learned' in a particular area.[102]

An important observation about the field of constitution-making is the fact that the literature is largely made up of present or former practitioners involved in constitution-making processes. For instance, the head of the constitution-building unit at International IDEA, Sumit Bisarya, has published academic articles as well as policy documents.[103] Cheryl Saunders, a leading scholar in the field, has been a member of the board of advisors of International IDEA.[104] Tom Ginsburg, another major figure in the field of constitution-making, has published in academia and for international organisations.[105] Maartje de Visser has noted that 'the work of the [Venice] Commission appears to have largely escaped academic notice' and that literature on this particular actor comes mostly from its members.[106] While these accounts are important as they offer insights in what remains a process conducted largely behind closed doors, they lack the external point of view that a socio-legal approach endeavours to achieve.

A law and society approach is fundamentally an empirical way of studying the law. Herbert Kritzer defines empirical legal research as the 'use of systematically collected data, either qualitative or quantitative, to describe or otherwise analyse some legal phenomenon'.[107] In particular, empirical research is useful to examine the different legal actors present during the production of norms. While this kind of research is now prevalent in the United States, it has its roots in Europe, dating back to Émile Durkheim and Max Weber.[108] The present inquiry uses qualitative legal research, a method that is particularly adept at examining, as Lisa Webley puts it, 'whether or not a particular social phenomenon exists and if so, the nature of the phenomenon'.[109] In the discipline of constitutional law, early scholars were convinced of the importance of undertaking empirical analysis. Léon Duguit's remark from a 1901 work is particularly evocative:

> Legal science, if it exists, is not in a separate world, but in the world of realities; it does not have for objects fictions or abstractions, but concrete

> facts. Having disregarded it, legal scholars have been exhausted for centuries in purposeless and profitless scholastic controversies.[110]

Maurice Hauriou similarly called for not limiting legal analysis to the 'final product' but also examining the social conditions from which legal norms emerge.[111] Thus, while primarily informed by the law and society movement of the 1960s, this book stands on the shoulders of a legal tradition that has existed for over a century.

Despite the increasing popularity of the law and society approach, few studies have examined the production of constitutional norms from an empirical standpoint. While there is a wealth of scholarship in law and society that centres on the production of legal norms in contexts of democratic transition[112] – and other transnational contexts more generally[113] – there is little that focuses on the creation of constitutional norms. There are particular works in the sub-field of sociology that studies constitutions that have examined the role that constitutions play in the social realm;[114] however, these are not concerned with the creation of legal norms. Finally, there have been quantitative studies of constitution-making,[115] but few have approached the topic using qualitative empirical analysis.[116]

Scope of the present study

This book aims to shed light on the transnational dimension of constitution-making by focusing on the external actors involved in the process. The scope is limited to constitution-making that takes place in the context of democratic transition. The particular legal object under scrutiny is the 'constitution' and the 'constitution-making process'. Here, constitutions are understood in their formal sense as a 'fundamental document that sets out the rules regulating the government of the state and which has a specially protected legal status'.[117] Constitutions are legal documents that are granted special status following a particular adoption procedure; the focus here is on modern written constitutions, and thus the scope is restricted to formal constitutions.[118] Constitution-making refers both to a political practice by a certain set of actors with the aim of adopting a new constitution, as well as to the legal phenomenon of creating constitutional norms. For the purposes of this study, 'the creation of constitutional norms', 'constitution-making', and 'the making of constitutions' are all understood to refer to the adoption of a formal constitution, regardless of legal continuity. Partial constitutional amendments are beyond the scope of the present inquiry.[119]

Within the constitution-making process, this book focuses largely on the constitutional drafting stage, which occurs after the agenda-setting stage and before the adoption of the constitution (i.e., 'ratification' and 'implementation' stages).[120] When making a new constitution, different phases can be distinguished. Generally, the agenda-setting phase occurs first where political actors decide on the procedure and the institutional shape of the entire constitution-making process.[121] For instance, they may choose between a committee of appointed experts or the election of a national constituent assembly.[122] The 'deliberation' phase follows, where constitution-makers hear from experts and debate on substantive issues; in some cases, this can involve a participatory element, with consultation from 'the people'.[123] The next stage is 'drafting', where principles from prior stages are developed into an actual text, and a draft constitution is produced. Next comes the 'ratification' stage,[124] which has received perhaps the most attention from constitutional scholars.[125] Finally, comes the 'implementation' stage, which 'extends for an indefinite period from the time the Constitution is passed'[126] and can also involve adopting particular legislation thus creating the institutions enshrined in the constitution. Constitutional drafting has received little attention from comparative constitutional scholars,[127] but it is the most important phase for understanding the involvement of external actors in constitution-making.[128] While external involvement occurs during all phases of the constitution-making process, examination of these areas will be saved for future inquiries.

This book is centred on a particular dimension of constitution-making: the transnational one. The term 'transnational' is used here to refer to elements that extend beyond the borders of the constitutional legal order (i.e., the state). It refers specifically to the dynamic that exists between different levels of governance, in contrast with the term 'global' that refers to 'legal ordering that covers all nations and localities'.[129] The added value of 'transnational' over 'international' is that the former still preserves space for the state; as Halliday and Shaffer put it, 'the nation-state remains central to law-making, law recognition and law enforcement'.[130]

The transnational dimension of constitution-making is approached through the lens of the legal actors involved. Constitutions are made within existing transnational regulatory webs that encompass different legal actors.[131] This book uses the term 'external actors' to refer to actors whose interventions extend beyond national borders; the contrast is thus drawn between 'external' actors and 'national' or 'domestic' actors.[132] These external actors are transnational in the sense that they extend beyond the public/private dichotomy, as well beyond the national/international dichotomy.[133] External actors include: international governmental organisations (IGOs) as well as international non-governmental organisations (INGOs), which encompasses research centres, advocacy groups, and political foundations. States themselves (e.g., representatives from a country's foreign office) are included under the label 'external actors' when they are involved in the constitutional drafting process of other states.

Finally, this book focuses on the creation of constitutional norms during a particular political context: democratic transition. In broad strokes, a 'democratic transition' refers to the dynamic process where a political system is transformed in such a way as to increase the exercise of power by its people through, for instance, more inclusivity or transparency (among other values) – this includes cases where a country moves from an authoritarian regime towards a political system that includes some of the key signifiers of democracy (including – but not limited to – universal suffrage, the rule of law, and a human rights framework).

Several choices have been made from a temporal standpoint. To cover the full evolution of the development enterprise, the timeframe of this book focuses on two prolific periods of constitution-making: constitution-making during decolonisation (roughly 1940–1960) and post-Cold War constitution-making (1990–2023). The dismantling of colonial empires resulted in the rise of nation-states and thus extensive constitutional activity. In 1973, Ivo Duchacek noted that 'over two-thirds of the [world's] existing national constitutions were drafted and promulgated in the last three decades'.[134] There were 56 independent countries in 1910, and by the mid-1970s, 142 independent states could be counted.[135] Within the context of constitution-making undertaken during decolonisation, the question arises, are metropoles really external actors? From the standpoint of international law, the relationship between metropoles and colonies was a domestic affair; they were considered to be a single unit, thus metropoles could not be external actors. However, the logic of differentiation that characterised the relationship between the metropole and its colonies – or at least between metropoles and non-white colonies – qualifies them as external actors.[136] The post-Cold War period was another golden era of constitution-making. Following the fall of the Berlin Wall, Eastern and Central European countries adopted new constitutions; there was also a wave of democratisation throughout Africa.[137] Aside from the sheer volume of new constitutions adopted during these two periods, they are significant and illustrative as constitution-making during decolonisation mostly took place before there was any prohibition from international law to intervene in constitutional affairs.

In order to analyse the transnational dimension of constitution-making, this book relies on different data than those traditionally used by legal scholars. To adopt an external perspective on law, it was necessary to gather extensive data to paint the most comprehensive picture possible of how transnational involvement in constitution-making occurs.

The analysis of external actor involvement relies on a diverse set of primary and secondary sources. Primary sources include project and annual reports of external actors, drawing heavily on institutional documentation available freely online or that was provided upon request; the institutional documentation available varied depending on the external actor. Concerning international organisations, annual reports, project reports, evaluations, and general content on websites were used. UNDP project reports are available online, while other actors such as International IDEA do not publish significant documents online. Concerning INGOs, the variation in accessible information was even starker. European-based INGOs, such as Democracy Reporting International (DRI), publish annual reports and monitoring reports on their websites. Information that was published on the website and social media of these organisations was also relevant to this study. These sources were complemented by testimonies from experts involved in constitution-making process that have been published in scientific journals or are publicly available online; these constitute an internal perspective on the subject matter.[138]

There was only limited data available for this topic. With regard to expertise, it was particularly difficult to gather primary sources as involvement tends to be informal in nature even if in certain recent cases foreign expertise has been institutionalised in constitution-making processes. To this end, this study relies on secondary sources, drawing on work from historians who have studied the role of constitutional scholars in constitution-making during decolonisation. Barbara Perry's article 'Constitutional Johnny Appleseeds: American Consultants and the Drafting of Foreign Constitutions' provides an extensive account of academics that were involved in constitutional assistance in the 1960s up to the 1980s, which was an invaluable resource for mapping the constellations of external actors.[139]

Limitations of the study

This study involves several limitations that stem from the particular legal phenomenon studied, constitution-making, and the socio-legal approach chosen.

There are challenges arising from the legal object analysed: constitutions. Studying how constitutions are made is a complex undertaking, particularly in a context of democratic transition. This study develops a particular lens to better understand the phenomenon but in no way claims that it offers a complete picture of the constitution-making process; so many elements are at play when a new constitution is made, such that there are other dynamics and concepts that can further explain the involvement of external actors.[140] This overview is not exhaustive and merely aims to show general patterns of transnational constitution-making by discussing the diverse set of external actors involved. Cases of constitution-making are illustrative of global trends, and this study does not account for the involvement of all external actors in every constitution-making process. One reason for this is the unevenness in primary and secondary sources available from different time periods or different geographic areas. For instance, constitutional legal historians have investigated constitution-making in the context of decolonisation with regard to the British Empire,[141] yet few have done the same for the French or Belgian Empires.[142] Similarly, the period between decolonisation and post-Cold War has been left aside, given the lack of sources. This is not to say that no transnational constitution-making occurred between 1960–1990, just that there is a dearth of primary and secondary sources. Focusing on constitution-making in the context of decolonisation and post-Cold War constitution-making allows for the broad trends of external actor involvement to be sketched.

It is important to highlight that while external actors were involved in constitution-making processes that took place within contexts of decolonisation and post-Cold War, how much constitution-makers were actually influenced by them may have varied according to the particular context. From a methodological standpoint, the question of impact is very difficult to measure, given that it is a multifaceted process and it is difficult to know who or what had more impact on the final product. For this reason, this book is focused on the process rather than the outcome. Finally, it is worth bearing in mind that the external actors will encounter resistance on the ground, and while this is not the focus of the current project, it is acknowledged and calls for further investigation.[143]

Why read this book

This book aims to contribute to the current understanding of constitution-making. It focuses on the transnational dimension of this legal phenomenon by examining the involvement of external actors during a particular stage of constitution-making: constitutional drafting. It sheds light on constitution-making by unveiling how this fundamental legal object actually gets made, who is involved in its making, and how external actors are involved in the process. Finally, by developing a new analytical lens to approach the study of constitution-making, this work has significant theoretical contributions.

For constitutional scholars, this work contributes from a methodological, theoretical, and empirical standpoint. For comparative constitutional scholars, this book provides a new way to approach legal questions. The socio-legal approach developed in this book aims to encourage scholars to engage in interdisciplinary dialogue to further understanding of the multifaceted legal phenomenon that is the making of constitutional norms. Further, this methodological approach is particularly valuable in a field characterised by blurry lines between policy and practice. The contribution is also theoretical, as this study contends that the concept of constituent power, which continues to provide the foundation for much of the literature, is inadequate to capture external actor involvement. To analyse the making of constitutional norms and to capture a more detailed picture of constitution-making during democratic transitions from a transnational perspective, a new analytical lens is required. This book develops such a lens – coining the term 'the development enterprise' – which enables the study of a broader range of external actors involved in constitution-making, expanding the scope of analysis beyond those commonly addressed in the literature.

Further, special focus is undertaken to examine a particular legal actor that has hitherto received limited attention from comparative constitutional law: the expert. This book reveals tacit underlying assumptions guiding external actors involved in constitution-making. It also sheds light on the figure of the expert, an actor that is present in constitution-making processes, as well as other types of law-making such as drafting legislation or developing international norms. Finally, this study has empirical contributions, as it details the involvement of external actors in constitution-making both today and in the context of decolonisation. Despite receiving little attention from constitutional scholars, constitution-making in the context of decolonisation is far from anecdotal and in fact marks the beginning of the 'development enterprise'.

For law and society scholars, this book contributes empirically by improving the current understanding of the circulation of legal ideas and by highlighting the figure of the expert as an important actor to take into account when thinking about norm creation. It also calls for the legal object 'constitution' to be taken seriously, as well as closely examining the politics of expertise at the constitutional level, contributing to research interested in expertise more broadly, whether in international relations or in public law.

For constitution-makers and practitioners, this book provides important insights. First, it urges caution against the romanticisation of the constitution-making process – it shows that this process is multifaceted by nature, involving a plethora of national and transnational actors. It also details the practical implications of constitution-making by illuminating the power dynamics at play during the legal process, as well as the many avenues through which involvement takes place. This book calls attention to the 'background of common sense', by bringing to light the paradigm of 'liberal legalism', which is ubiquitous both in the literature and among external actors. Finally, this book has a normative contribution: building on insights from scholarship devoted to legal reforms in the context of development, it highlights the limits and pitfalls of international expertise. Once again, this is a contribution with theoretical and practical utility.

Chapter overview

From constitution-making in the context of decolonisation to the most recent case in Chile, this book argues that the current dominant approach to study this complex legal phenomenon fails to capture its transnational dimension, which results in a myopic perspective. By developing a new analytical lens, the 'development enterprise', which allows for a more comprehensive view of transnational involvement, the theoretical and empirical contributions of this study set the stage for future scholarship on constitution-making, legal reform, and expertise.

The first part of the book is devoted to theoretical discussions by explaining why the current approach is insufficient, before introducing an alternative conceptual lens. **Chapter 1** demonstrates that the concept of constituent power cannot adequately address the transnational dimension of constitution-making. This chapter provides a close examination of constituent power as it constitutes the theoretical backbone of the majority of the literature on constitution-making. The chapter demonstrates that constituent power as a concept, generally defined as the power to create and modify the constitution, involves two different functions. First, the concept sustains a particular political theory: liberal constitutionalism. Second, the concept serves to justify the constitutional legal order for legal positivist scholarship. These two functions are contradictory: the theory of law (legal positivism) that the concept of constituent power sustains claims to be autonomous from the political field, yet we see how the concept also prescribes a particular political model. As such, it prevents a close examination of external actor involvement in constitution-making.

To be able to accommodate external actor involvement, an antifoundationalist understanding of constitution-making is required. Drawing on the work of Angélica Bernal, an antifoundationalist approach broadens the scope of analysis beyond the adoption of the constitution to include other phases of constitution-making, including the under-studied yet crucially important stage of constitutional drafting. This approach emphasises the political assumptions that underpin external actor involvement and foregrounds a particular legal actor in the drafting stage: the expert. To develop this theory, this chapter draws on interdisciplinary scholarship on legal reform in the context of structural economic and political reforms in Third World territories, which has transferrable insights relevant to transnational constitution-making, as these reforms are themselves characterised by a transnational dimension. **Chapter 2** details the paradigm of liberal legalism, one dimension of the development enterprise, while **Chapter 3** discusses the other dimension, centring on the figure of the expert in legal reform.

The second part of the book uses the development enterprise lens to examine external actor involvement in constitution-making. **Chapter 4** exposes the continuity of this involvement throughout history, revealing that despite the diversity of external actors, they were – and continue to be – largely moved by the same rationale (i.e. liberal legalism) where constitutions are understood as a legal tool that can accelerate social change. It is a particular kind of constitution that is deemed capable of catalysing change: the Western liberal constitution. While showing continuity, the analytical lens of the development enterprise also points to a shift in external actor involvement – during decolonisation these actors were involved in the overall constitution-making process; after this period, their involvement became heavily concentrated in the constitutional drafting stage. **Chapter 5** examines the figure of the expert within constitution-making, an actor that is revealed to be an integral part of the process and one that must be taken seriously. The chapter focuses on the involvement of constitutional experts during decolonisation and post-Cold War constitution-making. Finally, the **Conclusion** discusses the main results of the study and paves the way for future avenues of research. This book provides an alternative theory, to the constituent power theory which is currently the cornerstone of constitutional scholarship. Throughout this book, the development enterprise has proven to be a useful lens to understand the transnational dimension of constitution-making, revealing the continuity of the rationale of liberal legalism, as well as the centrality of the figure of the expert.

Notes

1 Harshan Kumarasingham (ed), *Constitution-Maker: Selected Writings of Sir Ivor Jennings* (CUP 2015) 23.
2 Alicia Pastor y Camarasa, 'Demystifying How Constitutions Are Made: External Actors' Modes of Actions in the 2014 Tunisian Constitution' [2022] Michigan Journal of Law & Society 51, 95.
3 ibid.
4 Adriaan Lanni and Adrian Vermeule, 'Constitutional Design in the Ancient World' (2012) 64 Stanford Law Review 907, 910.
5 Marc Belissa, 'Rousseau, la Corse et la Pologne' [2009] Annales Historiques de la Révolution Française 238.
6 Maartje De Visser, 'A Critical Assessment of the Role of the Venice Commission in Processes of Domestic Constitutional Reform' (2015) 63 The American Journal of Comparative Law 963; Vijayashri Sripati, *Constitution-Making Under UN Auspices: Fostering Dependency in Sovereign Lands* (OUP 2020).
7 Bruce Cain, 'Symposium: What, if Anything, Do We Know About Constitutional Design?' [2009] Texas Law Review Symposium 1265.
8 David Law, 'Constitutions' in Peter Cane and Herbert Kritzer (eds), *The Oxford Handbook of Empirical Legal Research* (OUP 2010) 379.
9 See Ngoc Son Bui, 'Contextualizing the Global Constitution-Making Process: The Case of Vietnam' (2016) 64 The American Journal of Comparative Law 931; Gregory Shaffer, Tom Ginsburg and Terence Halliday (eds), *Constitution-Making and Transnational Legal Order* (CUP 2019).
10 Ulrich Preuss, 'Constitutional Powermaking for the New Polity: Some Deliberations on the Relations Between Constituent Power and the Constitution' (1992) 14 Cardozo Law Review 639.
11 Angelica Maria Bernal, *Beyond Origins: Rethinking Founding in a Time of Constitutional Democracy* (OUP 2017) 226.
12 Jon Elster, 'Forces and Mechanisms in the Constitution-Making Process' (1995) 45 Duke Law Journal 362, 364.
13 András Jakab, Arthur Dyevre and Giulio Itzcovich, *Comparative Constitutional Reasoning* (CUP 2017) 10.
14 Philipp Dann and Zaid Al-Ali, 'The Internationalized Pouvoir Constituant – Constitution-Making Under External Influence in Iraq, Sudan and East Timor' (2006) 10 Max Planck Yearbook of United Nations Law 423.
15 This paper is consistently quoted by literature. See Andrew Arato, 'Constitution-Making' in Anthony Lang and Antje Wiener (eds), *Handbook on Global Constitutionalism* (Edward Elgar Publishing 2017) 285; Chaihark Hahm and Sung Ho Kim, *Making We the People: Democratic Constitutional Founding in Postwar Japan and South Korea* (CUP 2015) 32; Christina Murray and Cindy Wittke, 'International Institutions, Constitution-Making and Gender' in Helen Irving (ed), *Constitutions and Gender* (Edward Elgar Publishing 2017) 108; Katrin Seidel, *Involvement and Impact of External Actors on Constitution Making in South*

Sudan and Somaliland: A Comparative Study (Global Cooperation Research Papers 2017) 5.

16 Claude Klein, *Théorie et pratique du pouvoir constituant* (Presses Universitaires de France 1996); Martin Loughlin, 'The Concept of Constituent Power' (2014) 13 European Journal of Political Theory 218; Martin Loughlin and Neil Walker, *The Paradox of Constitutionalism: Constituent Power and Constitutional Form* (OUP 2007); Chris Thornhill, 'Contemporary Constitutionalism and the Dialectic of Constituent Power' (2012) 1 Global Constitutionalism 369; Joel Colón-Ríos, *Constituent Power and the Law* (OUP 2020).

17 Cheryl Saunders, 'Constitution-Making in the 21st Century' [2012] International Review of Law 1, 3.

18 Bernal (n 11) 2.

19 Using the term does not imply by any means any type of hierarchy between the 'First', 'Second', and 'Third World', but rather it is used to refer to this broad elusive analytical category. The term was coined in 1952 by French demographer Alfred Sauvy, as a reference to the *Tiers Etat*. Leslie Wolf-Phillips elaborates: 'The use of *Tiers Monde* in this analogical context would express ideas of neglect, exploitation and revolutionary potential'. Leslie Wolf-Phillips, 'Why "Third World"? Origin, Definition and Usage' (1987) 9 Third World Quarterly 1311–12.

20 Frederick Cooper, 'Modernizing Bureaucrats, Backward Africans, and the Development Concept' in Frederick Cooper and Randall Packard (eds), *International Development the Social Sciences: Essays on the History Politics of Knowledge* (U of California P 1997); Ruth Craggs, 'Development in a Gobal-Historical Context' in Vandana Desai and Rob Potter (eds), *The Companion to Development Studies* (Routledge 2014); Harshan Kumarasingham, 'Liberal Ideals and the Politics of Decolonisation' (2018) 46 The Journal of Imperial and Commonwealth History 815; Thomas Pfister and Anna Horvath, 'Reassessing Expert Knowledge and the Politics of Expertise' (2014) 27 Innovation: The European Journal of Social Science Research 311.

21 David Kennedy, *A World of Struggle: How Power, Law, and Expertise Shape Global Political Economy* (Princeton UP 2018) 91.

22 'The "West" does not refer to the geographical zone of Western Europe and North America, but to an *historical* construct that connotes a "developed" society'. Stuart Hall, 'The West and the Rest: Discourse an Power' in Stuart Hall and others (eds), *Modernity: An Introduction to Modern Societies* (Blackwell Publishers 1996) 186.

23 See Matthew R Hartz, 'Constitutional Provisions in the Occupier's Interest: Lessons from Article 9 of the Japanese Constitution' (2012) 45 New York University Journal of International Law and Politics 861; Edmund Spevack, *Allied Control and German Freedom: American Political and Ideological Influences on the Framing of the West German Basic Law (Grundgesetz)* (LIT Verlag 2001); Noah Feldman, 'Imposed Constitutionalism' (2004) 37 Connecticut Law Review 857; Ulrich K Preuss, 'Perspectives on Post-Conflict Constitutionalism: Reflections on Regime Change Through External Constitutionalization' (2007) 51 New York Law School Law Review 466, 474–81; Marie Guimezanes, 'Les transitions constitutionnelles "internationalisées": Étude de droit interne' [2015] Revue française de droit constitutionnel 801, 804; Stefan Kadelbach, 'Constitution-Making in Occupied Countries' in Gunter Frankenberg (ed), *Order from Transfer Comparative Constitutional Design and Legal Culture* (Edward Elgar Publishing Limited 2013); Andrew Arato, *Constitution Making Under Occupation: The Politics of Imposed Revolution in Iraq* (Columbia UP 2009).

24 Zaid Al-Ali, 'Constitutional Drafting and External Influence' in Tom Ginsburg and Rosalind Dixon (eds), *Comparative Constitutional Law* (Edward Elgar Publishing 2011); Kevin Cope, 'The Intermestic Constitution: Lessons from the World's Newest Nation' (2012) 53 Virginia Journal of International Law 667; Dann and Al-Ali (n 14) 32; Rosalind Dixon and Vicki Jackson, 'Constitutions Inside Out: Outsider Interventions in Domestic Constitutional Contexts' (2013) 48 Wake Forest Law Review 149; Tom Ginsburg, 'Constitutional Advice and Transnational Legal Order' in Gregory Shaffer, Terence C Halliday and Tom Ginsburg (eds), *Constitution-Making and Transnational Legal Order* (CUP 2019); Murray and Wittke (n 15); Cheryl Saunders, 'International Involvement in Constitution Making' in David Landau and Hanna Lerner (eds), *Comparative Constitution Making* (Edward Elgar Publishing 2019).

25 Marie-Sophie Berger, 'La Commission de Venise et l'élaboration de la Constitution tunisienne du 27 janvier 2014' in *Mouvances du droit: Études en l'honneur du Professeur Rafâa Ben Achour Tome I* (Konrad Adenauer Stiftung 2015); Francesco Duranti, 'Constitution of Tunisia, Venice Commission and International Constitutionalism' in Loretta Dell'Aguzzo and Emidio Diodato (eds), *The 'State' of Pivot States in South-Eastern Mediterranean: Turkey, Egypt, Israel, and Tunisia After the Arab Spring* (Stranieri UP 2016); Visser (n 6).

26 Carina Barbosa Gouvêa, *As intervenções da ONU no processo de Constitution-Making nos estados em transição política: O papel das Nações Unidas no resgate da ordem democrática* (Juruá 2016).

27 Murray and Wittke (n 15) 124; Dixon and Jackson (n 24) 39.

28 Coel Kirkby, 'A Cure for Coups: The South African Influence on Fijian Constitutionalism' in Rosalind Dixon and Roux Theunis (eds), *Constitutional Triumphs, Constitutional Disappointments: A Critical Assessment of the 1996 South African Constitution's Local and International Influence* (CUP 2018); Pastor y Camarasa (n 2); Bui (n 9).

29 David Landau and Hanna Lerner, *Comparative Constitution Making* (Edward Elgar Publishing 2019). Chapters by Saunders (n 24); Joanne Wallis, *Constitution Making and State Building* (CUP 2014).

30 Emmanuel De Groof, *State Renaissance for Peace: Transitional Governance Under International Law* (CUP 2020); Ralph Wilde, *International Territorial Administration: How Trusteeship and the Civilizing Mission Never Went Away* (OUP 2010).

31 Anna Saunders, 'Constitution-Making as a Technique of International Law: Reconsidering the Post-War Inheritance' (2023) 117 American Journal of International Law 251, 253.

32 Gaurav Mukherjee, 'Shaping Sovereignties: The Role of International Financial Institutions in Constitution-Making' (2023) 117 American Journal of International Law Unbound 251.

33 Sripati (n 6); Vijayashri Sripati, 'The United Nation's Role in Post-Conflict Constitution-Making Processes: TWAIL Insights' (2008) 10 International Community Law Review 411; Vijayashri Sripati, 'UN Constitutional Assistance Projects in Comprehensive Peace Missions: An Inventory 1989–2011' (2012) 19 International Peacekeeping 93; Vijayashri Sripati, 'United Nations Constitutional Assistance in Statebuilding' in *Routledge Handbook of International Statebuilding* (Routledge 2013).

34 Kirsti Samuels, 'Post-Conflict Peace-Building and Constitution-Making' (2005) 6 Chicago Journal of Intternational Law 663; Christine Bell, 'Peace Agreements: Their Nature and Legal Status' (2006) 100 American Journal of International Law 373.

35 Romain Bertrand, 'Les organisations de "promotion de la démocratie" et la construction des bureaucraties électorales indonésiennes' [2008] Critique Internationale 51; Sara Kendall, '"Constitutional Technicity": Displacing Politics Through Expert Knowledge' (2015) 11 Law, Culture and the Humanities 363.
36 Quentin Deforge, 'Une expertise internationale sans "bonnes pratiques": Soutenir la professionnalisation du travail parlementaire dans la Tunisie d'après 2011' [2019] Critique Internationale 127, 299–302.
37 Amelia Odida, 'Making Policy, Problems, and Constitutions: Decolonising the UN Policy of Constitutional Assistance' (UCL (University College London) 2022) 149.
38 ibid.
39 Jan Aart Scholte, 'Defining Globalisation' (2008) 31 World Economy 1471, 1478.
40 Benoît Frydman, 'Les défis du droit global' in Caroline Bricteux and Benoît Benoît Frydman (eds), *Les défis du droit global* (Bruylant 2018). See Ankie Hoogvelt, *Globalization and the Postcolonial World: The New Political Economy of Development* (Palgrave Macmillan 2007).
41 Dixon and Jackson (n 24) 149, 166.
42 Mark Tushnet, 'The Inevitable Globalization of Constitutional Law' (2008) 49 Virginia Journal of International Law 985–86, 1006; Hanan Qazbir, *L'internationalisation du droit constitutionnel* (Dalloz 2015).
43 See Thomas Franck and Arun Thiruvengadam, 'International Law and Constitution-Making' (2003) 2 Chinese Journal of International Law 467, 469; Hélène Tourard, 'L'internationalisation des constitutions nationales' (PhD dissertation, Université Robert Schuman 1998).
44 South Africa, Constitution of South Africa (1996) Constitute Project Article 233.
45 Frederick Schauer, 'On the Migration of Constitutional Ideas' (2004) 37 Connecticut Law Review 907; David Law, 'Globalization and the Future of Constitutional Rights' (2008) 102 Northwestern University Law Review 1277.
46 Ngoc Son Bui, 'Globalization of Constitutional Identity' (2017) 23 Washington International Law Journal 463, 475; Maya Hertig Randall, 'L'internationalisation de la juridiction constitutionnelle: défis et perspectives' (2010) 129 Revue de droit suisse 221.
47 Thomas Franck, 'The Emerging Right to Democratic Governance' (1992) 86 American Journal of International Law 46; Michèle Olivier, 'The Emergence of a Right to Democracy – An African Perspective' in Carlo Panara and Gary Wilson (eds), *The Arab Spring New Patters for Democracy and International Law* (Martinus Nijhoff Publishers 2013).
48 Franck and Thiruvengadam (n 43).
49 Günter Frankenberg, 'Constitutional Transfer: The IKEA Theory Revisited' (2010) 8 International Journal of Constitutional Law 563.
50 Schauer (n 45); Vlad Perju, 'Constitutional Transplants, Borrowing, and Migrations' in Michel Rosenfeld and András Sajó (eds), *The Oxford Handbook of Comparative Constitutional Law* (OUP 2012).
51 Chaihark Hahm and Sung Ho Kim, 'To Make "We the People": Constitutional Founding in Postwar Japan and South Korea' (2010) 8 International Journal of Constitutional Law 800, 809.
52 See Bui (n 9) 978.
53 Philip Jessup, *Transnational Law* (Yale UP 1956) 2.
54 Christian Tietje and Karsten Nowrot, 'Laying Conceptual Ghosts of the Past to Rest: The Rise of Philip Jessup's Transnational Law Regulatory Governance of the International Economic System' in Christian Tietje, Karsten Nowrot and Alan Brouder (eds), *The Regulatory Governance of the International Economic System* (Institute for Economic Law 2006).

55 Jamie O'Connell, 'Common Interests, Closer Allies: How Democracy in Arab States Can Benefit the West' (2012) 48 Stanford Journal of International Law 341, 353.
56 Saunders (n 24) 75.
57 ibid 8.
58 Kadelbach (n 23); International Peace Conference, The Hague, Official Record, 'Hague Convention (IV) Respecting the Laws and Customs of War on Land and Its Annex: Regulations Concerning the Laws and Customs of War on Land' (18 October 1907) art 43 <https://ihl-databases.icrc.org/applic/ihl/ihl.nsf/0/1d1726425f6955aec125641e0038bfd6> accessed November 2020.
59 United Nations, *UN Charter* (United Nations 26 June 1945) 1 UNTS XVI.
60 ibid art 39.
61 International Court of Justice, *Nicaragua v United States of America, Merits* (International Court of Justice 27 June 1986) §258.
62 Human Rights Committee, *Marshall v Canada*, 4 November 1991, Communication No 205/1986, UN Doc CCPR/C/43/D/205/1986, point 5.4.
63 UN Human Rights Committee, *CCPR General Comment No 25: Article 25 (Participation in Public Affairs and the Right to Vote), the Right to Participate in Public Affairs, Voting Rights and the Right of Equal Access to Public Service, CCPR/C/21/Rev.1/Add.7* (UN Human Rights Committee 12 July 1996) §6.
64 Stephen Schnably, 'Emerging International Law Constraints on Constitutional Structure and Revision: A Preliminary Appraisal' (2007) 62 University of Miami Law Review 417.
65 Marie-Françoise Rigaux, *La théorie des limites matérielles à l'exercice de la fonction constituante* (Larcier 1987).
66 The definition of soft law has been widely discussed. In this book, the definition of Daniel Thürer is followed, who considers 'soft law as a phenomenon in international relations covers all those social rules generated by State[s] or other subjects of international law which are not legally binding but which are nevertheless of special legal relevance'. Daniel Thürer, 'Soft Law' in Anne Peters and Rüdiger Wolfrum (eds), *Max Planck Encyclopedia of Public International Law* (OUP 2000) §8. For an historical discussion of the emergence of the concept Alexandre Flückiger, *(Re)faire la loi: Traité de légistique à l'ère du droit souple* (Stämpfli Verlag 2019) 272–76.
67 David Fontana, 'The Rise and Fall of Comparative Constitutional Law in the Postwar Era' (2011) 36 Yale Journal of International Law 1, 104; Harold Hongju Koh, 'The Globalization of Freedom' (2001) 26 Yale Journal of International Law 305–6.
68 UNDP, *UNDP Guidance Note on Constitution-Making Support* (UNDP 2014); OHCHR, *Human Rights and Constitution-Making* (OHCHR 2018); Markus Böckenförde, Nora Hedling and Winluck Wahiu, *A Practical Guide to Constitution Building* (International IDEA 2011).
69 Marthe Fatin-Rouge Stéfanini (ed), *Internationalisation des constitutions et constitutionnalisation du droit international: Réflexions sur quelques interactions entre droit constitutionnel et droit international* (Les cahiers de l'institut Louis-Favoreu, Presses Universitaires d'Aix-Marseille 2015).
70 Murray and Wittke (n 15) 109; Saunders (n 24) 75; Visser (n 6) 992.
71 UNSG, *Guidance Note of the Secretary-General Regarding United Nations Assistance to Constitution-Making Processes* (UNSG 2009) 2.
72 ibid 3.
73 ibid 5.
74 ibid.

75 ibid 6.
76 ibid 2.
77 UNSG, *Guidance Note of the Secretary-General on United Nations Constitutional Assistance* (UNSG 2020).
78 ibid 2.
79 See Mihaela Anca Ailincai, 'La soft law est-elle l'avenir des droits fondamentaux?' (2017) 20 Revue des droits et libertés fondamentaux 21; Andrew Guzman and Timothy Meyer, 'International Soft Law' (2010) 2 Journal of Legal Analysis 171.
80 Eric C Ip, 'Globalization and the Future of the Law of the Sovereign State' (2010) 8 International Journal of Constitutional Law 636, 643. See Gregory Shaffer and Mark A Pollack, 'Hard Versus Soft Law in International Security' (2011) 52 Boston College Law Review 1147.
81 Charles Roger, *The Origins of Informality: Why the Legal Foundations of Global Governance Are Shifting, and Why It Matters* (OUP 2020) 1.
82 Flückiger still considers that the legislation holds a central role. See Flückiger (n 66) x.
83 ibid 34.
84 In this study, legal actors refer to actors involved in the making or the implementation of legal norms. It includes lawmakers, public administrations, and private actors.
85 Rodney Bruce Hall and Thomas J Biersteker, *The Emergence of Private Authority in Global Governance* (CUP 2002).
86 Sabino Cassese, *A World Government?* (Global Law Press 2018); Sufyan Droubi and Jean d'Aspremont, *International Organisations, Non-State Actors, and the Formation of Customary International Law* (Manchester UP 2020); Peer Zumbansen, 'Comparative, Global and Transnational Constitutionalism: The Emergence of a Transnational Legal-Pluralist Order' (2012) 1 Global Constitutionalism 16.
87 Roger Cotterrell, 'What Is Transnational Law?' (2012) 37 Law & Social Inquiry 500, 518.
88 Gregory Shaffer, *Transnational Legal Ordering and State Change* (CUP 2012) 6.
89 Cotterrell (n 87) 501; Craig Scott, '"Transnational Law" as Proto-Concept: Three Conceptions' (2009) 10 German Law Journal 859.
90 Sripati (n 6) 411. See Abrak Saati, 'Participatory Constitution-Making as a Transnational Legal Norm: Why Does It Stick in Some Contexts and Not in Others' (2017) 2 UC Irvine Journal of International Transnationall & Comparative Law 113.
91 Ginsburg (n 24) 49–50.
92 Lynn Mather, 'Law and Society' in Keith Whittington, Daniel Kelemen and Gregory Caldeira (eds), *The Oxford Handbook of Political Science* (OUP 2011).
93 Elizabeth Mertz, Stewart Macaulay and Thomas Mitchell, *The New Legal Realism: Volume 1: Translating Law-and-Society for Today's Legal Practice* (CUP 2016) xiv.
94 Theodore Eisenberg, 'Why Do Empirical Legal Scholarship' (2004) 41 San Diego Law Review 1741.
95 Mertz, Macaulay and Mitchell (n 93) 4.
96 Donald Horowitz, 'Constitution-Making: A Process Filled with Constraint' (2006) 12 Review of Constitutional Studies 1.
97 Elster (n 12) 370.
98 Yash Ghai, 'A Journey Around Constitutions: Reflections on Contemporary Constitutions' (2005) 122 South African Law Journal 804, 325.

99 Véronique Champeil-Desplats, *Méthodologies du droit et des sciences du droit* (Dalloz 2016) 11.
100 ibid 12. [My own translation].
101 Olivier Corten, *Méthodologie du droit international public* (Éditions de l'Université de Bruxelles 2009) 34.
102 Zinaida Miller, 'Effects of Invisibility: In Search of the "Economic" in Transitional Justice' (2008) 2 The International Journal of Transitional Justice 266.
103 Sumit Bisarya, 'No Strings Attached? Constraints on External Advice in Internationalized Constitution-Making' in Emmanuel De Groof and Micha Wiebusch (eds), *International Law and Transitional Governance* (Routledge 2020); Sumit Bisarya, *Advice on Applying Mediation Fundamentals in UN Constitutional Assistance* (UNDPPA November 2022).
104 International IDEA, 'Board of Advisers' (Undated) <www.idea.int/about-us/board_of_advisers> accessed 11 February 2021. Christina Murray works for the Mediation Support Unit. United Nations Peacemakers, 'Standby Team of Senior Mediation Advisers' (Undated) <https://peacemaker.un.org/mediation-support/stand-by-team> accessed 11 February 2021, as well as Xavier Philippe who has collaborated with Democracy Reporting International and UNDP. Xavier Philippe, 'Le rôle des organisations non gouvernementales dans les processus constituants postconflictuels: Expertise ou plaidoyer' in Xavier Philippe and Natasa Danelciuc-Colodrovschi (eds), *Transitions constitutionnelles et constitutions transitionnelles* (Institut Universitaire Varenne 2014).
105 Tom Ginsburg, *Constitutional Design for Territorially Divided Societies* (International IDEA August 2018); Shaffer, Ginsburg and Halliday (n 9).
106 Visser (n 6) 964.
107 Herbert Kritzer, 'The (Nearly) Forgotten Early Empirical Legal Research' in Peter Cane and Herbert Kritzer (eds), *Oxford Handbook of Empirical Legal Research* (OUP 2010) 883.
108 Mark Suchman and Elizabeth Mertz, 'Toward a New Legal Empiricism: Empirical Legal Studies and New Legal Realism' (2010) 6 Annual Review of Law and Social Science 555–56.
109 Lisa Webley, 'Qualitative Approaches to Empirical Legal Research' in Peter Cane and Herbert Kritzer (eds), *The Oxford Handbook of Empirical Legal Research* (OUP 2010) 948.
110 Léon Duguit, *L'Etat, le droit objectif et la loi positive* (Fontemoing 1901) 614. [My own translation].
111 Maurice Hauriou, *Précis de droit constitutionnel* (Librarie du Recueil Sirey 1929); Quoted in Champeil-Desplats (n 99) 173.
112 See Jamie Rebecca Rowen, '"We Don't Believe in Transitional Justice": Peace and the Politics of Legal Ideas in Colombia' (2017) 42 Law & Social Inquiry 622; Heinz Klug, *Constituting Democracy: Law, Globalism, and South Africa's Political Reconstruction* (CUP 2000).
113 Yves Dezalay and Bryant Garth, *The Internationalization of Palace Wars: Lawyer, Economists, and the Contest to Transform Latin American States* (U of Chicago P 2002). See Mikael Madsen, 'The International Judiciary as Transnational Power Elite' (2014) 8 International Political Sociology 332; Antoine Vauchez, *Brokering Europe: Euro-Lawyers and the Making of a Transnational Polity* (CUP 2015).
114 For an overview of the different sociological perspectives see Mikael Madsen, 'Sociological Approaches to Constitutional Law' (2020) iCourts Working Paper Series, No 212, 2020, 1. See Kim Lane Scheppele, 'Constitutional Ethnography: An Introduction' (2004) 38 Law & Society Review 389; Chris Thornhill, *A*

Sociology of Constitutions: Constitutions and State Legitimacy in Historical-Sociological Perspective (CUP 2011).

115 Tom Ginsburg and Mila Versteeg, 'Why Do Countries Adopt Constitutional Review?' (2014) 30 The Journal of Law, Economics, & Organization 587.

116 Bui (n 9); Melissa Crouch, 'Pre-Emptive Constitution-Making: Authoritarian Constitutionalism and the Military in Myanmar' (2020) 54 Law & Society Review 487; François Bastien, *Le régime politique de la Ve République* (La Découverte 1999) 11; David Law, 'Constitutional Archetypes' (2016) 95 Texas Law Review 153; Ngoc Son Bui, *Constitutional Change in the Contemporary Socialist World* (OUP 2020).

117 Dawn Oliver and Carlo Fusaro, *How Constitutions Change: A Comparative Study* (Hart Publishing 2011) 1.

118 Armel Le Divellec, 'Le style des Constitutions écrites dans l'histoire moderne: Une esquisse sur les trois types de l'écriture constitutionnelle (XVIIe–XXe siècles)' (2013) 9 Jus Politicum 1, 5.

119 Some include them in the scope of their analysis: see Sripati (n 6); Visser (n 6).

120 Saunders (n 17) 8 distinguishes between 'deliberation, drafting, ratification, and the initial phases of implementation'. Jennifer Widner, 'Constitution Writing in Post-Conflict Settings: An Overview' (2007) 49 William & Mary Law Review 1513 distinguishes between 'drafting – consultation – deliberation – adoption – ratification'.

121 Saunders (n 17) 4.

122 See Andrew Arato, 'Forms of Constitution Making and Theories of Democracy' (1995) 17 Cardozo Law Review 191.

123 See Abrak Saati, 'The Participation Myth: Outcomes of Participatory Constitution Building Processes on Democracy' (PhD dissertation, Umeå universitet 2015); Saati (n 90).

124 See Jeffrey Lenowitz, 'Why Ratification? Questioning the Unexamined Constitution-Making Procedure' (PhD dissertation, Columbia University 2013).

125 See for instance, Coel Kirkby and Christina Murray, 'Constitution-Making in Anglophone Africa: We the People?' in Muna Ndulo and Mamoudou Gazibo (eds), *Growing Democracy in Africa: Elections, Accountable Governance, and Political Economy* (Cambridge Publishers 2016).

126 Saunders (n 17) 9.

127 Gabriel Negretto, *Redrafting Constitutions in Democratic Regimes: Theoretical and Comparative Perspectives* (CUP 2020).

128 See Rosalind Dixon, 'Constitutional Drafting and Distrust' (2015) 13 International Journal of Constitutional Law 819.

129 Terence Halliday and Gregory Shaffer, 'Transnational Legal Orders' in Terence C Halliday and Gregory Shaffer (eds), *Transnational Legal orders* (CUP 2015) 18.

130 ibid 13.

131 Shaffer (n 88) 8.

132 Cotterrell (n 87) 501.

133 The notion of 'transnational' preserves space for nation-states. As Halliday and Shaffer explain, 'the nation-state remains central to law-making, law recognition and law enforcement'. Halliday and Shaffer (n 129) 13 The term 'international' refers to a specific body of law (i.e. international law), which is not relevant in the case of constitution-making as it does not capture the phenomenon in its entirety, particularly with regard to the horizontal spread of constitutional ideas.

134 Ivo Duchacek, *Power Maps: Comparative Politics of Constitutions* (American Bibliographical Center-Clio Press 1973); Cited in Julian Go, 'Modeling the State:

Postcolonial Constituitions in Asia and Africa' (2002) 39 Southeast Asian Studies 558.

135 Go (n 134) 558.

136 See James Crawford, *The Creation of States in International Law* (OUP 2006) 300, 303; Antony Anghie, 'Finding the Peripheries: Sovereignty and Colonialism in Nineteenth-Century International Law' (1999) 40 Harvard International Law Journal 1; Emmanuelle Saada, 'France: The Longue Durée of French Decolonization' in Martin Thomas and Andrew Thompson (eds), *The Oxford Handbook of the Ends of Empire* (OUP 2019) 92; Thibault Guilluy, *Du 'Self-Government' des Dominions à la dévolution: Recherches sur l'apparition et l'évolution de la Constitution britannique* (Editions Panthéon-Assas 2014) 378.

137 Charles Manga Fombad, 'Constitutional Reforms and Constitutionalism in Africa: Reflections on Some Current Challenges and Future Prospects' (2011) 59 Buffalo Law Review 1007, 1009.

138 See Louis Aucoin, 'The Role of International Experts in Constitution-Making: Myth and Reality' (2004) 5 Georgetown Journal of International Affairs 89; Albert Blaustein, 'Constitution Drafting: The Good, the Bad, and the Beautiful' (1991) 2 Scibes Journal of Legal Writing 49; Jean Du Bois de Gaudusson, 'Le rôle de l'expertise constitutionnelle dans la transition constitutionnelle' in Xavier Philippe and Natasa Danelciuc-Colodrovschi (eds), *Transitions constitutionnelles et constitutions transitionnelles* (Institut Universitaire Varenne 2014); Ghai (n 98); Murray and Wittke (n 15); Philippe (n 104); Alison Quentin-Baxter, 'Making Constitutions, from the Perspective of Constitutional Adviser' (2002) 33 Victoria University Wellington Law Review 239; Christina Murray, 'Making and Remaking Kenya's Constitution' in Tom Ginsburg and Sumit Bisarya (eds), *Constitution Makers on Constitution Making: New Cases* (CUP 2022); Tom Ginsburg, 'Some Advice on Constitutional Advice' in *European Yearbook of Constitutional Law 2021: Constitutional Advice* (Springer 2022) 14.

139 Barbara Perry, 'Constitutional Johnny Appleseeds: American Consultants and the Drafting of Foreign Constitutions' (1992) 55 Albany Law Review 767.

140 See for instance Sripati who highlights the economic implications that drive UN Constitutional assistance as the Western liberal constitution is a tool to achieve economic exploitation in Third World Territories. Sripati (n 6).

141 See Harshan Kumarasingham, *Constitution-Making in Asia: Decolonisation and State-Building in the Aftermath of the British Empire* (Routledge 2016); Harshan Kumarasingham, 'Eastminster – Decolonisation and State-Building in British Asia' in Harshan Kumarasingham (ed), *Constitution-Making in Asia Decolonisation and State-Building in the Aftermath of the British Empire* (Routledge 2016).

142 Several email discussions with historians specialised in French colonial history have confirmed it. See Samia El Mechat and Florence Renucci, *Les décolonisations au XXe siècle: Les hommes de la transition. Itinéraires, actions et traces* (L'Harmattan 2014); Florence Renucci, 'La "décolonisation doctrinale" ou la naissance du droit d'Outre-mer (1946-début des années 1960)' [2011] Revue d'Histoire des Sciences Humaines 61.

143 See research of Odida (n 37).

Part 1

Crafting a new theory

From constituent power to the development enterprise

Chapter 1

The limits of constituent power for transnational constitution-making

In 2010, Tunisia embarked in a constitution-making process that captured the world's media and academic attention. A National Constituent Assembly was elected in 2011, tasked with drafting a new constitution, marking a new democratic era following decades of the authoritarian regime of Ben Ali. After a long arduous process, the Constitution was finally adopted in January 2014. At first sight and reading the literature on the topic, the Tunisian Constitution was a pure national product, the transnational dimension is scarcely mentioned.[1] However, empirical research revealed that the transnational dimension was not only significant in terms of the diversity of actors present ranging from UNDP to International IDEA but also in terms of means. For instance UNDP, who supported the process, had a budget of $18 million USD for its constitutional assistance project in Tunisia (2011–2014) alone while the National Constituent Assembly's annual budget was $11 million USD in 2012.[2] External actors were actively involved in the drafting of the Constitution by providing, for instance, one-on-one constitutional advising.[3] The involvement of external actors in Tunisia was mainly informal and hence escaped scrutiny. This is not to say that the National Constituent Assembly did not exercise its constituent power to draft a new constitution or that a constitutional text was imposed by foreign actors, such as in the case of occupied constitutionalism in 1947 Japan or 2005 Iraq. Rather, it calls for understanding constitution-making as multifaceted, where the transnational dimension must be taken seriously as it was not anecdotal.

Studying the transnational dimension of constitution-making first requires challenging the theoretical foundation that grounds current constitutional scholarship. This chapter sets out to demonstrate why the concept of constituent power is limited in its ability to address the transnational dimension of constitution-making, providing only a partial picture of how constitutions are actually made. The concept of constituent power is generally defined as 'the power to create and modify the constitution'.[4] The constituent power fulfils two different functions. First, it sustains a particular political theory: liberal constitutionalism.[5] To fix the rules in a written document such as the constitution is seen as a way to prevent arbitrary government,[6] which is one of

DOI: 10.4324/9781003386186-3

the basic tenets of constitutionalism.[7] While constitutionalism can be linked to different political doctrines and values, liberal constitutionalism refers to the political doctrine that hinges on 'a written constitution that includes an enumeration of individual rights, the existence of rights-based judicial review, a heightened threshold for constitutional amendment, a commitment to periodic democratic elections, and a commitment to the rule of law'.[8] It is this particular variety of constitutionalism that the concept of constituent power has historically served to support. Second, 'constituent power' serves as a non-legal concept that justifies the constitutional legal order for legal positivist constitutional scholarship.[9] Providing clarity on the use and meaning of constituent power is an important task, as Martin Loughlin reminds us that the concept is 'bound up with deeper disputes concerning the nature of legal, political and constitutional ordering'.[10]

Distinguishing between the two functions of constituent power, beyond providing greater conceptual clarity, helps to explain why the concept is limited in its utility to study the transnational dimension of constitution-making as it only addresses it partially. The two functions are difficult to hold at the same time, and somewhat contradictory, as the concept refers to a particular political theory (liberal constitutionalism), while at the same time sustains a theory of law (legal positivism) that strives to be autonomous from the political realm. By keeping the concept of constituent power central, the burgeoning field of comparative constitutional law narrows the scope of analysis, only capturing a segment of the complete range of external actors involved. Because the field is grounded in legal positivism, it mostly takes into account cases where external actor involvement is legally framed by international or national law. This results in a restricted and inaccurate picture of the legal phenomenon.

This chapter addresses the limitations of the notion of constituent power to study the transnational dimension from a theoretical standpoint. While it is acknowledged that the concept may have theoretical utility in addressing other dimensions of constitution-making, this remains beyond the scope of this inquiry. Similarly, this chapter recognises that 'the people', as the body with the authority to write the constitution, hold a significant role in constitution-making processes: through the formal adoption of the constitution by a constituent assembly, through a referendum, or through involvement in discussions during the process. Especially since the period of decolonisation, the participation of 'the people' is understood as a necessary condition of granting legitimacy to the newly adopted constitution.[11] This chapter argues, however, that conflating the 'power to make a constitution' and the 'process of constitution-making' is analytically flawed, particularly when it comes to the transnational dimension.

The first section proceeds chronologically by showing how the concept of constituent power first emerged with regards to a political practice and then came to sustain a particular political theory, liberal constitutionalism.

The second section discusses how constituent power serves as a foundation to a certain theory of law – legal positivism – that is prevalent among constitutional scholars and that sustains the constitutional legal order. The third section elucidates the tension that exists between the two functions of constituent power and teases out the inherent limitations of the concept to fully address external actors. The final section discusses Angelica Bernal's antifoundationalist theory that contributes to the theoretical backbone of this book.

Constituent power as a foundational concept for the liberal constitutional state

One function of the concept of constituent power is to serve and sustain a particular political theory: liberal constitutionalism. Historically situated within the creation of the liberal state,[12] the term 'constituent power' first emerged related to the practice of writing a constitution. Despite being attributed to the Abbey Emmanuel Joseph Sieyès,[13] legal historians locate the first use of the term 'constituent power' in a letter from the American revolutionary Thomas Young, an organiser of the 1773 Boston Tea Party.[14] On 11 April 1777, 12 years before the publication of Sieyès' pamphlet *Qu'est-ce-que le Tiers Etat*, Young wrote a letter to the 'Inhabitants of Vermont', signalling his support for the drafting of a constitution in their state:

> For my own part, I esteem the people at large the true proprietors of governmental power. They are the *supreme constituent power*, and of course their immediate Representatives are the supreme Delegate power; and as soon as the delegate power gets too far out of the hands of the *constituent power*, a tyranny is in some degree established.[15]

In early twentieth-century public legal scholarship, the use of the term constituent power was limited to describing the French experience of making a constitution. In Germany, Georg Jellinek (1851–1911) in *General Theory of the State* [Allgemeine Staatslehre] refers to constituent power using the French term in his text, as exemplified in this passage discussing the French revolution: 'Die Idee der Volkssouveranetat, die aus ihr entspringende, spater von Sieyes formulierte Lehre vom *pouvoir constituant*, das stets beim Volk bleibe'.[16] In contrast, when discussing the Constitution of the German Empire, he does not use the term constituent power. In the United Kingdom, Albert Dicey's 1885 text, *Introduction to the Study of the Law of the Constitution*, does not mention 'constituent power' at all. Dicey explains that the

> very language [therefore], expressing the difference between a "legislative" assembly which can change ordinary laws and a "constituent" assembly which can change not only ordinary but also constitutional and

> fundamental laws, has to be borrowed from the *political phraseology of foreign countries*.[17]

Constituent power has played and continues to play in legitimating and sustaining liberal constitutionalism. As Christopher Thornhill points out,

> the classical doctrine of constituent power revolved around the claim that constituent power forms an original and pre-legal wellspring for legitimate political order, in the exercise of which the sovereign subject of the people (or the nation) first enacts and authorizes the laws (the constitution) by which the people is then publicly and objectively bound.[18]

So understood, constituent power first sustains the idea of curtailing government by creating a higher law. It is grounded on a particular conception of political authority held by 'the people'.

Constitutions as a legal tool to limit government power

When making a constitution, which is the highest written norm that curtails political power, the concept of constituent power helps to create a particular kind of government that upholds the principles of liberal constitutionalism, grounded in the liberty of individuals.[19] A constitution becomes a legal manifestation of the political idea that the power of government can be constrained by a legal norm; it also implies that there is a special kind of norm required to perform that function, namely the constitution.

Invoking the concept of constituent power marked a move to the political doctrine of liberal constitutionalism, which centres on limiting the exercise of political power within a written constitution. This rests on the idea of creating a different legal order, the constitutional legal order, to constrain political power.[20] The doctrine of liberal constitutionalism influenced the 'Fathers' of the United States Constitution, which is generally treated as the first liberal constitutional state,[21] followed in 1789 by France (and its sister Republics) and the adoption of liberal constitutions beyond the European borders in Saint Domingue (1801), Haiti (1801), and Venezuela (1822).[22]

Liberal constitutionalism is inspired by John Locke's theory of the social contract and self-government, which holds that limiting governmental power is necessary to guarantee the natural rights of men; these rights were centred on liberty and private property.[23] Within this theoretical framework, laws are meant to constrain government, and constitutions were conceived of as the principal means of limiting governmental power, 'in accordance with natural law'.[24] Locke himself drafted the 1669 Constitution of the Colony of Carolina, one of the earliest pre-independence North American constitutions.[25] While for Locke the concepts of 'law' and 'constitution' were largely interchangeable, an important idea was established: law can curtail government.[26]

This idea had a significant influence on Thomas Jefferson, who considered Locke to be one of 'the greatest men that ever lived without any exception'[27] and became a guiding principle in the drafting of the Constitution of the United States.

Through the writing of constitutions, the idea of constituent power creates a distinctive legal norm, implying that another variety of fundamental norms ought to be distinguished from legislative norms. The Swiss jurist Emer de Vattel (1714–1767), whose theory influenced the American Revolution, first developed this distinction in his 1758 study *Droit des gens*.[28] Vattel defines the constitution as the 'fundamental regulation that determines the manner in which the public authority is to be executed' and goes on to explain that the fundamental law forms the constitution of a given state.[29] He ultimately distinguishes between law that comes from the legislature and fundamental law, anticipating the later distinction between 'constituent' and 'constituted'.[30] A central feature in liberal constitutionalism is that fundamental rules frame the exercise of political power as 'constitutions have an important limiting function as they contain the criteria for distinguishing between admissible and inadmissible forms of public power'.[31] This distinction is important, as the constituent power relates to a particular understanding of how political authority can be legitimately exercised. In this conception, written constitutions, as legal instruments that limit the power of the government, are necessary to guarantee the freedom of the people.

The people are sovereign

By enshrining the idea that sovereignty lies in the people, constituent power serves another central feature of liberal constitutionalism.[32] The concept of constituent power is imbued with a theory of sovereignty that answers the fundamental question of who holds political authority; this leads to a further question of who can create norms. In liberal constitutionalism, sovereignty is vested in the people, wherein lies the source of political authority. The concept of constituent power marks a shift from a classical conception of sovereignty to a modern one. Angelica Bernal discusses this change:

> no longer was the creation of political order to be the work of superhuman, divine beings, or something handed down over the ages by tradition and inherited by kings; political order and community was now an object of mortal making by and for the many.[33]

Even early monarchical constitutions were couched in the rhetoric of the people, where kings and queens would 'grant' the constitution in the name of the people. The Preamble of the 1791 Polish Constitution states that the monarch, Stanisław August, grants it 'representing the Polish people'.[34] The Brazilian imperial constitution of 1824 was also 'granted' by the Emperor Dom Pedro.[35] In 1893, the preamble of the draft Hawaiian Constitution notes:

> I, Liliuokalani, Queen of the Hawaiian Islands, in my capacity as Sovereign of this Kingdom, and as the representative of the people, and in accordance with their almost universal desire, and in conformity with their wishes . . . do proclaim and promulgate this constitution.[36]

With the 1788 Constitution of the United States and its 'We the People' Preamble, the 'people' became not only the sole holders of political authority but possessed the sole ability to exercise it.

Martin Loughlin traces the move from the 'traditional or sacred authority of the sovereign' to the 'people', arguing that constituent power emerged as a rational concept rooted in the radical idea that the 'ultimate source of political authority derives from an entity known as "the people"'.[37] With that said, the modern conception of constituent power has its roots within early modern political theory. Loughlin explains that its origin can be traced to a Calvinist reinterpretation of Jean Bodin's theory of sovereignty developed in 1576.[38] Bodin defined sovereignty as 'the most high, absolute and perpetual power over the citizens and subjects in a Commonweal'.[39] The Calvinist reinterpretation centred on a '"double sovereignty", with personal sovereignty (majestas personalis) being held by the ruler and real sovereignty (majestas realis) [vested] in the people'.[40]

The move towards treating the people as sole holders of sovereignty can be further located in the English Civil War (1642–1651), which occurred over a century before the political practice of writing liberal constitutions. Bernal situates this as the moment that 'began to carve out for the people a revolutionary function as a vehicle for repudiating an existing political authority'.[41] The Levellers are key to understanding this particular history – a group of English radicals, largely comprised of men who fought in the Civil War for Oliver Cromwell's New Model Army, they represented different religious sects but shared a strong belief in God making all men equal. Via a series of essays and pamphlets, including John Lilburne's seminal 'The Free Man's Freedom Vindicated' (1647), the Levellers demanded a series of reforms, including: universal male suffrage, religious tolerance, abolition of the House of Lords, short parliamentary periods, freedom of speech, and proportional parliamentary representation. In this regard, they are often treated as the first group to place the 'people' above those holding the power of government.[42]

Bernal points to the institutional innovation of assemblies of the people, which '[operated] outside existing formal institutions and representative bodies during moments of political crises',[43] resulting in the conception of 'the people' as an agent of revolution, ultimately outlining 'the first modern conception of a democratic or popular founding'.[44] This principle would be encapsulated in the United States Declaration of Independence, adopted in Philadelphia on 4 July 1776:

> That whenever any Form of Government becomes destructive of these ends, it is *the Right of the People to alter or to abolish it*, and to institute new Government, laying its foundation on such principles and organising its powers in such form, as to them shall seem most likely to effect their Safety and Happiness.[45]

In 1789, in the context of the French Revolution, in his political pamphlet *What is the Third Estate* [Qu'est-ce que le Tiers-Etat], Emmanuel-Joseph Sieyès (the Abbé Sieyès) developed a theory of constituent power as a tool to assert the sovereignty of the people.[46] Sieyès, elected deputy representing the *Tiers-Etat* in 1789, a social category which represented commoners, sought to assert the power of this group against its rival institution, the French monarchy.[47] Sieyès built this theory to respond to the political concern of removing the monarch from the process of establishing a new constitution:[48] 'if we have no constitution, it must be made, and only the nation has the right to make it'.[49] He further developed the idea that any constitution presupposes a constituent power: 'a constitution implies above all a constituent power'.[50]

Sieyès situates the origins of political power within individuals, and he outlines three periods through which political societies develop. In the first period, individual wills are atomised among isolated individuals wishing to unite, 'by this fact alone, they already constitute a nation: they enjoy all the rights of a nation and it only remains for them to exercise them . . . they are the origin of all power'.[51] The second period sees power move towards the community, the common will: 'individual wills still constitute its origin and form its essential components; but, taken separately, they would be powerless. Power exists only in the aggregate'.[52] The constitution and constituent power appear in the third period when the number of individuals makes it difficult to exercise their 'common will', which is exercised through government by proxy.[53] To organise the laws and procedure that will enable the representative government to function, a constitution becomes necessary.[54] The representative government must act within the confines of the constitution, which 'the nation has chosen to give it'.[55] Sieyès concludes, 'it is equally obvious that every government must have its constitution'.[56]

Another important idea follows from Sieyès' assertion. As the constituent power emanates from the nation, it cannot be limited in any way. The nation pre-exists the constituent power: 'The nation is prior to everything. It is the source of everything. Its will is always legal; indeed, it is the law itself. Prior to and above the nation, there is only natural law'.[57] The constituent power, which emanates from the nation, creates the constitution that frames the manner in which representatives of the nation function through legislative and executive power and is thus unbound.[58] In this regard, the nation bounds the way that representatives will exercise their power, which falls under the label of constituted power.[59] According to Sieyès, not only does the notion of constituent power belong to the people, but it ought to be exercised through representation:

> Thus a purely democratic Constitution becomes, not only impossible in a large society; even in the least extended State, it is way less appropriate to the needs of society, less leading to the aim of political union than the representative constitution, which is the second legitimate form of government.[60]

Here lies one of his major innovations as he distinguishes between the *pouvoir constituant*, which is unlimited and the *pouvoirs constitués*, which are limited in the exercise of their power.[61] The constituent power is thus exercised through a representative body, which embodies the nation.[62] In the French case it was the *Assemblée constituante* (1798–1791). As the nation cannot exercise its power by itself, this occurs through representation of a special kind.

The notion of constituent power, which emerged as a legal tool to achieve the political aim of Sieyès to remove the monarch from the making of the constitution, came to serve a different political theory: liberal constitutionalism. What began as an idealised, reductive representation of political reality, sustaining a certain conception of sovereignty ('by the people'), exercised through representation to curtail the power of government, came to form the basis of political legitimacy for modern liberal constitutions.[63]

Constituent power as the foundation of the constitutional legal order

The notion of constituent power further serves as a justification for legal positivism, which continues to dominate contemporary constitutional legal theory.[64] In this regard, the concept has become the foundation of the entire constitutional legal order. In constitutional legal scholarship, constituent power is not generally treated as a purely legal concept – as traditionally a distinction is made between the notion of *pouvoir constituant originaire* and of *pouvoir constituant dérivé*.[65] This distinction originates in French legal scholarship, where there have been vivid doctrinal discussions given France's tumultuous constitutional history, under the aegis of fourteen constitutions and five republics since 1789. In 1942, Roger Bonnard cemented the conception of the two varieties of constituent power, and this distinction continues to ground constitutional scholarship today.[66]

According to the dominant strand of constitutional legal scholarship, the *pouvoir constituant originaire* belongs to the factual realm, as it is exercised outside of any constitutional provisions; either because none exist, as is the case in the creation of a new state or because it is exercised after a revolution.[67] In contrast, the *pouvoir constituant dérivé* fully belongs in the legal realm and refers to the exercise of constituent power *within* the framework of the constitution, following the procedure established to amend it.[68] This dichotomy remains at the root of most constitutional scholarship.[69] This understanding is shared by most constitutional scholars regardless of their tradition.[70] This is a subtle but important point: the exercise of constituent power *does not* fall within the legal realm when it is exercised outside the modes of revisions laid down by the constitution.

This theoretical understanding does not take away the fact that the *pouvoir constituant originaire* results in the creation of a new constitution; consequently, it has empirically a legal dimension. The emergence of the Belgian constitution, which is still in force today, offers an illustrative example where the exercise of the *pouvoir constituant originaire* was a factual matter. Following protests that began on 25 August 1830, a series of pre-constitutional institutions were set in place, including the Central Committee whose ten members were responsible for the first constitutional draft; however, this Committee had seized power without any mandate.[71] The constitutional draft would be discussed and approved within only three months by the *Congrès National*, which counted 200 elected members.[72] The ten people who first exercised the *pouvoir constituant* were not bound by any pre-existing constitution. In a similar fashion, the members of the Congress were elected following a decree issued by an interim government which also operated without a mandate.[73] While the exercise of the constituent power belongs to the factual realm, it involved legal consequences; a by-product of this exercise of the constituent power following a revolution was the 1831 Belgian Constitution, still in force today. The concept of constituent power always has a legal dimension, but because constitutional scholars rely on a particular philosophy of law, legal positivism, they are unable to examine it from a legal perspective due to their understanding of what is 'legal'.

It is essential for legal positivist constitutional scholars to treat constituent power as a non-legal concept, as their school of thought 'fashions itself on the autonomy of legal ordering'.[74] Explicitly or implicitly, constitutional scholars heavily rely on a Kelsenian conception of constitutional law; what matters most is a norm's validity, and other concerns are outside the realm of legal analysis.[75] A norm is valid if – and only if – it is adopted according to the procedure set up in a higher norm, by an authority whose 'competence can only be based on a norm that authorises the issuing of norms'.[76] Translated to constitution-making, a constitution is valid if – and only if – it has been adopted by the institution with this particular competence. This means that a constitutional norm is only valid according to the procedure laid down in the constitution; in other words, exercising the revision power of the *pouvoir constituant dérivé*.

Kelsen's argument hinges on a 'basic norm' [Grundnorm], which is a logical presupposition that underpins the whole legal system: 'the common source for the validity of all norms that belong to the same order – it is their common reason of validity'.[77] He continues: 'the search for the reason of a norms' validity cannot go indefinitely like the search for the cause of an effect. It must end with a norm which, as the last and highest is presupposed'.[78] Applying this logic to constitutions, it is necessary to go back, in history, to discover the first 'basic norm':

> that cannot have been created in this way and whose validity, therefore, cannot be traced back to a positive norm created by a legal authority; we arrive, instead, at a constitution that became valid in a revolutionary way, that is, either by breach of a former constitution or for a territory that formerly was not the sphere of validity of a constitution and of a national order based on it.[79]

For legal positivists, the constituent power (understood as *pouvoir constituant originaire*) is a logical presupposition, a non-legal concept upon which the entire constitutional legal order is based.[80] Conceiving it as a non-legal concept overcomes the aporia that constitutional scholars face because they consider law through a criterion of validity. The constituent power answers the question of how to justify the basic norm – or norms – that are adopted outside revision powers. In this regard, the concept of constituent power fulfils its role as justifying the whole constitutional edifice. The French constitutional scholar Raymond Carré de Malberg vividly illustrates the non-legal treatment of constituent power in his 1920 opus, *Théorie générale de l'Etat*. According to Malberg, the question is raised when the state has to organise itself to create its first constitution;[81] he ties the legal status of the first constitution to the foundation of the state and considers it 'a pure fact resisting any legal qualification'.[82] Similarly, adopting a new constitution after a revolution is a factual question, with no legal content. Following Malberg's famous dictum 'beyond the Constitution, only fact remains', he unambiguously asserts that the 'legal notion of constituent power implies in itself a pre-existing order and a certain constitutional organisation'.[83]

The notion of constituent power thus plays a central role for constitutional scholars as it serves to found the constitutional legal order. This is not to say that it has not raised discussions regarding its difficulties.[84] David Dyzenhaus writes that 'the idea of constituent power is at best a distraction for legal theory, at worst, when it is deployed by the likes of Schmitt, subversive of the very ideals professed by those who invoke it to understand constitutionalism'.[85] However, the concept is still used today by constitutional scholarship, to sustain a certain theory of law and guide the study of other dimensions of constitutional law. The limitations related to the concept become more acute when the field of analysis is constitution-making in the context of democratic transitions.

Inherent limitations of analysing transnational constitution-making through the lens of constituent power

Examining the transnational dimension of constitution-making through the lens of constituent power has concrete analytical implications. Comparative constitutional law scholarship approaches constitution-making through both functions of constituent power, which leads to theoretical and empirical problems, particularly concerning the study of external actors. These problems are inherent to the concept of constituent power, thus preventing a more comprehensive understanding of transnational constitution-making. The field of comparative constitutional law hinges on both aspects of the notion of constituent power: as a justification for a particular political theory, as well as a theory of law.

Between liberal constitutionalism and legal positivism

There is a segment of the field of comparative constitutional law that is interested in understanding 'how constitutions get off the ground in the first place'.[86] Comparative constitutional scholars grasp constitution-making through the lens of constituent power; indeed, this constitutes the theoretical backbone of the entire field.[87] However, comparative constitutional scholarship does not differentiate between the two different functions of constituent power. As we have seen, the notion of constituent power serves both to justify the exercise of political authority in liberal constitutionalism, as well as to justify the constitutional legal order in legal positivism. As legal positivists, comparative constitutional scholars endeavour to strip away the political from the legal, but their object of study makes this particularly difficult: the creation of a new political order lies clearly within the realm of the political. This difficulty is even more acute in the context of a democratic transition, which is so closely tied to a certain conception of the state (the modern liberal constitutional state), and where the intended direction towards a certain political exercise of power is explicit.

A general overview of the field reveals the extent of this confusion. On one side, the field relies on a legal positivistic understanding of the law, divorcing the legal from the political, as a way to distinguish itself from political science, which until 1989 had been the discipline that studied constitution-making.[88] According to legal positivism, legal analysis is restricted to the validity of the norm; everything else is political. Translated to cases of constitution-making, the key concern is whether the constitution was adopted according to the rule(s) framing its adoption. It follows that comparative constitutional scholars focus the majority of their attention on one legal actor: namely, the actor granted the exercise of constituent power, the one who adopts the constitution. A significant share of the literature is thus devoted to examining the different procedures of adopting a constitution on a case-by-case basis, offering taxonomies of constitution-making bodies – distinguishing between constituent assemblies and roundtables and deciding whether the constitution ought to be adopted by referendum or not.[89]

Legal positivists understand that the constituent power is the justification of the whole constitutional legal order. As they are limiting themselves to analysis of the legal – the adoption of constitutional norms – they tend to avoid treating constituent power as a non-legal concept sustaining the constitutional legal order. Indeed, in a context of democratic transition, particularly in revolutionary settings, it highlights the dilemma of having a constitutional legal order grounded on a non-legal idea. Legal positivists are concerned with preserving legal continuity, as this keeps constitution-making within the realm of the legal. To illustrate, scholars pay significant attention to the notion of 'interim constitution', as a legal document, which operates as a bridge that guarantees legal continuity of the constitutional transition.[90]

At the same time, the field of comparative constitutional law relies on the notion of constituent power, often implicitly, as a justification for the exercise of political power.[91] After all, it is 'the people' that lend legitimacy to a constitution. As Hannah Lerner and David Landau point out, 'the dominant theory of constitution making continues to be constituent power theory. . . . The key underpinning of constituent power theory is that constitution making is a sovereign act of the people to remake their institutional order'.[92] Herein lies the contradiction. Despite embodying a theory of law that promotes the autonomy of the legal from the political, comparative constitutional scholars are ideologically invested in defending liberal constitutional democracy, an *inherently political project*.

The academic field of constitution-making, as a scientific legal discipline and not a political practice, emerged only recently, at the end of the Cold War and the fall of the Berlin Wall, during what is often referred to as the 'third wave' of democratisation.[93] At that time, a substantial number of constitutions were adopted in Eastern and Central Europe, as well as in Africa and South America.[94] It was the *practical* need to draft liberal constitutions that created the *academic* field.[95] Drafting new constitutions required constitution-makers to understand how a foreign norm would fit into their own constitutional system;[96] these 'new democracies' had to borrow 'constitutional norms from abroad'.[97] In this context, comparative constitutional law was used by constitution-makers to draft new constitutions and by other actors involved in the process such as academics who acted as advisors in these processes.[98] Comparative constitutional law was, at that point, deeply tied to the political project of liberal constitutionalism. The discipline of comparative constitutional law emerged at the end of World War II. It had been heavily ideological as 'foreign constitutional systems were often studied as part of Soviet legal studies, and, respectively studies on Western bourgeois state law'.[99] After the fall of the Soviet Union, there was no longer an alternative model and the field became almost exclusively shaped by liberal constitutionalism.[100]

Perhaps due to its origins as a field driven by practical necessity, comparative constitutional law is traditionally more interested in the concrete concerns of constitution-making rather than by theoretical debates. While the ideological underpinnings are generally implicit, they are further proven by the blurry distinction that exists between the academic legal scholars and practitioners of democratic assistance. Several instances of 'grey literature', namely organisational or governmental reports, are referenced as scientific sources. For instance, the oft-quoted *Framing the State in Times of Transition: Case Studies in Constitution Making* published in 2010 by the United States Institute of Peace, an American federal institution, explicitly positions itself as a liberal project.[101] Another instance of grey literature is the series of publications from International IDEA, published by academics but clearly oriented towards a liberal political position, which comes as no surprise as International IDEA is an international organisation that promotes 'democracy' worldwide.[102] This liberal orientation is further highlighted by scholars' concern with making liberal constitutions 'work'; there is a normative component underpinning the theoretical analysis. What matters is that the constitution-making process is able to uphold liberal ideals. Before proceeding any further, it should be noted that this book does not engage in a normative discussion of the liberal ideals of constitution-making. From a scientific standpoint, the fact that this normative component tends to go unacknowledged raises important questions.

According to the general creed, there should be increased participation in constitution-making processes, which will lead the process to be people-owned and thus last longer.[103] The descriptive accounts of the adoption of constitutions are imbued with normative undertones, such that they not only describe the constitution-making process but also prescribe what ought to be done to increase ownership of the constitution by the people or which institutional design is better suited to draft a new constitution.[104] Cheryl Saunders argues that different arrangements to adopt the constitution ought to be chosen with 'legitimacy and effectiveness in mind':

> Various different mechanisms are available for this purpose, alone or in combination with each other. Three of the most common are as follows. The first is an advisory body of some kind, constituted by experts or representatives or both. The second is an elected body, which may be either a regular legislature or a specially constituted Constitutional Assembly. The third is a referendum. Each of these mechanisms has strengths and weaknesses.[105]

While others, such as David Landau, warn against the practical issues emerging from the constitution-making process in the exercise of constituent power: 'the central challenge of constitution-making is not to achieve a higher form of law-making but rather to constrain unilateral exercises of power'.[106] Once again, we see the confusion between the two functions of the concept of constituent power. On one side, the field restricts itself to examining the adoption of the constitution, while on the other it engages in normatively loaded descriptions of the phenomenon. This has concrete analytical implications when it comes to studying external actors' involvement in constitution-making.

Implications for the analysis of external actors in constitution-making processes

The analytical implications of using the theory of constituent power limit the possibility of a comprehensive examination of external actors' involvement in constitution-making.

As legal positivists, comparative constitutional scholars tend to focus on one aspect of the constitution-making process: the adoption of the constitution. It follows that scholars end up addressing only a small portion of the external actors actually involved in the process. If the legal aspect of constitution-making is limited to its adoption and focus is only given to the actors formally adopting the norm, this conceals other important external actors involved in constitution-making.

Restricting the scope of analysis of constitution-making to its adoption leads scholars to focus on external actors whose involvement is legally framed, that is to say, when external actors involvement is authorised under international law.[107] Outside of these cases, the influence of external actors is treated as outside the study of constitution-making. As Andrew Arato notes, 'influence does not violate autochthony, and thus does not require authorisation, or limitations as to agency or scope'.[108] In the same vein, Zaid Al-Ali and Philip Dann reject cases from their analysis that involve external actors whose involvement has a 'marginal influence', which consists 'only of advice from external experts, which is sought voluntarily by the domestic actors while control over process and substance of the constitution remains clearly in the hands of the nation at hand'.[109] While Lerner and Landau have recently argued that the porosity of constitution-making 'could be viewed as a paradigm shift in the field',[110] these discussions primarily focus on international involvement after the 2005 Constitution of Iraq.[111]

Limiting analysis of external actors to those formally involved results in a restriction in the cases examined, mostly centring on Bosnia, Iraq, Kosovo, and South Sudan. Many other constitution-making processes are simply not addressed, despite the fact of external actors being present. This leads to a partial description of the legal phenomenon, as several actors involved are positioned outside the framework of analysis as they are not formally involved. Some of these actors include international non-governmental organisations, as well as other international organisations that are not formally involved.[112]

Only examining external actors that are formally involved in the adoption of constitutions has deep theoretical and descriptive consequences; primarily, it makes it impossible to develop a theory of external actor involvement that comprehensively describes the legal phenomenon of constitution-making. One specific aspect of constitution-making that is under-examined is constitutional drafting. With a legal positivistic lens, who drafts the constitutional text behind closed doors is not relevant. What is important from a legal standpoint is whether the constitution has been adopted according to the procedure put in place during the transition, often through some kind of interim constitution. The transnational element is and has been a core feature of constitution-making; however, constituent power, the very concept that forms the theoretical backbone, is inherently limiting when it comes to describing external involvement. This results in a restricted focus on cases where external actors are legally framed, with their involvement understood to be an exception to the rule where a constitution is made 'by the people, for the people', constituting them as exception to the dominant understanding of constitution-making leaving aside other cases where external actor involvement has taken place during constitution-making. Relying on a theoretical approach centred on the concept of constituent power prevents the development of a theory that can adequately capture the involvement of the complete range of external actors that are present during constitution-making.

A solution to this impasse could be the expansion of the exercise of constituent power from a legal perspective beyond the adoption of the constitution. This would allow analysis to capture more than the sole legal actor who adopts the constitution; as it stands, the field of comparative constitutional scholarship largely overlooks other legal actors that are involved in constitution-making processes. Making a new constitution is an expansive activity, encompassing a series of decisions from different legal actors, including: who will exercise the constituent power; how it will be organised; what the conditions of its representation are; and how the constitution will be drafted.

Focusing only on the legal actor that adopts the constitution inevitably leaves aside other important legal actors that are involved in constitution-making. Alexis Blouët has demonstrated the diversity of actors that exercise the constituent power, applying a conceptual framework outside of the legal positivist tradition – building on the work of Olivier Beaud's *La puissance de l'Etat* – to the making of the 2014 Egyptian Constitution.[113] Beaud challenges the idea that the *pouvoir constituant originaire* is non-legal, identifying two dimensions within the concept: one is the 'deconstituent power' (*déconstitutant*), which breaks the previous constitutional legal order and the power '*reconstituant*', which relates to the establishment of a new constitution.[114]

Beaud argues that it is only the latter that can bear legal content[115] and points out the fact that the institutional shape of the constituent power can be extremely diverse, especially related to pre-constitutional law.[116] Blouët's attempt to analyse the exercise of constituent power from a legal perspective in Egypt exposes the variety of legal actors that exercise this power. For example, while traditional analysis would centre on the National Constituent Assembly, Blouët focuses on the Supreme Council of the Armed Forces.[117] However, expanding legal analysis of the exercise of the constituent power to other stages of the constitution-making process beyond the adoption of the constitution does not solve the dilemma in the case of external actors. It still focuses on the adoption of a norm, even if it is more expansive; in the case of external actors, analysis based on constituent power would remain restricted to those formally adopting the norms.

Other alternative conceptions of constituent power have emerged, recognising the limiting assumptions of the concept, such as being nation-bound. Scholars have identified the tension inherent in the fact of empirical constitution-making not being a purely nation-bound exercise.

Chaihark Hahm and Sung Ho Kim, following a well-documented examination of constitution-making processes in Japan and Korea, explain:

> Constitutional founding is rarely a pristine domestic affair. The demise of the status quo ante, which necessitates a new founding, is often the result of a constellation of international factors. The emergence of a new international order also has deep repercussions for the constitution making of a state embedded within it.[118]

Similarly, Arato points out that historically, constitution-making has involved a 'myriad of external actors'.[119]

The literature has acknowledged the problems posed by constituent power in capturing the real-world phenomenon of constitution-making.[120] With regard to the transnational dimension, the main alternative comes from a strand of scholarship, 'global constitutionalism', which often erases the nation altogether and considers the constitutionalisation of a transnational or global order through a transnational constituent power. Anthony Lang and Antje Wiener, for instance, point out that there are a variety of constituent powers in the global order: 'various groups, agencies and modes of activism together can be understood as providing a kind of representative community for the international community as a whole'.[121] Nico Kirsch argues that the notion of constituent power ought to be understood as a *pouvoir irritant* in the post-national order,[122] while Alexander Somek wonders if constituent power could be a transnational concept.[123] Finally, Mathias Kumm defends a post-nationalist conception of constitutionalism, arguing that:

> The idea of constituent power as a normative concept has a limited but important role to play within the context of a post-nationalist,

> post-positivist conception of constitutionalism. Within such a conception, 'We the People' and 'the international community' are co-constitutive for state constitutions and international law as central components of an integrative conception of global public law.[124]

These proposals, however, remain unsatisfactory to address the research questions as the explanatory component is still missing; all that changes here is the normative underpinning from the nation state to the global. The concept of constituent power is a concept that serves a certain theory of law, largely understood as nation-bound. What these proposals show is that the concept serves another theory of law, global constitutionalism, but still does not clarify how constitutions are made; it simply treats the 'global' as the legal order and, in doing so, further mystifies the constitution-making process. The key problem is that these alternative proposals conflate analytically the power to make the constitution and the process of constitution-making.

Some scholars attempting to understand the dialectical nature of transnational constitution-making have moved away from the notion of constituent power altogether. For example, Kevin Cope has developed a third way of reconciling international–national frictions, via the concept of 'intermestic constitutionalism', assessing the involvement of the international community in the drafting of the Constitution of South Sudan. He argues, for instance, that the rights and freedoms provisions of the constitutions will be the by-product of international influence whereas 'structural provisions – for instance, federalism, separation of powers, and limited government – will reflect the institutional self-interests of the domestic drafters'.[125] To study the transnational dimension of constitution-making, a different theoretical framework is needed.

Towards an antifoundationalist approach to constitution-making

Relying on the concept of constituent power to anchor the analysis of external actor involvement leads to an incomplete picture of what is actually happening on the ground during constitution-making, as the scope is limited to external actors that are formally involved (i.e. legally framed). A law and society approach to constitution-making involves embracing an antifoundationalist approach, challenging the deeply entrenched foundationalist view that underpins the dominant understanding of constitutional democratic founding. Foundationalism posits founding as a single, authoritative moment that constitutes democratic states and fixes in its constitution the principles, rights, and values that guide its people.[126] This paradigm grounds the way scholars think about how constitutions are made: at a particular point in time, the constituent power, expressing the will of the people, creates the constitution that will govern the new democratic polity. Founding is thus conceived as a superlative moment in time that provides legitimacy to a newly adopted constitution.

Due to disciplinary tradition, the vast majority of constitutional scholarship is based on some kind of foundationalist perspective; this is particularly the case when it comes to the study of constitution-making. As a discipline, constitutional law has been deeply impacted by rationalism since its birth in the mid-nineteenth century.[127] From the beginning, the science of constitutional law has relied on ideas from eighteenth-century political theory in order to explain positive law.[128] Most textbooks of constitutional law still include early modern philosophical doctrines, such as Rousseau's social contract, Montesquieu's theory of the separation of power, and Sièyes' theory of representation.[129]

The constituent power carries inherent limitations related to its reliance on foundationalism. Angelica Bernal offers a forceful critique of foundationalist theories, highlighting the normative implications related to constitution-making.[130] Bernal argues that a foundationalist approach prevents a complete understanding of what happens when a constitution is made,[131] as it 'distorts the past, masks undemocratic politics in the present, and obscures the multiplicity of founding action and actors across time',[132] ultimately erasing certain actors that do not fit the narrative of an 'authoritative founding moment', distorting the process by casting it in an 'apolitical' light.[133] As Bernal explains:

> It is also a distorting picture. Most troubling, it renders flat contingency and power struggle in the making of political orders, and masks the disagreements, conflicts, injustices, violences, and exclusions present in the original founding events of constitutional democracies.[134]

Bernal contends that it is necessary to move away from the quasi-mythical figure of the founder – which in the context of constitution-making is the constituent power – to a more nuanced account of the deeply political dynamics and the broader range of actors immersed within.[135] In constitutional scholarship, when scholars refer to this 'founding moment' they refer to the *constituant* as a single, apolitical figure that expresses 'the will of the people'.

In the field of comparative constitutional law, Chaihark Hahm and Sung Ho Kim have raised similar conclusions about the 'short-sightedness' of the literature on constitution-making, following analysis of the making of the constitutions of Korea (1948) and Japan (1946). Their analysis runs counter to much of the field of comparative constitutional law as they challenge the 'conventional creed' regarding what constitutes 'the people', which underpins constitutional founding:

> Positing a solipsistic people that has no relation to external others or to its own past only hampers our understanding of the complex process

> through which a constitutional order is founded. It promotes the mistaken view that the legitimacy of a connotational order is necessarily negated or diminished by even the slightest hint of external forces.[136]

Challenging the concept of constituent power requires shifting to an antifoundationalist theoretical approach. This book embraces an antifoundationalist understanding of the creation of constitutional legal orders, relying on Bernal's framework of 'founding-beyond-origins'.[137] For Bernal, founding is not a fixed moment in time where principles and values emerge ex nihilo but is instead characterised by political action and struggle situated within existing institutions that impact the founding process itself.[138] This approach involves moving from the singular, quasi-mythical figure of the founder to more 'complex political dynamics and the broader range of actors immersed in them',[139] allowing not only an expanded scope of 'who counts as a founder' but also 'how foundings take shape'.[140] This theoretical backdrop offers theoretical and empirical benefits to the comparative constitutional scholar, allowing for a more comprehensive understanding of the transnational dimension of constitution-making and a broader scope of external actors to be included in analysis.

Conclusion

Studies of constitution-making that are centred on the notion of constituent power are inherently limited in terms of their ability to address external actor involvement. Because the concept grounds a particular theory of law, legal positivism, the scope of external actors is thus restricted to those whose involvement is legally framed. This book argues that the transnational dimension of constitution-making demands an alternative analytical approach. It does not call for rejecting the notion of constituent power altogether and acknowledges that the concept can be analytically useful to study other dimensions of constitution-making. Building on Angélica Bernal's antifoundationalist theory, this book offers an alternative conceptual lens to examine the involvement of external actors in the context of a democratic transition during an under-studied phase of constitution-making: constitutional drafting. The next chapters develop a new theoretical framework to study the transnational dimension of constitution-making and aims to challenge the current understanding of how constitutions are made, where the constituent power and the process of making a constitution are conflated, resulting in a partial picture of how the process unfolds on the ground.

Notes

1 Antoni Abat i Ninet and Mark Tushnet, *The Arab Spring: An Essay on Revolution and Constitutionalism* (Edward Elgar Publishing 2015) 145–58, 167–84; Rafâa Ben Achour and Sana Ben Achour, 'La transition démocratique en Tunisie: Entre légalité constitutionnelle et légitimité révolutionnaire' (2012) 4 Revue française

de droit constitutionnel 715; David Mednicoff, 'A Tale of Three Constitutions: Common Drives and Diverse Outcomes in Post-2010 Arab Legal Politics' (2014) 28 Temple International & Comparative Law Journal 215.

2 Alicia Pastor y Camarasa, 'Demystifying How Constitutions Are Made: External Actors' Modes of Actions in the 2014 Tunisian Constitution' [2022] Michigan Journal of Law & Society 51.

3 ibid.

4 Yaniv Roznai, '"We the People", "Oui, the People" and the Collective Body: Perceptions of Constituent Power' in Gary Jeffrey Jacobsohn and Miguel Schor (eds), *Comparative Constitutional Theory* (Edward Elgar Publishing 2018) 295.

5 While it is commonly referred simply as 'constitutionalism' this chapter refers to 'liberal constitutionalism'. First it allows us to contrast with other types of constitutionalism (such as authoritarian constitutionalism). Second it shows the link between constitutionalism and liberalism. The notion of constituent power also sustains another political ideology – which would be the populist strand with Carl Schmitt and Antonio Negri representing these positions.

6 The notion of constitutionalism also relates to the merge between the formal and material constitution. See Pascal Mahon and Sophie Weerts, 'La procédure d'adoption et de révision de la Constitution fédérale' (2020) 3 Verfassungsrecht der Schweiz/Droit constitutionnel suisse 1883.

7 Constitutionalism does not per se require the existence of a written constitution, but a written constitution is seen as a way to materialise what unites different understandings of constitutionalism; constitutionalism 'is concerned with the fundamental principle that governmental power requires constraint in the interests of social order'. Andrew Godden and John Morison, *Constitutionalism* (OUP 2017) §2.

8 Tom Ginsburg, Aziz Huq and Mila Versteeg, 'The Coming Demise of Liberal Constitutionalism?' (2018) 85 The University of Chicago Law Review 239.

9 The concept of constituent power also serves as a foundation for other legal philosophies such as natural law. See the discussion by Joel Colón-Ríos, *Constituent Power and the Law* (OUP 2020) 151–58.

10 Martin Loughlin, 'The Concept of Constituent Power' (2014) 13 European Journal of Political Theory 218–19.

11 For a descriptive and critical account of the emerging standard of participation and constitution-making see the work of Abrak Saati, 'Participatory Constitution-Making as a Transnational Legal Norm: Why Does It Stick in Some Contexts and Not in Others' (2017) 2 UC Irvine Journal of International, Transnational & Comparative Law 113.

12 Loughlin (n 10) 219.

13 Indeed, Sieyès himself considered it to be a wholly French invention. During a speech on the topic of the 1791 French Constitution, he claimed that, 'a sensible and useful idea was introduced in 1788: Namely the distinction between constituent power and constituted powers. This idea belongs among the discoveries that have moved science forward, and it is owed to the French'. Emmanuel Joseph Sieyès, *The Essential Political Writings* (Brill 2014) 159.

14 Will Adams, *The First American Constitutions: Republican Ideology and the Making of the State Constitutions in the Revolutionary Era* (Rowman & Littlefield Publishers 2001) 63. Martin Loughlin traces back the use of the term 'constituent power' to mid-century England. See Martin Loughlin, 'Constituent Power Subverted: From English Constitutional Argument to British Constitutional Practice' in Martin Loughlin and Neil Walker (eds), *The Paradox of Constitutionalism Constituent Power and Constitutional Form* (OUP 2007) 28.

15 Letter of Thomas Young to the Inhabitants of Vermont, a Free and Independent State, bounding on the River Connecticut and Lake Champlain. Philadelphia, 11 April 1777 [Emphasis added] in Zadock Thompson, *History of Vermont, Natural, Civil, and Statistical, in Three Parts* (Chauncey Goodrich 1842) 106.
16 Georg Jellinek, *Allgemeine Staatslehre* (Verlag von 0 Haring 1914) 522; Georg Jellinek, *L'Etat moderne et son droit: Deuxième partie [Allgemeine Staatslehre]* (V Giard & E Brière 1913) 193. [My own translation].
17 Albert Dicey, *Introduction to the Study of the Law of the Constitution* (Macmillan and Co 1965) 85. [Emphasis added].
18 Chris Thornhill, 'Contemporary Constitutionalism and the Dialectic of Constituent Power' (2012) 1 Global Constitutionalism 369–70.
19 Ulrich Preuss, 'Constitutionalism' in Edward Craig (ed), *Routledge Encyclopedia of Philosophy* (Routledge 1998) 1.
20 Andrea Buratti, *Western Constitutionalism: History, Institutions, Comparative Law* (Springer 2019) 2.
21 David Dyzenhaus, 'Constitutionalism in an Old Key: Legality and Constituent Power' (2012) 1 Global Constitutionalism 229.
22 Armel Le Divellec, 'Le style des Constitutions écrites dans l'histoire moderne: Une esquisse sur les trois types de l'écriture constitutionnelle (XVIIe–XXe siècles)' (2013) 9 Jus Politicum 1, 13–14.
23 John Locke, *Second Treatise of Government and a Letter Concerning Toleration* (OUP 2016) 40.
24 Bruno Aguilera-Barchet, *A History of Western Public Law* (Springer 2015) 351.
25 United States of America, The Fundamental Constitutions of Carolina (1 March 1669) The Avalon Project Yale University.
26 Carlos Miguel Pimentel, 'Du contrat social à la norme suprême: L'invention du pouvoir consituant' [2009] Jus Politicum 1.
27 Letter to John Trumbull cited in Barbara Arneil, *John Locke and America: The Defence of English Colonialism* (OUP 1996) 187.
28 Gordon Wood, *The Creation of the American Republic, 1776–1787* (Norton 1993) 9, 274.
29 Emer de Vattel, *Le droits des gens ou principes de la loi naturelle appliqués à la conduite et aux affaires des nations et des souverains* (Imprimerie de la Société Typographique 1773) 31–32.
30 ibid 36–37; Olivier Beaud, *La puissance de l'Etat* (Presses Universitaires de France 1994) 206.
31 Rainer Grote, 'Definition of Constitutions' in Rainer Grote (ed), *Max Planck Encyclopedia of Comparative Constitutional Law* (OUP 2017) §8.
32 Preuss (n 19) 1. See also Chaihark Hahm and Sung Ho Kim, *Making We the People: Democratic Constitutional Founding in Postwar Japan and South Korea* (CUP 2015) 5.
33 Angelica Maria Bernal, *Beyond Origins: Rethinking Founding in a Time of Constitutional Democracy* (OUP 2017) 78.
34 Poland, Constitution of Poland (1791) Constitute Project.
35 Le Divellec (n 22) 9.
36 Hawaii Nation, 'Draft Constitution of 14 January 1893' (Unknown) <www.hawaii-nation.org/constitution-1893.html> accessed October 2023.
37 Loughlin (n 10) 219.
38 ibid 219–20.
39 Quoted in Martin Loughlin, *The Idea of Public Law* (OUP 2003) 136.
40 Loughlin (n 10) 219–20.
41 Bernal (n 33) 79.

42 See Edmund Morgan, *Inventing the People: The Rise of Popular Sovereignty in England and America* (WW Norton 1988) 208–11.
43 Bernal (n 33) 79.
44 ibid 80.
45 National Archives, 'Declaration of Independence: A Transcription' (4 July 1776) <www.archives.gov/founding-docs/declaration-transcript> accessed July 2018. [Emphasis added].
46 Emmanuel Joseph Sieyès, *Qu'est-ce que le Tiers-Etat?* (Librairie Droz 1970).
47 Lucia Rubinelli, *Constituent Power: A History* (CUP 2020) 44–45.
48 Alexis Blouët, 'Le pouvoir pré-constituant: Contribution à l'étude de l'exercice du pouvoir constituant originaire à partir du cas de l'Egypte après la révolution du 25 janvier (Février 2011–Juillet 2013)' (PhD dissertation, Université Paris 1 Panthéon Sorbonne 2018) 21–22.
49 Sieyès (n 13) 87.
50 Emmanuel Joseph Sieyès, *Préliminaire de la Constitution: Reconnoissance et exposition raisonnée des droits de l'homme et du citoyen* (Chez Baudouin 1789) 35. [My own translation].
51 Sieyès (n 13) 87–88.
52 ibid 88.
53 ibid.
54 ibid.
55 ibid 89.
56 ibid 88–89.
57 ibid 89.
58 ibid.
59 ibid.
60 Emmanuel Joseph Sieyès, *Observations sur le rapport du comité de Constitution concernant la nouvelle organisation de la France* (Chez Baudouin 1789) 35. [My own translation].
61 Dieter Grimm, *Constitutionalism: Past, Present, and Future* (OUP 2016) 12.
62 Sieyès (n 46) 181.
63 Chaihark Hahm and Sung Ho Kim, 'To Make "We the People": Constitutional Founding in Postwar Japan and South Korea' (2010) 8 International Journal of Constitutional Law 800.
64 Tamara El Khoury, 'Pouvoir Constituant' in Rainer Grote (ed), *Max Planck Encyclopedia of Comparative Constitutional Law* (OUP 2017) 1.
65 For clarity's sake, in this book when we refer to constituent power, we refer to the *pouvoir constituant originaire*; we will use the expression 'revision power' to refer to the *pouvoir constituant dérivé*.
66 Roger Bonnard, *Les actes constitutionnels de 1940* (Librairie générale de droit et de juriprudence 1942) 7, 14.
67 ibid 7.
68 ibid 14.
69 Contra see Beaud (n 30) 223.
70 Colón-Ríos (n 9) 4.
71 Vincent Dujardin, 'Les droits constitutionnels originaires' in Marc Verdussen and Nicolas Bonbled (eds), *Les droits constitutionnels en Belgique* (Bruylant 2011) 40.
72 The National Congress will first meet on 10 November 1830 and will adopt the Constitution on 7 February 1831.
73 John Gilissen, 'Le caractère collégial des premières formes de gouvernement et d'admnistration de l'Etat belge (1830–1831)' (1981) 3 Belgisch Tijdschrift voor Nieuwste Geschiedenis 609, 612.

74 Loughlin (n 10) 219.
75 Andrew Arato, *Post Sovereign Constitution Making: Learning and Legitimacy* (OUP 2016) 1.
76 Hans Kelsen, *Pure Theory of Law* (The Lawbook Exchange 2005) 194.
77 ibid 195.
78 ibid 194.
79 ibid 200.
80 Arato (n 75) 1.
81 Raymond Carré de Malberg, *Contribution à la théorie générale de l'Etat spécialement d'après les données fournies par le droit constitutionnel français: Tome Premier* (Sirey 1922) 484.
82 ibid 66. [My own translation].
83 ibid 500. [My own translation].
84 See proposals from Arato (n 75) 4; Amal Sethi, 'Looking Beyond the Constituent Power Theory: The Theory of Equitable Elite Bargaining' [2023] Global Constitutionalism 1.
85 Dyzenhaus (n 22) 257.
86 Mark Tushnet, 'Comparative Constitutional Law' in Mathias Reimann and Reinhard Zimmermann (eds), *The Oxford Handbook of Comparative Law* (OUP 2017) 1234.
87 David Landau and Hanna Lerner, *Comparative Constitution Making* (Edward Elgar Publishing 2019) 1; Claude Klein and András Sajó, *Constitution-Making: Process and Substance* (OUP 2012) 421.
88 Tushnet (n 86) 1228.
89 For an overview of the state of the field see David Landau and Hanna Lerner, 'Introduction to Comparative Constitution Making: The State of the Field' in David Landau and Hanna Lerner (eds), *Comparative Constitution Making* (Edward Elgar Publishing 2019).
90 See Silvia Suteu, *Eternity Clauses in Democratic Constitutionalism* (OUP 2021).
91 The field of comparative constitutional law has engaged very little in the fertile scholarly discussions that have animated constitutional theory more broadly in recent years, regarding the constituent power in revolutionary contexts or the dilemmas that the constituent power poses for democratic founding. See Beaud (n 30); Colón-Ríos (n 9); Claude Klein, *Théorie et pratique du pouvoir constituant* (Presses Universitaires de France 1996); Nimer Sultany, *Law and Revolution: Legitimacy and Constitutionalism After the Arab Spring* (OUP 2017); Loughlin (n 10); Thornhill (n 18); Geneviève Nootens, 'Constituent Power and People-as-the-Governed: About the "Invisible" People of Political and Legal Theory' (2015) 4 Global Constitutionalism 137; Zoran Oklopcic, *Beyond the People: Social Imaginary and Constituent Imagination* (OUP 2018); Andreas Kalyvas, 'Popular Sovereignty, Democracy, and the Constituent Power' (2005) 12 Constellations 223.
92 Landau and Lerner (n 89) 5.
93 Tushnet (n 86) 1228.
94 See Samuel Huntington, 'Democracy's Third Wave' (1991) 2 Journal of Democracy 12.
95 Michel Rosenfeld and András Sajó, 'Introduction' in Michel Rosenfeld and András Sajó (eds), *The Oxford Handbook of Comparative Constitutional Law* (OUP 2012) 7.
96 ibid 10.
97 ibid 2.
98 ibid 7, 9.

99 ibid 6.

100 It is evidenced by the concern of the field of the rise of 'illiberal' constitutionalism. See Timea Drinoczi and Agnieszka Bien-Kacala, 'Illiberal Constitutionalism: The Case of Hungary and Poland' (2019) 20 German Law Journal 1140; Silvia Suteu, 'The Populist Turn in Central and Eastern Europe: Is Deliberative Democracy Part of the Solution?' (2019) 15 European Constitutional Law Review 488.

101 Laurel Miller and Louis Aucoin, *Framing the State in Times of Transition: Case Studies in Constitution Making* (US Institute of Peace 2010). Cited for instance by Andrew Arato, 'Conventions, Constituent Assemblies, and Round Tables: Models, Principles and Elements of Democratic Constitution-Making' (2012) 1 Global Constitutionalism 173, 182; Landau and Lerner (n 89) 1; Cheryl Saunders, 'Constitution-Making in the 21st Century' [2012] International Review of Law 1, 6.

102 See studies by constitutional scholars quoting reports from International IDEA. Carina Barbosa Gouvea and Jayme Benvenuto, 'United Nations Assistance to Constitution-Making Processes: Pre-Constituent and Constituent phases' (2019) 75 Revista da Faculdade de Direito da Universidade Federal de Minas Gerais 65, 68; Donald Horowitz, 'Constitution-Making: A Process Filled with Constraint' (2006) 12 Review of Constitutional Studies 1, 3; Cheryl Saunders, 'International Involvement in Constitution Making' in David Landau and Hanna Lerner (eds), *Comparative Constitution Making* (Edward Elgar Publishing 2019) 73.

103 Contra see Tom Ginsburg, Zachary Elkins and Justin Blount, 'Does the Process of Constitution-Making Matter?' (2009) 5 Annual Review of Law and Social Science 201; Klein and Sajó (n 87) 424.

104 Arato (n 101); Coel Kirkby and Christina Murray, 'Constitution-Making in Anglophone Africa: We the People?' in Muna Ndulo and Mamoudou Gazibo (eds), *Growing Democracy in Africa: Elections, Accountable Governance, and Political Economy* (Cambridge Publishers 2016); Tushnet (n 86) 1228.

105 Saunders (n 101) 6–7.

106 David Landau, 'Constitution-Making Gone Wrong' (2012) 64 Alabama Law Review 923.

107 Marie Guimezanes, 'Les transitions constitutionnelles "internationalisées": Étude de droit interne' [2015] Revue française de droit constitutionnel 801.

108 Andrew Arato, 'Constitution-Making' in Anthony Lang and Antje Wiener (eds), *Handbook on Global Constitutionalism* (Edward Elgar Publishing 2017) 285.

109 Philipp Dann and Zaid Al-Ali, 'The Internationalized Pouvoir Constituant – Constitution-Making Under External Influence in Iraq, Sudan and East Timor' (2006) 10 Max Planck Yearbook of United Nations Law 423, 429.

110 Landau and Lerner (n 89) 7.

111 ibid.

112 Christina Murray and Cindy Wittke, 'International Institutions, Constitution-Making and Gender' in Helen Irving (ed), *Constitutions and Gender* (Edward Elgar Publishing 2017) 124.

113 Blouët (n 48).

114 Beaud (n 30) 223.

115 ibid.

116 ibid 223, 266.

117 Blouët (n 48) 230.

118 Hahm and Kim (n 63) 813.

119 Arato (n 108) 287.

120 Sultany (n 91).

121 Anthony Lang and Antje Wiener, 'A Constitutionalising Global Order: An Introduction' in Anthony Lang and Antje Wiener (eds), *Handbook on Global Constitutionalism* (Edward Elgar 2017) 3.
122 Nico Krisch, 'Pouvoir Constituant and Pouvoir Irritant in the Postnational Order' (2016) 14 International Journal of Constitutional Law 657.
123 Alexander Somek, 'Constituent Power in National and Transnational Contexts' (2012) 3 Transnational Legal Theory 31, 26.
124 Mattias Kumm, 'Constituent Power, Cosmopolitan Constitutionalism, and Post-Positivist Law' (2016) 14 International Journal of Constitutional Law 697, 711.
125 Kevin Cope, 'The Intermestic Constitution: Lessons From the World's Newest Nation' (2012) 53 Virginia Journal of International Law 667, 683.
126 Bernal (n 33) 1.
127 On the tradition of constitutional scholarship influenced by empiricism in France see Julien Lainé, 'Empirisme et conceptualisme en droit constitutionnel' (PhD dissertation, Université Lille II 2011) 12.
128 ibid 36.
129 Julien Lainé has done an in-depth study of French textbooks of constitutional law, particularly on Montesquieu's theory of the separation of powers.
130 Bernal (n 33) 3.
131 ibid 2.
132 ibid 4.
133 ibid 2.
134 ibid.
135 ibid 10.
136 Hahm and Kim (n 32) 65. See also Oklopcic (n 91).
137 Bernal (n 33) 2.
138 Bernal's framework also allows to engage with other aspects of the political dynamics that are beyond the scope of this inquiry, such as examining the involvement of civil society or of different political actors present in the constitution-making process.
139 Bernal (n 33) 10.
140 ibid 11.

Chapter 2

Unpacking liberal legalism

In 1960, at the request of the emperor Haïlé Sellassié, René David, one of the figureheads of the discipline of comparative law, was invited alongside two other foreign experts to draft the new Ethiopian Civil Code. In his conference made at the *Société de législation comparée* on 3 April 1962, he details his experience in drafting the Civil Code. He explains how Ethiopian law was in a pre-codification state of a disorganised state: 'there was no code, very few laws (3); there were in Ethiopia no compendia of jurisprudence or works of doctrine'.[1] He continues explaining:

> If this be true in developed countries, it must be even more so in countries like Ethiopia, that are less developed, where everyone, and especially government leaders, wish to work a revolution that will close this gap.[2]

David sees the role of law as a catalyser for Ethiopia to reach civilisation and considers codification to be a tool to 'catch up' on its European counterpart. This understanding of the role of the law in legal reforms, which still pervades today, is what this chapter aims to unpack.

This chapter discusses liberal legalism, one of the pillars of the analytical framework – labelled 'the development enterprise' – used in this book to examine external actors' involvement in constitution-making. Motivating this analytical framework is David Kennedy's argument that it is essential to expose the implicit 'background of common sense' and the fact that 'background ideas about the world – often experienced as "facts" rather than "ideas"– shape the world before people set to work on the problems they see with the knowledge they have'.[3] The development enterprise is characterised by two core features that sustain it across time: the paradigm of liberal legalism and the figure of the expert. A paradigm refers to 'basic assumptions in social thought contain[ing] a cognitive map of relations among social phenomena',[4] which may or may not be empirically based.[5] Within the development enterprise, this refers to a particular set of beliefs about how law can impact economic and political change. Following the paradigm of liberal legalism, legal reforms are treated as a catalyst to reach liberal democracy

DOI: 10.4324/9781003386186-4

that can be achieved through importing rational modern law.[6] So understood, these reforms had to be undertaken because they followed a process of rationalisation. According to liberal legalism, as the West had already undergone a process of rationalisation, by mimicking the legal framework of the West a Third World territory could also reach political and economic development in the same manner.[7] As such, law is essential to the development enterprise as it is necessary to implement and translate political doctrines into tangible policy.[8] As David Kennedy explains, public law was key to achieving the goal of political and economic development:

> Industrialization demanded the creation of numerous public law institutions, established by statute and implemented by public law bureaucracies. . . . Legislation was necessary to establish tariffs, subsidies, exchange controls, marketing boards, and all the other elements of the system. A vastly expanded administrative apparatus, with rule making, licensing, and other legal authority would need to be set up.[9]

The actor that carries out this process of rationalisation is the 'expert'. Offering legal expertise to accelerate these social goals was the raison d'être of the development enterprise and continues to play a role in channelling the paradigm of liberal legalism that is shared by external actors.[10] The figure of the expert is developed in the next chapter.

To establish the analytical lens of the development enterprise, this chapter draws from a variety of literatures that broadly relate to legal reform often of a legislative nature, undertaken in the context of structural economic and political reforms in Third World territories. It puts into dialogue scholars from social sciences from, in particular, history of colonialism, development studies, and Third World Approaches to International Law (TWAIL). These literatures are particularly relevant to the present study since legal reform in development settings has been characterised by foreign involvement.

Because the development enterprise constitutes the central analytical lens of this book, several caveats are in order. The chapter focuses on the transnational dimensions of the development enterprise. The history of legal reform is more complex and includes periods of resistance and agency from political and legal actors from Third World territories. However, these discussions remain outside the scope of the present study.[11] While aspects of the development enterprise have been examined by different disciplines – from economics to sociology, political science to history – this book pays closest attention to those that have emerged in the realm of political science, as the literature regarding political development is particularly useful.[12] On that note, while there is a clear relationship between political and economic development, the focus of this study is largely political development. Further, while this book acknowledges the changes that have occurred with the political independence of territories that were previously colonised, it aims to emphasise the pervading traits characterising transnational involvement in legal reforms.

A final caveat is particularly crucial to bear in mind: this chapter deals with the paradigm of liberal legalism, which is characterised by latent, implicit principles and aims concealed behind a more explicit, public-facing discourse. In this regard, the 'civilising mission' is an illustration of the implicit-explicit levels of discourse, as the idea of a benevolent 'civilising mission' served to legitimise colonialism and to extract resources from Third World territories.[13] Similarly, the violence and suppression that characterised these 'missions' occurred under the banner of 'civilising'.[14] The following discussion aims to understand and expose the set of explicit beliefs and the particular paradigm that underpinned (and indeed continues to underpin) legal reforms in Third World territories.

A key contribution of this book is to provide an alternative understanding of the transnational dimension of constitution-making by offering a new conceptual lens, which captures the complete range of external actors involved in the process, as well as their often tacit rationales. Further, the development enterprise reveals the continuity of the paradigm of liberal legalism that underpins legal reform, despite its different rebrandings: from colonisation to today's rule of law reform agenda, the same understanding of 'law as rational' and an 'instrumental means to achieve social change' remains intact.

This chapter unpacks the paradigm of liberal legalism and examines its pervasiveness from colonisation through the 'development decades' (1960s–1970s) and to the post-Cold War period. The chapter situates liberal legalism within a broader understanding of the modernisation rationale and outlines the colonial lineage of the modernisation project. It first discusses the different manifestations that liberal legalism has taken in legal reform and then explores what is at the core of an instrumentalist understanding of the law (i.e. the belief that law is predictable because it is rational). The core of liberal legalism is the idea that because the West is considered rational, Third World territories can also achieve political and economic development by mimicking Europe and North America.

Law as an instrument for social change

Liberal legalism, a term coined by David Trubek and Marc Galanter, refers to the idea that 'rules are consciously designed to achieve social purposes or effectuate basic social principles'.[15] As a paradigm, it assumes a certain understanding of the relationship between legal systems and development, which leads to the idea that development can be achieved through legal reforms. With that said, simply because some scholars and practitioners hold an instrumentalist understanding of the law as a catalyst for social change, it does not follow that this materialises empirically.[16] Legal reforms are at the centre of the development enterprise as this is the method used to develop broader policies with regard to development. As John Merryman comments, 'law is widely *perceived* as the proper medium for social reform'.[17] This instrumentalist conception of the law has been reproduced over time – explicitly and implicitly – and has characterised legal reforms in Third World countries since the beginning of the colonial civilising mission. While the actors involved and the modes through which these reforms have been administered have varied, they are embedded within an instrumentalist understanding of the law, which remains a red thread connecting the successive rebrandings of legal reform despite different critiques voiced over the past decades.[18] The pervasiveness of the paradigm of liberal legalism is illustrated through the different manifestations that an instrumentalist understanding of the law has adopted, from colonisation to today's promotion of the rule of law.

The entrenched instrumentalist understanding of the law shared by most legal scholars in the early twentieth century served as a justification for the 'civilising mission'. Legal scholars believed that there could be a certain kind of law that could achieve social progress.[19] This is particularly visible with regard to the birth of comparative law, a legal discipline that would later play a key role in legal reforms. The founders of comparative law considered that the goal of the discipline was to improve different legal branches (e.g. property law) by seeking points of convergence and divergence, to then strengthen their respective domestic legislation.[20] A fountainhead of comparative law, Edouard Lambert, sought social solutions in a *droit commun législatif*; searching for a *ius commune* to draft a '*droit commun de l'humanité*' [a common law of humanity].[21] The underlying idea was to find legal principles that would lead to progress; through comparison, a dominant model would emerge. Comparing law meant comparing legislation from different countries on a similar topic, in a laundry list-like fashion.[22] Without surprise, only legislation from Western European and North American countries were compared. Behind the idea that there existed 'perfect laws' that could pave the way towards social progress, was the conviction that European countries were already civilised and that modern European law was *the* key marker of civilisation.

Legal reform was a tool of the colonial *mission civilisatrice*. As it was assumed that law could achieve social change, the law was treated as an essential feature of colonial administration. Scholars and colonial administrators thought that modern written law should be brought to the colonies as it was 'rational' and thus more advanced, in contrast with customary laws.[23] The Western canon was treated as superior, since one of the features of modern Western law, as Galanter explains, is that the 'application of law is reproducible and predictable'.[24] Actors of the 'civilising mission' – including colonial administrations and legal scholars – noted crucial differences between Western, formal, 'rational' legal systems and non-Western, customary, 'irrational' legal systems;[25] these comparisons resulted in a conceptual relationship forged between 'formal and civilised' and 'informal and uncivilised'.[26] Following the understanding of actors of the 'civilising mission', Europe had become civilised through the rationalisation of law, since modern law emerged in Europe through a process of codification and formalisation;[27] because it was deemed superior, colonies could become civilised by importing this law. To be sure, other legal systems existed – for instance, in India or the Maghreb region[28] – but they were considered 'uncivilised' and because they were unfamiliar to Westerners they were ignored and invisibilised.[29] Legal reforms, via the imposition of a legal system, were seen as a way to fulfil the 'civilising mission' across a broad range of non-legal areas, including the economy, morality, and family structures.[30] By importing modern law to the colonies, not only would legal development ensue but also political, economic, and social development.

In a post-colonial context, legal reforms were thought to bring economic and political development, which translated to, respectively, free market economies and liberal democracies.[31] Following decolonisation, metropoles lost their grip on shaping the legal systems of their former colonies directly, yet in order to achieve 'development', law was still the principal means of achieving social goals. The law and development movement, composed of scholars and practitioners, emerged in the United States in the late 1960s, and shared a similar instrumentalist understanding of the law.[32] Its goal was to help newly founded countries achieve political and economic development, again understood as achieving free market economies and liberal democracies.[33] To meet these goals, legal reforms were seen as essential vectors, as law was conceived of as an 'instrument for change'.[34]

The paradigm of liberal legalism persisted when the law and development movement fell out of favour at the end of the 1980s and carries on into the contemporary rule of law movement, where law and development's core ideas were rebranded into 'good governance' and 'rule of law and development', including an instrumentalist understanding of the law.[35] Despite the rebranding, both movements were characterised by the same optimism of carrying out economic and political development through law in the newly decolonised countries in Africa and Asia, as well as in Latin America.[36] The instrumental understanding of the law as a means to achieve social change is grounded in the idea that law is a rational means to reach political development and is thus anchored in Max Weber's theory of rationalisation.

Rational law to reach political and economic development

The paradigm of liberal legalism sees legal reforms as a means of achieving social change because the rationality of the law leads to a predictable process, where political and economic development can be accelerated. At the core of liberal legalism's instrumentalist understanding of the law lies its rationality. This section first introduces Max Weber's theory of rationalisation, before sketching out the pervasiveness of legal rationality throughout legal reform, particularly with regard to political development.

Weber, rationalisation, and the law

According to liberal legalism, it is due to law's rational character that legal reforms become a means of achieving political and economic development, which can be accelerated thanks to science and rationality. In this context, the notion of rationalisation, as discussed by Max Weber, can help to further elucidate the tenets of liberal legalism. Weber himself did not explicitly define 'rationalisation', yet it appears throughout his works *Economy and Society* and *The Protestant Ethic and the Spirit of Capitalism*. Weber uses the term 'rationalisation' to refer to 'an increase in instrumentally rational action',[37] arguing that the 'process of rationalization of action is the substitution for the unthinking acceptance of ancient custom, of deliberate adaptation to situations in terms of self-interest'.[38] So understood, rationalisation is a historical drive where 'one can, in principle, master all things by calculation'.[39] In the 'Author's Introduction' of *The Protestant Ethic*, Weber notes that rationalisation can take different forms in different areas of life:[40]

> There is, for example, rationalization of mystical contemplation, that is of an attitude which, viewed from other departments of life, is specifically irrational, just as much as there are rationalizations of economic life, of technique, of scientific research, of military training, of law and administration. Furthermore, each one of these fields may be rationalized in terms of very different ultimate values and ends, and what is rational from one point of view may well be irrational from another.[41]

For Weber, law plays a central role within the process of rationalisation, related to economic development: 'the development of economic rationalism is partly dependent on rational technique and law'.[42] In law, the process of rationalisation is analysed through various stages, from charismatic to rational law.[43] The rationalisation of law creates a more predictable legal process, which, in turn, leads to 'the most important conditions for the existence of economic enterprise intended to function with stability and, especially, of capitalistic enterprise, which cannot do without legal security'.[44] Weber's idea here is that modern written laws, alongside bureaucratic management, 'reinforce the elements of predictability in the socio-political environment that encumbers industrial capitalism by means of introducing formal equality of citizenship, a rule-bound legislation of legal norms, an autonomous judiciary, and a depoliticized professional bureaucracy'.[45]

Within the context of the development enterprise, rational law (via legal reform) helps to accelerate social change in a predictable manner. Law is thus the structure that enables the free market system to emerge. As Trubek notes, echoing Weber, 'modern law does not bring about political development; it merely supports the centralized bureaucratic state which depends for its legitimacy on a belief that its decisions are rational'.[46]

In the law and development movement, as Yong-Shik Lee explains, 'Modern law was believed to be the functional prerequisite of an industrial economy, and law was seen as a force which can be molded and manipulated to alter human behavior and achieve development'.[47] Because political development was understood to facilitate economic development and law was treated as a catalyser for political development, it also came to be seen as a key enabler of economic development.[48] Law not only creates the right conditions to increase foreign direct investment but can also 'direct or evoke economic activity regarded as desirable for the national economy by regulating credit, land tenure', thus having the right legal framework can 'accommodate – indeed, facilitate – the social change that in most developing lands must accompany economic growth'.[49] For instance, implementing an independent judicial system with laws regulating corporate activity (i.e. foreign investment) would 'directly affect economic growth'.[50] To wit: modern law was seen as a prerequisite for both political development (understood as liberal democracy) and economic development (understood as free market economies).[51]

New bottles, old wine: the many shapes of legal rationality in the development enterprise

Legal reforms in the development enterprise are characterised by a shared understanding that rational law accelerates political and economic development. The paradigm of liberal legalism shows the pervasiveness of this instrumentalist understanding of the law; an understanding that has evolved since colonisation, moving away from a public administration approach towards a public policy approach. The understanding of law as a means of achieving social change has remained while the legal vessel chosen to carry out the intended legal reform has shifted from being included in legislation to being embedded within a broader framework of the public policy approach.[52] The examination of the different transposition of legal rationality through successive phases of legal reform with regard to development is informed by Alexandre Flückiger's succinct comments regarding the transformation of legal rationality and its impact on 'legislative drafting'.[53]

Liberal legalism treats law as accelerating the different stages of development, as predicted by the process of rationalisation of the political sphere. This idea has persisted from the colonial era to today, even if the manifestations of legal rationality have changed over time. During colonisation and the development decades, legislation was the vessel chosen to implement desired social change. As Sally Engle Merry points out, 'colonial legal officials saw themselves as bringing civilization and the rule of law to peoples whose customs (since they were typically seen to lack law) were arbitrary, capricious, and irrational'.[54] Legal reforms were carried out through specific 'thematic legislation', referred to as 'framework laws' [*lois-cadres*]. In the British Empire, this was implemented through the Colonial Development and Welfare Act of 1940, while in France a framework law was adopted in 1956 to 'ensure the evolution of the territories' of the French Union.[55]

In the aftermath of decolonisation, a similar logic pervaded. Following independence, as Paul Proehl and Henry Richardson point out, 'law-as-legislation' was understood as an 'obvious tool of social engineering to meet the pressing problems of nationhood presented by independence and to reach development goals'.[56] In a similar vein, René David notes the urgency of importing foreign law to Ethiopia:

> Ethiopia cannot wait 300 or 500 years to construct in an empirical fashion a system of law which is unique to itself. The development and modernization of Ethiopia necessitate the adoption of a 'ready-made' system; they force the reception of a foreign system of law in such a manner as to assure as quickly as possible a minimal security in legal relations.[57]

Following the end of the Cold War, a shift in thinking can be observed. Legal reform in development began to be characterised by a public policy approach, where public governance is achieved by 'governing by objectives'.[58] The framework law, understood as a legal norm adopted by a given parliament dealing with a social problem, loses the spotlight. As Alexandre Flückiger explains, legislation becomes part of a broader scheme to achieve a particular social objective, and within the legal framework lie a variety of legal norms, including legal recommendations, strategic plans, memoranda, and executive orders.[59] An instrumentalist understanding of the law still continues, as the law is thought to achieve a particular social aim. For instance, with regard to legislative drafting, Flückiger refers to *légistique matérielle*, which aims to offer to the creator of a legal norm all of the different options available to best solve the social problem at hand.[60] This suggests that within legal reform we have to look beyond traditional hard law norms to discover the process of creating laws. While the manifestations change, we see here that an underlying instrumentalist understanding of the law persists throughout time.

A final piece of the puzzle is missing to fully grasp the paradigm of liberal legalism. In addition to an instrumentalist approach to law, the paradigm of liberal legalism implicitly holds that the desired model for social change lies in the West. Thus, it belongs to a broader idea that by imitating the Western legal structures, a Third World country can achieve political development faster. Weber himself believed that rationalisation is a unique feature of the West and that it is through the rationalisation process that the West reached its current stage of development.[61] Weber further points out the 'specific and peculiar rationalism of Western culture',[62] arguing that

> When we find again and again that, even in departments of life apparently mutually independent, certain types of rationalization have developed in the Occident, and only there, it would be natural to suspect that the most important reason lay in differences of heredity.[63]

The paradigm of liberal legalism captures this Weberian logic and treats modern law, due to its rationality, as the key enabler of Western Europe and North America to achieve economic and political development. In short, liberal legalists argue that the 'Third World should copy modern legal systems',[64] which lead to development.[65]

The West as the ultimate stage of development

To understand the *liberal* side of liberal legalism, it is important to address the often implicitly assumed yet little discussed assumption that by imitating the legal framework of the West, Third World countries will achieve economic and political development. The West is understood as both a goal of political development and a means of reaching said development. A broader paradigm underpinning liberal legalism, the modernisation rationale, and its colonial lineage explains why the West is treated as *the* standard to mimic.

The colonial lineage of the modernisation rationale

Liberal legalism is the legal dimension of a broader paradigm, the modernisation rationale, which has an explicit colonial lineage. The modernisation rationale is the belief that Western states have achieved political and economic development through a process of rationalisation, guided by science and rationality and rooted in the paradigm shift related to 'social changes initially brought about by the Enlightenment project of modernity', which itself centres on the radical idea that humans can exert control over their social environments.[66] Shifting towards 'modernity' involved moving away from religious beliefs to 'scientific ideas and the principles of rationality', as opposed to mythological or religious beliefs; indeed, this is a cornerstone of the political project of modernisation.[67] Since humans were believed to have control over their environment, they could shape such an environment, and law quickly became a core tool at their disposal to achieve these social changes. At its essence, the modernisation rationale understands that the West's level of development – social, political, and economic – was a direct consequence of following science and reason. To be sure, this rationale obfuscates the history of exploitation, appropriation, and violence that has led to the so-called degree of economic and political development.

Explaining Western political and economic development through science implied positing the West as superior to the rest of the world. Thus, the political project of modernisation was deeply embedded within another political project, which had been ongoing for a few centuries already: colonisation. Historians have argued that the modernisation rationale is intimately tied to colonialism, as it emerged in the context of colonial empire.[68] An excellent illustration of the relationship between modernisation and colonialism is the early use of the term 'civilisation', which served as a justification for colonial enterprise. Alice Conklin explains that 'civilisation' was first used in France in the mid-eighteenth century by French philosophers to denote the triumph of French 'rationalism' over the 'barbarism' that characterised much of the world. As such, the term 'civilisation':

> connote[s] the triumph and development of reason, not only in the *constitutional*, political, and administrative domain, but in the moral, religious, and intellectual spheres as well – a word that would capture the essence of French achievements compared to the uncivilized world of savages, slaves, and barbarians.[69]

Similarly, Tyler Stovall has shown how the history of the British and French Empires is characterised by the relationship between modernity and colonialism: 'Their rise and fall coincided with but also crucially contributed to ideas of modernity, illustrating the truism that colonialism has been intrinsic to the making of the modern world'.[70] Positing the West as the standard of civilisation, which is at the core of the modernisation rationale, lasted long after colonisation, through to the 'development era'.[71]

From the 'mission civilisatrice' to development

The modernisation rationale has undergone successive rebrandings, with its goal explicitly changing from reaching 'civilisation' to 'development' to 'good governance'. The emergence of the idea of development is commonly attributed to the inaugural speech of President Harry Truman in 1948.[72] Actually, the idea of development was born directly from the civilising mission, which emerged in the mid-nineteenth century and was later rebranded through the lens of development when the ties of colonialism were shredded and former colonies achieved formal political independence.[73] Despite the rebranding, the core idea remains that the West is the standard to replicate.

The shift from the civilising mission to development was rooted in the idea that the West represents the final stage of political and economic development, which was achieved through a rational process. This shift can be understood as proceeding through three different periods. In the early nineteenth century, the idea emerged of the civilising mission, embedded within the political discourse of modernisation developed by the metropoles, where the coloniser had a duty towards their colonies to civilise them.[74] The civilising mission related to a variety of aspects, ranging from family to health and education, but in our case we are interested in its political aspect.[75] The connection between the 'civilising' and 'modernisation' projects was that both would bring social progress and 'a more civilized society'[76] to any Third World territory that mimicked the West; indeed, doing so would mean that 'modernisation would be accomplished in at most a few decades'.[77] Because the West believed itself to possess a higher degree of civilisation, this led to the entitlement to civilise others; the civilising mission served to legitimise colonialism itself. In 1885, French Prime Minister Jules Ferry justified the colonial expansion of France in terms of a 'duty to civilise': 'I repeat that there are for superior races a right, because there is a duty for them. They have the duty to civilise inferior races'.[78]

From the civilising mission grew the idea of colonial development. Ruth Craggs points out that at the close of the nineteenth century colonial empires started putting 'more emphasis on development on humanitarian grounds for native colonial communities', which 'provided the mandate for European powers to help these territories develop through following a path towards Western modernity'.[79] In the British Empire, this translated in the 1929 Colonial Development Act, which aimed for the first time to 'authorise the making of advances for aiding and developing agriculture and industry in certain colonies and territories'.[80] This marked a significant shift, at least discursively, with the metropoles now serving their colonial territories and not vice versa.[81] In 1940, the Colonial Development and Welfare Act 'ushered in state-led large-scale development for the purposes of improving welfare' in British colonies,[82] with a shift to development *tout court* occurring soon after when colonial powers – chiefly the United Kingdom and France – were losing power; this marked the total move away from the idea of the civilising mission and towards 'development'.[83]

The idea of development emerged in a context with colonies calling explicitly for self-determination.[84] Colonial empires conceived of development as an 'idea that would reinvigorate colonialism'.[85] Development provided, as Frederick Cooper writes, the 'progressive basis for continued colonial rule'.[86] The link between colonialism and development is clearly illustrated by the continuity that existed between civil servants of the Minister of the Colonies who went on to work in development-related organisations.[87] While the terminology changed from 'barbarian' or 'uncivilised' to 'under-developed', two important underlying ideas remain. First, there still exist justifications for intervention by former metropoles to combat 'under-development' or 'misery'.[88] Second, similar to the civilising mission, the move to development is also characterised as being grounded in science and rationality. As Cooper explains: 'Framed as a single idea of "development" bringing together the raising of African standards of living and the reconstruction of the British economy, of "responsible" trade unions and respectable politicians, of "scientific" ideas applied by knowledgeable experts'.[89] This idea of rational development continues to pervade, even if the use of the term 'civilisation' has disappeared.

Political development equals liberal democracy

In the political realm, the modernisation rationale translates to the idea that a 'developing' country ought to adopt Western liberal constitutional democracy in order to achieve political development. This was, after all, the model adopted in the West, which is considered to be the peak of political development. Within the paradigm of liberal legalism and the development enterprise, political development simply equates to (Western) liberal democracy. As David Trubek explains, 'modern law is also viewed as an essential element in political development. In the core conception, such development means not only the creation of a strong, central state, but also the construction of a pluralist, *liberal*-democratic government'.[90]

Throughout the development enterprise, from the colonial era to today, this idea pervades where 'political development as liberal democracy' appears in the background of the successive stages of development legal reform. During colonisation, the civilising mission translated politically in 'helping' colonies reach liberal democracy, which was considered to be the ultimate stage of political evolution.[91] As Sally Engle Merry explains, the rule of law was a 'gift' from the metropole to its colonies, with the metropole benevolently transforming the culture of the colonies to reach civilisation:

> the oppositions were painted in images of family and moral order: the 'mother country' and 'young nations'; the colonized as 'half-devil, half-child' in contrast to the dutiful but unappreciated white adult male colonizer in Kipling's famous poem, 'The White Man's Burden'.[92]

In the British Empire, a major rationale for colonisation was the fight against slavery,[93] in particular on the African continent.[94] As Harshan Kumarasingham points out regarding 'Britain's liberal empire', 'the quest across the Empire was for political liberalism and to share in the responsibility and mantle of government'.[95] Similarly, the French Empire, following the Third Republic (1875), ascertained its 'civilising mission' through the idea of the liberal empire. Alice Conklin explains that, 'when France began to enlarge its holdings in Africa and Indochina, French publicists, and subsequently politicians, declared that their government-alone among the Western states had a special mission to civilize the indigenous peoples now coming under its control'.[96]

Following decolonisation, the underlying idea that Western liberal democracy is the standard to replicate persisted. From the 1960s to the 1980s, political development was thought to be achieved by adopting the correct legal framework; this is visible in the law and development movement, which is also characterised by an instrumentalist understanding of the law. In this case, legal reform is synonymous with liberal reform, with scholars and practitioners believing that a 'modern legal system would not only support more efficient and effective policies; it also would, almost by its nature, protect rights and further core liberal values'.[97] At the end of the Cold War, the rule of law movement emerged as the new hegemonic school of thought guiding legal reforms for democratic promotion. The understanding of the type of legislation needed to achieve legal reform had changed, moving from programmatic laws to governing by objective; however, the idea that political development is synonymous with Western liberal democracy remained.[98] As Thomas Carothers explains, 'the value of rule-of-law work are two controlling axioms: the rule of law is necessary for economic development and necessary for democracy'.[99] In other words, it involves an instrumentalist understanding of the law to achieve political development, which again equates to liberal democracy.[100]

Conclusion

This chapter has unpacked the paradigm of liberal legalism and revealed it to be the belief that law is a means of achieving social change because it leads to a process of rationalisation. This relies on the assumption that political and economic development can be reached through scientific and rational means, positioning North America and Western Europe as sites where such development has occurred. The rationale of this paradigm is that, by mimicking Western legal frameworks, a Third World territory can reach development more quickly in a predictable and rational manner. The paradigm of liberal legalism is one of the two core features of the theory developed in this book – the development enterprise – to analyse the transnational dimension of constitution-making. This chapter has shown the colonial lineage of the paradigm of liberal legalism that has pervaded legal reform in Third World territories. To bring about this process of rationalisation through law, the development enterprise relies on a particular type of actor: the expert.

Notes

1 Rene David, 'Sources of the Ethiopian Civil Code' (1967) 4 Journal of Ethiopian Law 341.
2 ibid 343.
3 David Kennedy, *A World of Struggle: How Power, Law, and Expertise Shape Global Political Economy* (Princeton UP 2018) 89.
4 David Trubek and Marc Galanter, 'Scholars in Self-Estrangement: Some Reflections on the Crisis in Law and Development Studies in the United States' [1974] Wisconsin Law Review 1062, 1069.

5 See Laura Nader, 'Promise or Plunder? A Past and Future Look at Law and Development' (2007) 7 Global Jurist I.
6 Kevin Davis and Michael Trebilcock, 'The Relationship Between Law and Development: Optimists Versus Skeptics' (2008) 56 The American Journal of Comparative Law 895, 901.
7 See discussion of the term 'Third World' in Introduction.
8 David Kennedy, 'The "Rule of Law", Political Choices, and Development Common Sense' in David M Trubek and Alvaro Santos (eds), *The New Law and Economic Development: A Critical Appraisal* (CUP 2006) 102.
9 ibid.
10 Trubek and Galanter (n 4) 1094.
11 See for instance, Jamie Rowen, *Searching for Truth in the Transitional Justice Movement* (CUP 2017); Mark Fathi Massoud, 'Work Rules: How International NGOs Build Law in War-Torn Societies' (2015) 49 Law & Society Review 333, 335; Yves Dezalay and Bryant Garth, *The Internationalization of Palace Wars: Lawyer, Economists, and the Contest to Transform Latin American States* (U of Chicago P 2002) 7; Romain Bertrand, 'Les organisations de "promotion de la démocratie" et la construction des bureaucraties électorales indonésiennes' [2008] Critique Internationale 51, 72.
12 Robert Bates, 'Political Development' in Carol Lancaster and Nicolas Van de Walle (eds), *The Oxford Handbook of the Politics of Development* (OUP 2018).
13 Bipan Chandra, 'Colonialism, Stages of Colonialism and the Colonial State' (1980) 10 Journal of Contemporary Asia 272, 274. See Ewout Frankema and Frans Buelens, *Colonial Exploitation and Economic Development: The Belgian Congo and the Netherlands Indies Compared* (Routledge 2013); Antony Anghie, 'The Evolution of International Law: Colonial and Postcolonial Realities' (2006) 27 Third World Quarterly 739; Ntina Tzouvala, *Capitalism as Civilisation: A History of International Law* (CUP 2020).
14 Both the French and the British Empire engaged in large state-violence acts. See Harshan Kumarasingham, 'Liberal Ideals and the Politics of Decolonisation' (2018) 46 The Journal of Imperial and Commonwealth History 815, 817; Terence Halliday and Lucien Karpik, 'Political Liberalism in the British Post-Colony' in Terence Halliday, Lucien Karpik and Malcolm Feeley (eds), *Fates of Political Liberalism in the British Post-Colony: The Politics of the Legal Complex* (CUP 2012); Alice Conklin, *A Mission to Civilize: The Republican Idea of Empire in France and West Africa, 1895–1930* (Standford UP 1997) 9.
15 Trubek and Galanter (n 4) 1071.
16 David Trubek, 'Toward a Social Theory of Law: An Essay on the Study of Law and Development' (1972) 82 The Yale Law Journal 1, 19.
17 John Henry Merryman, 'Comparative Law and Social Change: On the Origins, Style, Decline & Revival of the Law and Development Movement' [1977] The American Journal of Comparative Law 457, 466. [Emphasis added].
18 Wouter Vandenhole, 'Law and Development Revisited: From Self-Estrangement to Revival – Review of MJ Trebilcock and MM Prado, Advanced Introduction to Law and Development' (2015) 9 Human Rights & International Legal Discourse 112, 114–16.
19 Ralf Michaels, 'The Functional Method of Comparative Law' in Mathias Reinmann and Reinhard Zimmermann (eds), *Oxford Handbook of Comparative Law* (OUP 2006) 346.
20 Bénédicte Fauvarque-Cosson, 'Deux siècles d'évolution du droit comparé' (2011) 63 Revue internationale de droit comparé 527, 529.

21 ibid 530. See for instance, Edouard Lambert, *Etude de droit commun législatif ou de droit civil comparé: Première série* (T Giord et E Brière 1903).
22 See Félix Moreau, *Régime parlementaire et principe représentatif: Procès-verbaux des séances et documents. Congrès International de droit comparé tenu à Paris du 31 juillet au 4 août 1900* (Librairie générale de droit et de jurisprudence 1905) 343, 357.
23 James Tully, 'The Imperialism of Modern Constitutional Democracy' in Martin Loughlin and Neil Walker (eds), *The Paradox of Constitutionalism: Constituent Power and Constitutional Form* (OUP 2007) 318.
24 Marc Galanter, 'The Modernization of Law' in Myron Weiner (ed), *Modernization: The Dynamics of Growth* (Basic Books 1966) 155.
25 Trubek (n 16) 5.
26 Sally Engle Merry, 'Colonial and Postcolonial Law' in Austin Sarat (ed), *The Blackwell Companion to Law and Society* (Blackwell Publishing 2004) 572.
27 ibid 569.
28 See Harith Al-Dabbagh, 'Le droit comparé comme instrument de modernisation: L'exemple des codifications civiles des Etats arabes du Moyen-Orient' (2013) 43 Revue de Droit: Université de Sherbrooke 388, 387–441; Jean-Louis Halpérin, *Profils des mondialisations du droit* (Dalloz 2009) 118–29.
29 Thibault Guilluy, 'Visions of Constitutionalism: The Implementation of Representative Institutions in the British Colonies' in Kelly Grotke and Markus Prutsch (eds), *Constitutionalism, Legitimacy, and Power: Nineteenth-Century Experiences* (OUP 2014) 286.
30 Legal anthropologists have shown how this process was more complex than pure imposition. See for instance, Merry (n 26) 570. Similarly colonial elites instrumentalised the discourse of the metropoles to defend their political interests in context of decolonisation. See Sarah Stockwell, 'Imperial Liberalism and Institution Building at the End of Empire in Africa' (2018) 46 The Journal of Imperial and Commonwealth History 1009–10.
31 David Greenberg, 'Law and Development in Light of Dependency Theory' (1980) 3 Research Law & Society 129–30.
32 Yong-Shik Lee, 'General Theory of Law and Development' (2017) 50 Cornell International Law Journal 415, 421.
33 Trubek (n 16) 8.
34 Elliot Burg, 'Law and Development: A Review of the Literature and a Critique of "Scholars in Self-Estrangement"' [1977] The American Journal of Comparative Law 492, 505; Greenberg (n 31) 130.
35 Thomas Carothers, 'The Problem of Knowledge' in Thomas Carothers (ed), *Promoting the Rule of Law Abroad: In Search of Knowledge* (Carnegie Endowment for International Peace 2006) 15; David Trubek, 'Law and Development: 40 Years After Scholars in Self Estrangement – A Preliminary Review' (2014) 66 University of Toronto Law Journal 301, 310; David Mednicoff and Joanna Springer, 'The Rule of Law and Political Liberalization in the Arab Gulf' in Michael Hudson and Mimi Kirk (eds), *Gulf Politics and Economics in a Changing World* (World Scientific 2014).
36 Carothers (n 35) 15.
37 Richard Swedberg and Ola Agevall, *The Max Weber Dictionary: Key Words and Central Concepts* (Stanford UP 2016) 286.
38 Max Weber, *Economy and Society: An Outline of Interpretive Sociology* (U of California P 1978) 30.
39 Max Weber, *From Max Weber: Essays in Sociology* (Routledge 1991) 139.
40 Max Weber, *The Protestant Ethic and the Spirit of Capitalism* (Routledge 2005) xxxix.
41 ibid xxxviii.
42 ibid xxxix.

43 Weber (n 39) 882.
44 ibid 883.
45 Kim Sung Ho, 'Max Weber' in Zalta Edward and Uri Nodelman (eds), *The Stanford Encyclopedia of Philosophy* (Metaphysics Research Lab 2019).
46 Trubek (n 16) 15.
47 Lee (n 32) 421.
48 Greenberg (n 31) 130.
49 Herbert Merillat, 'Law and Developing Countries' (1966) 60 American Journal of International Law 71–72.
50 ibid 74.
51 Brian Tamanaha, 'The Primacy of Society and the Failures of Law and Development' (2011) 44 Cornell International Law Journal 209, 214–16.
52 Sophie Weerts, 'Droit' in Nils Soguel and others (eds), *Comprendre et concevoir l'administration publique, le modèle IDHEAP* (EPFL Press 2023).
53 Alexandre Flückiger, *(Re)faire la loi: Traité de légistique à l'ère du droit souple* (Stämpfli Verlag 2019).
54 Merry (n 26) 572.
55 France, 'Loi relative aux mesures propres à assurer l'évolution des territoires relevant du ministère de la France d'outre-mer' [23 June 1956] Journal officiel de la République française 5781.
56 Henry Richardson III and Paul Proehl, 'Crossroads for Law in Africa' (1970) 18 UCLA Law Review 219, 221.
57 Rene David, 'Civil Code for Ethiopia: Considerations on the Codification of the Civil Law in African Countries' (1962) 37 Tulane Law Review 187.
58 Jan-Erik Lane, *New Public Management* (Routledge 2000) 34. See François Giovalucchi and Jean-Pierre De Sardan, 'Planification, gestion et politique dans l'aide au développement: Le cadre logique, outil et miroir des développeurs' [2009] Revue Tiers Monde 383.
59 Flückiger (n 53) xi.
60 ibid 43.
61 Sung Ho (n 45); Swedberg and Agevall (n 37) 286.
62 Weber (n 40) xxxviii.
63 ibid xlii.
64 Trubek (n 35) 303–5.
65 Greenberg (n 31) 130.
66 Paul Senior, Chris Crowther-Dowey and Matt Long, *Understanding Modernisation in Criminal Justice* (Open UP 2007) 19.
67 ibid.
68 Mary Gilmartin, 'Colonialism/Imperialism' in Carolyn Gallaher and others (eds), *Key Concepts in Political Geography* (Sage 2009) 115.
69 Conklin (n 14) 14. [Emphasis added].
70 Tyler Stovall, 'Empires of Democracy' in Graham Huggan (ed), *The Oxford Handbook of Postcolonial Studies* (OUP 2013) 68.
71 Kennedy (n 8) 98.
72 See The Avalon Project, 'Inaugural Address of Harry S Truman' (20 January 1949) <https://avalon.Law.yale.edu/20th_century/truman.asp> accessed July 2020.
73 Ruth Craggs, 'Development in a Gobal-Historical Context' in Vandana Desai and Rob Potter (eds), *The Companion to Development Studies* (Routledge 2014) 37; Ronaldo Munck and Denis O'Hearn, *Critical Development Theory: Contributions to a New Paradigm* (Zed Books 1999); Michael Havinden and David Meredith, *Colonialism and Development: Britain and Its Tropical Colonies, 1850–1960* (Routledge 1996); Michael Cowen and Robert Shenton, *Doctrines of Development* (Routledge 1996).

74 Conklin (n 14) 11–12.
75 ibid 6.
76 Senior, Crowther-Dowey and Long (n 66) 19.
77 Chandra (n 13) 272.
78 Assemblée Nationale, 'Jules Ferry (1885): Les fondements de la politique coloniale (28 juillet 1885)' <http://www2.assemblee-nationale.fr/decouvrir-l-assemblee/histoire/grands-discours-parlementaires/jules-ferry-28-juillet-1885> accessed February 2020. [My own translation].
79 Craggs (n 73) 34.
80 Colonial Development Act 1929 of 26 July 1929.
81 Frederick Cooper, 'Modernizing Bureaucrats, Backward Africans, and the Development Concept' in Frederick Cooper and Randall Packard (eds), *International Development the Social Sciences: Essays on the History Politics of Knowledge* (U of California P 1997) 64.
82 Craggs (n 73) 34.
83 Frederick Cooper, *Colonialism in Question: Theory, Knowledge, History* (U of California P 2005) 146.
84 Cooper (n 81) 70.
85 ibid 64.
86 ibid 70.
87 See David John Morgan, *The Official History of Colonial Development: Developing British Colonial Resources, 1945–1951* (Macmillan 1980); Overseas Development Institute, *Colonial Development: A Factual Survey of the Origins and History of British Aid to Developing Countries* (Overseas Development Institute 1964); John Michael Lee, *Colonial Development and Good Government: A Study. of the Ideas Expressed by the British Official Classes in Planning Decolonization 1939–1964* (Clarendon Press 1967).
88 Gilbert Rist, *Développement: Histoire d'une croyance occidentale* (Les Presses de Sciences Po 1996) 141.
89 Cooper (n 81) 81.
90 Trubek (n 16) 8. [Emphasis added].
91 Stovall (n 70) 72.
92 Merry (n 26) 572. This lies at the level of political discourse; while metropoles were allegedly exporting the rule of law, as Halliday explains: '[they] reserved for itself two exceptions: one based on the threat to social order, the other premised on racial and ethnic, religious and linguistic differences between the colonizing and subaltern populations' Halliday and Karpik (n 14) 4.
93 Stovall (n 70) 72–73.
94 Conklin (n 14) 16.
95 Kumarasingham (n 14) 815.
96 Conklin (n 14) 1.
97 Trubek (n 35) 303–5.
98 Tamanaha (n 51) 215.
99 Carothers (n 35) 17.
100 ibid 18.

Chapter 3

The figure of the expert

The idea that complex social problems should be entrusted to experts is not new. In 1865, Henri de Saint-Simon observed that 'all social functions necessarily [should] be entrusted to those men who are most capable of exercising them in conformity with the general aims of the community'.[1] Two centuries later, James Gardner noted the involvement of legal experts in development settings: 'Such lawyers would serve as problem solvers, architects of democracy, and social engineers for developing countries'.[2]

This chapter centres on the figure of the expert, the protagonist of the development enterprise. To bring about development via legal reform in Third World countries, the expert acts as a channel to transmit the knowledge acquired in the West. It is not just any kind of expert that is able to provide the legal knowledge necessary to achieve development – it is the *foreign* expert. The expert who offers legal expertise is key to understanding the full picture of transnational involvement during constitution-making. Offering legal expertise to accelerate these social goals was the raison d'être of the development enterprise.

The analytical lens is built by bringing together scholarship in international relations, history, political science, sociology, and anthropology – fields that have studied expertise in the international realm.[3] This chapter relies on studies of expertise in international relations grounded in an interpretative approach. The literature interested in expertise can be divided between functionalist and interpretative approaches. Functionalists tend to take at face value the authority of the expert in the political realm. For instance, in political science, scholars have noted the significant role that 'epistemic communities' play in shaping governance, as well as in the creation of international norms.[4] These studies often take for granted the self-appointed label by actors who identify as experts. As Jan Eijking notes, functionalists do not differentiate between expertise in the field of politics or other fields such as chemistry. For functionalists 'using experts in politics, on this view, does not affect the substance of expertise itself'.[5] Interpretative approaches, on the other hand, do not take 'expertise' for granted.[6]

DOI: 10.4324/9781003386186-5

Before proceeding any further, several caveats must be mentioned. First, it is important to note that while the involvement of 'local experts' has been acknowledged within the development enterprise, this particular subject is beyond the scope of the present study.[7] Second, the figure of the expert is an elusive actor, and there is widespread confusion and conflation among different terms – including expert, scholar, specialist, professional.[8] Indeed, the term expert itself has a broad range of definitions that cross disciplinary boundaries. The goal here is not to categorise who counts as an expert and who does not but instead to sketch this figure that pervades the development enterprise and that is not defined by organic criteria (for instance, being a university professor). Thomas Pfister and Anna Horvath highlight how the 'institutionalized boundaries between experts and nonexperts are regularly contested and reimagined'.[9]

The development enterprise and the antifoundationalist approach that underpins it serve to elucidate the transnational dimension of constitution-making in the context of democratic transition. Expanding the scope of analysis from the adoption of the legal norm to the whole process of legal reform, it thus exposes a whole set of legal actors that have been invisibilised by the lens of constituent power that continues to ground comparative constitutional scholarship. This chapter examines the root of the scientific discipline mobilised by actors involved in legal reforms, comparative law, and the role comparative legal scholars have played in successive legal reforms – from colonisation to rule of law reforms. Expertise is an important subject, as the advice of legal experts ends up setting the framework of what is possible within a constitution-making process and thus has practical consequences as certain options are not even considered.

While this is beyond the scope of the present study, it is important to note that if a certain kind of expertise is treated as legitimate by international actors, other types of knowledge, holding a different vision of what is possible, are disregarded.[10] As Briony Jones writes, the politics of knowledge affects what is 'imagine[d] to be possible in policy and practice'.[11] Expertise provided by external actors carries its own set of epistemic limitations that are grounded in liberal legalism. While critical scholars have provided meaningful critiques of the Western-centric, legalistic, state-led, institutional approach set forth by international experts in the context of transitional justice, constitution-making has not received the same scrutiny.[12]

The chapter first introduces the reason why the expert is key to the development enterprise: because social problems are redefined as technical ones. It then turns to the figure of the expert in the development enterprise, particularly in its legal dimension.

Framing problems in the development enterprise

Recasting social problems as technical problems

The central role of the expert in the development enterprise is largely due to the fact that social problems are reframed as technical ones. Pervading issues – from healthcare to governance to education[13] – are conceived as too complex to be left to amateurs.[14] It is the ostensible complexity of these problems that leads to them being recast as technical and thus the purview of the expert.[15] For instance, following this idea it would be inconceivable to ask people's opinion on issues related to macroeconomics or nuclear energy.[16] Because these issues are technical issues, they require a certain type of actor who holds specialised knowledge.

In the development enterprise, the figure of the expert as the holder of specialised knowledge to address social problems looms large in the background, from colonisation to 'development discourse'. During colonisation, the expert was a key player sent from the metropoles to the colonies to ostensibly raise the standards of living.[17] The social problem of 'uncivilised territories' required technical solutions to reach civilisation. As Frederick Cooper explains, officials could 'read European history as a process of finding rational solutions to complex social problems'.[18] The range of expertise on display included farming, agriculture, and medicine but also political and legal science.[19]

The duty to civilise carries in itself the idea that the metropoles held a certain knowledge that colonies did not. Following the modernisation rationale, Europe had reached a certain knowledge through rational means and thus the expert became key to colonial development and later development *tout court*. As Cooper writes, 'development is something to be done to and for Africa but not with it'.[20] From the beginning of the twentieth century, as Timothy Mitchell explains, development was understood as a 'politics of techno-science', where the defaults of nature and of society would be mended by 'bring[ing] the expertise of modern engineering, technology, and social science'.[21] The successive waves of development similarly relied heavily on the figure of the expert, captured in the idea that development is a natural unfolding of a universal social process in which 'human agent[s] could facilitate but which was driven by history'.[22] This is similarly illustrated in the waves of economists, engineers, and agronomists that were sent to Latin America, Africa, and Asia,[23] the idea being that problems could be solved in similar manners in different areas of the developing world. As Ferguson notes, 'many aspects of 'development' interventions remain remarkably uniform and standardised form place to place'.[24] In the same vein, Autesserre when discussing expertise in context of peace-building talks about fungible expertise, that is 'what works in one context will function just as well in another'.[25]

Legal experts to the rescue

The paradigm of liberal legalism sees social problems as solvable if the right law is adopted; social problems linked to political development are understood as technical legal problems. This means that these problems are divorced from political issues, and experts are thus necessary to provide local political actors with the answers and technical know-how. Throughout the development enterprise in its legal dimension, the lawyer is seen as the 'expert', a 'problem solver' of social problems. During colonisation and the civilising mission, this involved transferring legal norms and institutional design from the metropole to the colonies.[26] Legal experts who came from the metropole would bring 'modern rational' (written) law to Third World countries where law was deemed uncivilised and thus ensure the progress of economic and political development.[27]

From the 1960s onward, lawyers were similarly treated as problem-solvers to formulate solutions to the social problems encountered in a given society.[28] As James Gardner points out, the 'legal engineer' offered a 'model of professional omnipotence' and would 'serve as problem solvers, architects of democracy, and social engineers for developing countries'.[29] These legal engineers would engage in training their counterparts in the Third World to become 'technicians of democracy'.[30] Justice William Douglas argued that a key contribution of the West to developing nations was the provision of expertise: 'These newly developing nations need our help – not only our money and machines and food, but also the great capital of knowledge accumulated by our professors'.[31]

From the early 1990s, a broad range of subfields related to 'democracy promotion' were established, all hinging on the idea that political development could be achieved through legal reform. In a nutshell, adopting the right legal framework would facilitate a successful democratic transition. Areas such as elections, parliamentary monitoring, and peace-building came to be seen as purely technical. More recently, the field of transitional justice emerged transnationally along similar lines.[32] It is perceived by international actors not only as a mechanism to deal with the crimes of the past but also as a facilitator to ensure a democratic political transition, contributing to the establishment of the rule of law.[33] For instance, adopting the right institutional framework for a transitional justice process (i.e. a truth commission) is thought to increase the chances of a successful transition to democracy or to peace.[34]

The expert as holder of technical knowledge

Throughout the development enterprise, the 'legal engineer' looms large in the background, helping to solve social problems that are reconceived as technical ones that can be solved thanks to the experts' specialised knowledge grounded in rationality. While the term has now faded away, the instrumentalist understanding of the law, where social problems could be solved if the appropriate legal framework was put in place, remains very much alive. Because social problems are seen as technical, the legal expert is key to the whole endeavour, as they possess the necessary specialised knowledge.

Knowledge from training

The development of scientific, rational knowledge led to a special status granted to those with particular qualifications. The expert is able to address social problems because they possess specialised knowledge that is grounded in reason and science. For instance, in the case of infant mortality caused by cholera, a public health expert is able to solve this due to their specialised knowledge acquired through formal training. One characteristic of the expert is that they hold specialised knowledge that grants them authority to address social problems. But what does it mean to hold specialised knowledge?

It means that the expert possesses knowledge that others (i.e. amateurs) do not.[35] Expertise is characterised by passing through a certain kind of formal education; the specialised knowledge acquired through formal training is scientific knowledge (for the process of rationalisation).[36] It is the nature of rational scientific knowledge that distinguishes the expert from other holders of formal specialised knowledge, such as a priest. The figure of the expert emerges in a clearly defined form in the early nineteenth century, where the demands of a modernising economy called for actors who held specialised knowledge acquired through formal training.[37] As Frank Fischer points out, 'expert knowledge is indeed one of the most distinctive features of modern society'.[38] The expert then became fully formed within the context of a modern emphasis on 'knowledge gained by formal training and education',[39] becoming the 'technical specialist who was regarded as educated because he had passed through difficult schools'.[40]

When it comes to legal reforms, the expert holds specialised legal knowledge because of their formal training through university and because of their positionality, as someone knowledgeable of modern rational law. As David Trubek notes, with regard to the law and development movement, 'the foreigner from a "developed," "modern" nation has a special expertise to offer the "traditional," "underdeveloped" one: He has seen the future and he knows how it works. Thus, he is indispensable to legal development'.[41] Legal reforms have been carried out in the development enterprise by 'legal engineers', belonging to a hybrid field of practitioners and academics who are generally inserted within the discipline of comparative law. During colonisation, the tradition of legal expert and foreign aid was under the purview of colonial powers,[42] with metropoles drafting the legal framework of their colonies.[43] Several societies of comparative law were involved in providing legal expertise to implement the legal framework of the colonies.[44] For instance, in the United Kingdom, associations such as the Society of Comparative Legislation and International Law (1894) or the Empire Parliamentary Association (1911) were connected to the Colonial, Dominions, Commonwealth Relations and Successor Offices.[45] The French counterpart, the *Société de législation comparée*, had similar ties between its members and French political power, while not specifically engaging in their involvement in the colonies.[46]

During the transition period from colonisation to development, a number of French law professors were also involved in shaping the new paradigm aimed at 'developing' the colonies.[47]

From the 1960s through to the 1980s, the United States came to the fore of legal reform through the creation of the law and development movement, composed of a wide array of academics from different disciplines – such as comparative law, sociology, and area specialists – who all had extensive on-the-ground experience.[48] The United States government, along with the Ford and Rockefeller Foundations, sponsored legal reform projects throughout the Third World.[49] 'Legal missionaries', a term coined by James Gardner, went up and down Africa, Asia, and Latin America to 'aid' in legal reform programs.[50] Despite the fact that they did not always refer to themselves as comparativists, they acted as such.[51] These legal experts saw themselves as bringing 'modern rational' law to Third World territories in order to help them achieve economic and political development.

Both legal experts involved in legal reforms and comparative scholars have moved on from the idea of a *ius commune* and embodied the new paradigm of comparative law that emerged following World War II: functionalism.[52] Legal comparativists compare legal systems, analysing what was the legal solution given to a given problem. As Ugo Mattei, one of the leading comparativists, writes,

> In the world of legal globalization, transfers of knowledge are needed not only within different areas of a given legal system but also between different legal systems . . . [where] problem-solving experience acquired in one system of law understandable and possibly transferable to another.[53]

Similarly, with regard to legal reform in the Third World, proponents of the law and development movement see law as a channel to solve certain social problems. From the 1990s, the successor to the law and development movement, the rule of law promotion field,[54] relied on a hybrid network of academics and practitioners[55] as 'experts' for its legal reform agenda, which still remains in a similar functionalist framework.

Knowledge from participation

Holding specialised knowledge from training must also be supplemented by participation. To be an expert, one needs to not only 'know' but participate. As Harry Collins and Robert Evans explain: 'Where there is participation – i.e. experience – there can be expertise; where there is no participation there can be no expertise because there has been no opportunity to acquire the relevant tacit knowledge'.[56] In that sense, what characterises the figure of the expert is not only the possession of a certain scientific knowledge but also practical involvement. In this sense, academic scholars studying specific areas of social problems in development are not considered as experts within the purview of the development enterprise, as they do not participate in the process. What is important to note here is that this definition of the expert is not an organic criterion (i.e. belonging to an academic institution or international organisations) but an empirical one. Thus one of the key characteristics of the figure of the expert is its elusiveness, as it encompasses such a broad array of actors, ranging from civil servants from international organisations or former metropoles, to academic professors in advisory capacities.

Because the expert has participated in other processes, it gives them a certain knowledge that others do not hold. In the development enterprise, the specialised knowledge implicitly hinges on the fact that the expert comes from the 'developed' world; it follows that there is a hierarchy of the right knowledge to address social problems, rooted in the civilising mission but still prevalent today.[57] While today this hierarchy of knowledge is implicit, it still persists.[58] Séverine Autesserre has shown through her work on peace-building how it is viewed as a technical issue involving a 'set of technical problems to be solved by experts', with checklists and toolkits.[59] Autesserre reveals that because problems associated with peace-building are framed as technical, a hierarchy is established between foreign and local knowledge.[60] She explains that local knowledge 'entails an intimate understanding of the place's history, key actors, and political, social, cultural, and economic dynamics', and thematic knowledge refers to 'an in-depth understanding of particular aspects of intervention work'.[61] The thematic knowledge ranges from public finance to development to conflict-resolution.[62] The foreign expert, with their credentials, has particular expertise, as opposed to local knowledge which is generally perceived as 'less sophisticated and more parochial'.[63] In a similar vein, Briony Jones points out how the nature of expertise in shaping transitional justice tends to be 'legal, foreign and based on models to be replicated elsewhere',[64] leading to expertise being understood as 'professionalized and internationally mobile knowledge rather than knowledge that is situated in activist commitments and knowledge of local context'.[65]

The purported rational nature of experts' knowledge makes them as a key actor of the development enterprise as they are able to solve social problems that have been redefined as technical ones. Alongside economists and engineers, the legal expert has been a key figure of the development enterprise throughout colonisation, the development decades, as well as the new movement of rule of law promotion. Because these experts hold specialised technical knowledge (i.e. a comprehensive understanding of 'modern rational' law) they see themselves as bringing about economic and political development via the establishment of legal reforms. The emphasis on the technical character of their knowledge is important as it elucidates a further important dimension of the figure of the expert: the fact that they see themselves as political outsiders.

The expert as political outsider

'Apolitical' ideology

Another key characteristic of the figure of the expert is the fact that they see themselves as political outsiders. Because social problems are conceived as technical ones, external actors justify why experts should be entrusted with addressing social problems in foreign countries.

The nature of experts' knowledge as rational and scientific implies that they remain outside the realm of political action. A consequence of defining social problems as technical is that public affairs (*la chose publique)* become the purview of 'impartial' experts and not interest-driven politicians. The idea here is that modern social problems are so complex that only science can answer to them; in other words, only those with specialised knowledge should be entrusted with addressing these technical problems as opposed to leaving them to politicians, who do not have sufficient knowledge to tackle them.[66] One of the most vocal proponents of this conception of expertise was the eighteenth-century French theorist Henri de Saint-Simon, who argued that 'political decisions should be made on the basis of knowledge, not the parochial interests of untutored value preferences of politicians'.[67] Fischer refers to Saint-Simon's position as an 'apolitical ideology',[68] where the decision-making process is presented as free from politics and instead guided by a rational and scientific process.[69] In this way, the figure of the expert is conceived as not only *outside* of political action but *above* the political process.[70] The expert is detached from 'pulling the trigger' of political decision-making and is 'one step removed from decision-making as they advise a client, and it is the client who is in charge of making the decision'.[71]

In terms of legal experts, the 'clients' are local political actors. Following this conception, the legal engineer involved in legal reforms in Third World territories is divorced from actual political decision-making, and it is this removal from the process that constitutes their position as an expert and not a different kind of actor. From a strictly procedural standpoint, legal experts are not the ones adopting the law itself. Instead, the legal reform is adopted by local politicians, thus granting the entire process a stamp of democratic legitimacy (if one follows a legal positivist approach). For legal positivists, the author of a norm is the one that has adopted it; it does not matter what happens during other parts of the process of the creation of the law. Legal experts see themselves as remaining outside of the political realm, as they are not the one actually adopting the law. This justification means that legal experts do not see themselves as infringing on the sovereignty of the Third World nations in which they provide their expertise.

At the service of the 'common good'

Another important distinction here is that experts contrast themselves with local politicians based on their commitment to the 'common good' instead of political interests and partisan judgements.[72] Because of the expert's removal from politics and because they act towards the 'common good' they receive a particular claim to authority.[73] As Jan Eijking points out those working for international organisation, 'internationality gets equated with an expertise-based sort of impartiality'.[74] In a way, this conception translates into legal reforms in the sense that the experts are removed from internal political battles. Situating experts outside the political realm is key to the development enterprise, as it constitutes the primary justification for the international expert's involvement in domestic legal reform. Because the legal expert is understood to have specialised technical knowledge, divested from politics, guided towards the common good, they have been welcomed to be involved in legal reforms in Third World territories, which otherwise would be a process that is left up to local actors, following the principles of sovereignty and democratic legitimacy.

The idea that technocratic involvement is moved by the common good has existed since the genesis of the development enterprise. During the civilising mission, metropoles sent experts to the colonies in the name of the common good.[75] Science was seen as the solution to accelerate the process of becoming civilised.[76] Ruth Craggs explains that the goal of colonial policy in the twentieth century was to 'both support colonialism and to improve the welfare of local populations'.[77] In a similar manner, throughout the process of decolonisation, former metropoles and international organisations set up development policies ostensibly framed around the common good.[78] Former metropoles relied on former colonial experts to implement these development policies, relying 'on the input of colonial experts of various kinds – such as agriculturalists, other technical advisors, and colonial district officers'.[79] These professionals, in turn, ended up forming a part of the staff of international organisations created after World War II, such as UNDP and the World Bank.[80] Because of the multilateral nature of these international organisations, they were understood to be divested from national self-interests, which had previously guided metropoles' colonial development policies. David Webster notes that technical assistance provided by the UN 'seemed a fair and non-colonial way of development through skills sharing, promising continued links between North and South after the end of colonialism on the basis of cooperation rather than exploitation'.[81]

Similar technocratic projections exist in development cooperation today. Development professionals today continue to see themselves as 'neutral experts' and their work as non-ideological and apolitical.[82] Kennedy writes that experts see their role as 'purveyors of something more like science, understood to pose more nuanced choices and more neutral and objective criteria'.[83] This conception of neutrality and technicality at the service of the common good is related to their entitlement to be involved in development.[84]

Behind these discursive practices, critical scholarship in international relations has criticised the technocratic projection of the experts' work at large, arguing that all expertise is inherently political.[85] In development settings the same logic prevails as the technocratic dimension of transnational involvement serves as a justificatory discursive tool to legitimate this involvement. Jan Eijking, for instance, shows how this discursive logic was used by imperial powers to generate a technocratic claim to internationality. In his case study of the Suez Canal, he shows the co-constituted nature of expertise and claims to the international that produces legitimacy for foreign involvement.[86] As he put it: 'if involvement of technical or scientific judgement is in demand, expertise can get attached to internationality by being performed as inherently universal, loyal to no nation, mobile by scientific necessity, acting on behalf of human progress, and so on'.[87] James Ferguson has unpacked the same logic in *The Anti-Politics Machine* examining development work in Lesotho: apolitical and technical aims justify state intervention.[88] In the development enterprise, legal experts see themselves as advising on specific technical issues, not political ones. David Kennedy notes that experts 'typically refrain from the language of interests or ideologies. They speak professional vernaculars of best practice, analytic rigor, empirical necessity, good sense, and consensus values'.[89] In the international law realm, Anne Orford shows how, with regard to the responsibility to protect, international executive rule was purported by Hammarskjöld on grounds of political neutrality.[90]

Apolitical ideology with political consequences

It is important to highlight that the apolitical ideology of expertise as it is what justifies the involvement of external actors in the first place. Behind technocratic projections and technicity lie real political consequences.[91] David Kennedy explains that 'experts act politically when they distribute resources among groups and individuals'.[92] The content of expertise is grounded, consciously or not, on a particular 'background of common sense' about how the world is and ought to be,[93] which in the development enterprise is liberal legalism. Again, this is of political nature as the expertise delivered presents in universal terms what is a contested interpretation of reality, 'point[ing] to the hidden contestations and political nature of the expertise'.[94] Kennedy characterises knowledge struggles of experts where 'the technical, the ideological and the partisan are everywhere linked together'.[95]

At the international level, Anne Orford highlights how neutrality with regard to UN responsibility to protect proves to be impossible in practice as 'it will require choosing between competing institutional claimants to authority'.[96] In legal reforms, regardless of how expert conceive their work, scholars have highlighted how providing expertise in legal reforms that affect the political arena is political and has political consequences.[97] With regard to legal reforms closer to constitution-making, as are transitional justice, post-conflict building or election reforms, critical scholars have well challenged the technocratic justification for foreign involvement and highlighted how the provision of expertise by international actors is deeply political.[98] A critical scholar in the transitional justice field, Dustin Sharp observed that transitional justice reform, despite being projected in technocratic terms, 'carries heavy implications for the distribution of power (political, legal, social, etc.) in the post-conflict context'.[99] It leads Patricia Lundy and Mark Mc Govern to point out how international assistance always has political implications, as such there is no such thing as 'apolitical foreign actors'.[100] In the context of post-conflict strategies, Chandra Sriram has noted how institutional reform, which includes 'rewriting constitutions', involve struggles for power.[101] In this sense, expertise that is provided in these situations is neither neutral nor apolitical. Finally, Quentin Deforge has shown how international actors crafted and built a technocratic expertise in the field of parliamentary support.[102] Deforge's research highlights in detail how building a depoliticised technical expertise is the fruit of political struggle that is itself embedded in politics. Similarly, by tracing the process of depoliticisation, Quentin Deforge has shown how framing social and political questions as technical opened the door to foreign involvement. Deforge's research focuses on 'governance activities' with the aim of unpacking how 'international actors have managed to establish themselves in domestic political spaces to deal with problems considered to fall within internal affairs of States'.[103] Through an impressively documented historical analysis of USAID and UN involvement in election support and parliamentary building, he shows how in these institutions elections and parliamentary building were framed as 'technical' questions, 'conceived as "separated from the political", aiming to diffuse technical knowledge to improve the efficiency of administrations'.[104]

Conclusion

This chapter has discussed the figure of the expert, the second core feature of the development enterprise. To share the West's rational law with the rest of the world, the expert becomes an essential component of the development enterprise. As this chapter has shown, legal experts act as channels to spread the paradigm of liberal legalism to Third World territories. The expert is also directly related to legal reforms, as sharing legal expertise is the raison d'être of the development enterprise. While the expert is an elusive figure, this chapter has pointed out two defining features: first, the expert is seen as possessing specialised technical knowledge; second, the expert's involvement is understood outside of the realm of politics, where the expert ostensibly acts in a 'neutral' manner towards the 'common good'. The analytical lens developed in this chapter is particularly useful to grasp the transnational dimension of constitution-making, as it expands the scope of analysis to capture the process that unfolds prior to the adoption of a particular norm.

Notes

1 Oeuvres de Saint-Simon et d'Essfansin (1865–78) xix, pp. 199–200 cited in Friedrich Hayek, 'The Counter-Revolution of Science' (1941) 8 Economica 119, 126.
2 James Gardner, *Legal Imperialism: American Lawyers and Foreign Aid in Latin America* (U of Wisconsin P 1980) 256.
3 In political science, the role of expertise in democratic settings has been widely discussed, particularly with regard to legitimacy. Frank Fischer, *Technocracy and the Politics of Expertise* (Sage 1990); Frank Fischer, *Climate Crisis and the Democratic Prospect: Participatory Governance in Sustainable Communities* (OUP 2017); Frank Fischer, *Democracy and Expertise: Reorienting Policy Inquiry* (OUP 2009); Thomas Pfister and Anna Horvath, 'Reassessing Expert Knowledge and the Politics of Expertise' (2014) 27 Innovation: The European Journal of Social Science Research 311; Giulia Pastorella, 'Technocratic Governments: Power, Expertise and Crisis Politics in European Democracies' (PhD dissertation, The London School of Economics and Political Science (LSE) 2016).
4 Peter Haas, 'Introduction: Epistemic Communities and International Policy Coordination' (1992) 46 International Organization 1, 3, 21; Antonin Cohen, 'Legal Professionals or Political Entrepreneurs? Constitution making as a Process of Social Construction and Political Mobilization' (2010) 4 International Political Sociology 107.
5 Jan Eijking, 'Historical Claims to the International: The Case of the Suez Canal Experts' (2023) 67 International Studies Quarterly 1, 3.
6 Quentin Deforge, 'Une expertise internationale sans "bonnes pratiques": Soutenir la professionnalisation du travail parlementaire dans la Tunisie d'après 2011' [2019] Critique Internationale 127; Annabelle Littoz-Monnet, *Governing Through Expertise: The Politics of Bioethics* (CUP 2020); Marieke Louis and Lucile Maertens, *Why International Organizations Hate Politics: Depoliticizing the World* (Routledge 2021) 2. For a summary of the debates in the literature. See Eijking (n 5) #12090.
7 See Yves Dezalay, Didier Bigo and Antonin Cohen, 'Enquêter sur l'internationalisation des noblesses d'Etat: Retour réflexif sur des stratégies de double jeu. Entretien avec Yves Dezalay' [2015] Cultures & Conflits 15; Boris Petric, *Where Are All Our Sheep? Kyrgyzstan, a Global Political Arena* (Berghahn Books 2015).
8 Christian Quast, 'Towards a Balanced Account of Expertise' (2018) 32 Social Epistemology 379, 397; Harald Mieg and Julia Evetts, 'Professionalism, Science, and Expert Roles: A Social Perspective' in Anders Ericsson and others (eds), *The Cambridge Handbook of Expertise and Expert Performance* (CUP 2018) 142; Reiner Grundmann, 'The Rightful Place of Expertise' (2018) 32 Social Epistemology 372, 377.
9 Pfister and Horvath (n 3) 312.
10 Séverine Autesserre, *Peaceland: Conflict Resolution and the Everyday Politics of International Intervention* (CUP 2014) 70–90.
11 Briony Jones, 'The Performance and Persistence of Transitional Justice and Its Ways of Knowing Atrocity' [2020] Cooperation and Conflict 1–2.
12 Rosemary Nagy, 'Transitional Justice as Global Project: Critical Reflections' (2008) 29 Third World Quarterly 275.
13 Fischer, *Democracy and Expertise: Reorienting Policy Inquiry* (n 3)18.
14 Fischer, *Technocracy and the Politics of Expertise* (n 3) 23.
15 ibid.
16 ibid 22.

17 Frederick Cooper, 'Modernizing Bureaucrats, Backward Africans, and the Development Concept' in Frederick Cooper and Randall Packard (eds), *International Development the Social Sciences: Essays on the History Politics of Knowledge* (U of California P 1997) 81.
18 ibid.
19 ibid 65.
20 ibid.
21 Timothy Mitchell, *Rule of Experts: Egypt, Techno-Politics, Modernity* (U of California P 2002) 22.
22 Cooper (n 17) 64.
23 Herbert Merillat, 'Law and Developing Countries' (1966) 60 American Journal of International Law 71–72.
24 James Ferguson, *The Anti-Politics Machine: 'Development', Depoliticization and Bureaucratic Power in Lesotho* (Routledge 1990) 258.
25 Autesserre (n 10) 77.
26 Sally Engle Merry, 'Colonial and Postcolonial Law' in Austin Sarat (ed), *The Blackwell Companion to Law and Society* (Blackwell Publishing 2004) 569.
27 Modern rational law had been used from early colonial times as a tool of modernisation as it was used in the process of 'formalisation', during which customary law was codified in the colonies. Other forms of law existed in other parts of the world, and these were translated into written codes. See Harith Al-Dabbagh, 'Le droit comparé comme instrument de modernisation: L'exemple des codifications civiles des Etats arabes du Moyen-Orient' (2013) 43 Revue de Droit: Université de Sherbrooke 388, 395; Jean-Louis Halpérin, *Profils des mondialisations du droit* (Dalloz 2009); Maaike Voorhoeve, 'Judicial Discretion in Tunisian Personal Status Law' in Maaike Voorhoeve (ed), *Family Law in Islam Divorce, Marriage and Women in the Muslim World* (IB Tauris 2012).
28 David Trubek, 'Toward a Social Theory of Law: An Essay on the Study of Law and Development' (1972) 82 The Yale Law Journal 1, 38.
29 Gardner (n 2) 256.
30 ibid 11.
31 William Douglas, 'Lawyers of the Peace Corps' (1962) 48 American Bar Association Journal 909; cited in David Trubek and Marc Galanter, 'Scholars in Self-Estrangement: Some Reflections on the Crisis in Law and Development Studies in the United States' [1974] Wisconsin Law Review 1062, 1067.
32 Jamie Rowen, *Searching for Truth in the Transitional Justice Movement* (CUP 2017) 22–37.
33 Dustin Sharp, 'Addressing Dilemmas of the Global and the Local in Transitional Justice' (2014) 29 Emory International Law Review 71, 78; Nicolas Michel and Katherine Del Mar, 'Transitional Justice' in Andrew Clapham and others (eds), *The Oxford Handbook of International Law in Armed Conflict* (OUP 2014) 841.
34 See contra Nagy (n 12).
35 Quast (n 8) 398.
36 Michael Barnett, 'International Paternalism and Humanitarian Governance' (2012) 1 Global Constitutionalism 485, 508.
37 ibid.
38 Fischer 1990 (n 3) 13.
39 Barnett (n 36) 508.
40 Friedrich Hayek, *The Counter-Revolution of Science: Studies on the Use and Abuse of Reason* (Liberty Fund Inc 1952) 110.
41 Trubek (n 28) 18.
42 Gardner (n 2) 35.

43 ibid 12.
44 Anne Peters and Heiner Schwenke, 'Comparative Law Beyond Post-Modernism' (2000) 49 International & Comparative Law Quarterly 800, 804.
45 Anne Thurston Pugh, *Records of the Colonial Office, Dominions Office, Commonwealth Relations Office, and Commonwealth Office* (Her Majesty's Stationery Office 1995) 129.
46 Pierre Allorant and Walter Badier, 'La société de législation comparée: Boîte à idées du parlementarisme libéral de l'Empire libéral à la République opportuniste' (2017) 13 Revue électronique d'histoire du droit 1.
47 Florence Renucci, 'La "décolonisation doctrinale" ou la naissance du droit d'Outre-mer (1946-début des années 1960)' [2011] Revue d'Histoire des Sciences Humaines 61–62.
48 Elliot Burg, 'Law and Development: A Review of the Literature and a Critique of "Scholars in Self-Estrangement"' [1977] The American Journal of Comparative Law 492, 498.
49 For an historical documented analysis of the emergence of the law and development movement see Quentin Deforge, 'La fabrique transnationale du politique: Une sociologie historique du champ réformateur de la "gouvernance" (1961–2019)' (PhD dissertation, Université Paris-Dauphine 2019).
50 Gardner (n 2) 282.
51 John Henry Merryman, 'Comparative Law and Social Change: On the Origins, Style, Decline & Revival of the Law and Development Movement' [1977] The American Journal of Comparative Law 457, 482. See Jedidiah Kroncke, 'Law and Development as Anti-Comparative Law' (2012) 45 Vanderbilt Journal of Transnational Law 477.
52 Bénédjcte Fauvarque-Cosson, 'Deux siècles d'évolution du droit comparé' (2011) 63 Revue internationale de droit comparé 527, 531.
53 Ugo Mattei, 'Three Patterns of Law: Taxonomy and Change in the World's Legal Systems' (1997) 45 The American Journal of Comparative Law 5–6.
54 Thomas Carothers, 'The Problem of Knowledge' in Thomas Carothers (ed), *Promoting the Rule of Law Abroad: In Search of Knowledge* (Carnegie Endowment for International Peace 2006) 15.
55 Kevin Davis and Michael Trebilcock, 'The Relationship Between Law and Development: Optimists Versus Skeptics' (2008) 56 The American Journal of Comparative Law 895.
56 Harry Collins and Robert Evans, 'A Sociological/Philosophical Perspective on Expertise: The Acquisition of Expertise Through Socialization' in Anders Ericsson and others (eds), *The Cambridge Handbook of Expertise and Expert Performance* (CUP 2018) 23.
57 Ruth Craggs, 'Development in a Gobal-Historical Context' in Vandana Desai and Rob Potter (eds), *The Companion to Development Studies* (Routledge 2014) 39.
58 ibid 38.
59 Autesserre (n 10) 77, 90.
60 ibid 72.
61 ibid 69.
62 ibid.
63 ibid 84.
64 Jones (n 11) 1.
65 ibid.
66 Bastien François has highlighted how in the late 1950s in France existed this idea that politics had to be in hands of technicians. François Bastien, *Le régime politique de la Ve République* (La Découverte 1999) 11.

67 Claude Henri de Rouvroy, comte de Saint-Simon (commonly known as Henri de Saint-Simon) quoted in Pastorella (n 3) 37.
68 Fischer 1990 (n 3) 21.
69 ibid.
70 ibid 24.
71 Grundmann (n 8) 378.
72 Autesserre (n 10) 75. See Pfister and Horvath (n 3) 311.
73 Michael Barnett, *The International Humanitarian Order* (Routledge 2009) 58.
74 Eijking (n 5) 4.
75 Cooper (n 17) 65.
76 Prabhakar Singh, 'The Scandal of Enlightenment and the Birth of Disciplines: Is International Law a Science?' (2010) 12 International Community Law Review 5–6.
77 Craggs (n 57) 37.
78 Uma Kothari, 'From Colonialism to Development: Reflections of Former Colonial Officers' (2006) 44 Commonwealth & Comparative Politics 118, 125.
79 Craggs (n 57) 38.
80 See Joseph Hodge, *Triumph of the Expert: Agrarian Doctrines of Development and the Legacies of British Colonialism* (Ohio UP 2007) 38; Kothari (n 78).
81 David Webster, 'Development Advisors in a Time of Cold War and Decolonization: The United Nations Technical Assistance Administration, 1950–59' (2011) 6 Journal of Global History 249–50.
82 David Kennedy, 'The "Rule of Law", Political Choices, and Development Common Sense' in David M Trubek and Alvaro Santos (eds), *The New Law and Economic Development: A Critical Appraisal* (CUP 2006) 97.
83 ibid.
84 Eva-Maria Muschik, 'Managing the World: The United Nations, Decolonization, and the Strange Triumph of State Sovereignty in the 1950s and 1960s' (2018) 13 Journal of Global History 121–22.
85 See Hélène Dufournet, 'Quand techniciser c'est faire de la politique "sans le dire": Récit d'une "technicisation réussie" au ministère de la Défense' (2014) 3 Gouvernement et action publique 29; Marion Fresia, 'La fabrique des normes internationales sur la protection des réfugiés au sein du comité exécutif du hcr' [2012] Critique Internationale 39; Timothy Mitchell, 'The Work of Economics: How a Discipline Makes Its World' (2005) 46 European Journal of sociology/Archives Européennes de Sociologie 297; Pfister and Horvath (n 3); Irène Théry, 'Expertises de service, de consensus, d'engagement: Essai de typologie de la mission d'expertise en sciences sociales' [2005] Droit et société 311; Lisa Stampnitzky and Delphine Ettinger, 'Experts, états et théorie des champs: Sociologie de l'expertise en matière de terrorisme' [2013] Critique Internationale 89.
86 Eijking (n 5) 2.
87 ibid.
88 Ferguson (n 24) 262.
89 David Kennedy, *A World of Struggle: How Power, Law, and Expertise Shape Global Political Economy* (Princeton UP 2018) 114.
90 Anne Orford, *International Authority and the Responsibility to Protect* (CUP 2011) 192.
91 On the political nature of comparative law see Gunter Frankenberg, 'Stranger Than Paradise: Identity & Politics in Comparative Law' [1997] Utah Law Review 259–63.
92 Kennedy (n 82) 95.
93 Kennedy (n 89) 89.

94 Jones (n 11) 7.
95 Kennedy (n 89) 3.
96 Orford (n 90) 193.
97 See Kennedy (n 82); Ferguson (n 24); Louis and Maertens (n 6); Lucile Maertens and Raphaëlle Parizet, '"On ne fait pas de politique!" Les pratiques de dépolitisation au PNUD et au PNUE' [2017] Critique Internationale 41.
98 See a more in-depth discussion in chapter 5.
99 Sharp (n 33) 82.
100 Patricia Lundy and Mark McGovern, 'Whose Justice? Rethinking Transitional Justice from the Bottom Up' (2008) 35 Journal of Law and Society 265. See Sandrine Lefranc, 'Convertir le grand nombre à la paix: Une ingénierie internationale de pacification' (2007) 80 Politix 7; Kieran McEvoy and Lorna McGregor, *Transitional Justice from Below: Grassroots Activism and the Struggle for Change* (Hart Publishing 2008); Rowen (n 32).
101 Chandra Lekha Sriram, 'Justice as Peace? Liberal Peacebuilding and Strategies of Transitional Justice' (2007) 21 Global Society 579, 588.
102 See Deforge (n 49) 27.
103 ibid 22. [My own translation].
104 ibid 37–38. [My own translation].

Part 2

External actors in constitution-making as a development enterprise

Chapter 4

Tracing external actor involvement from decolonisation to post-cold war constitution-making

In a report for the United Nations Department of Political and Peacebuilding Affairs (UNDPPA) titled *Advice on Applying Mediation Fundamentals in UN Constitutional Assistance*, Sumit Bisarya observed that 'until the mid-twentieth century, it was not unusual for external actors to draft constitutions, either in part or in full'.[1] Sir Kenneth Roberts Wray, who participated in many pre-independence constitutional conferences as a legal advisor in Britain's Colonial Office, echoed this idea, writing that he did not understand 'the urge to have a new constitution produced in such way that it can claim to be an entirely local product'.[2] Many decades later, a new sentiment surrounds external involvement, with scholars and practitioners alike distancing themselves from the era when constitutions were imposed on local actors. The 2020 Guidance Note holds as one of its core principles that 'Constitution making is a sovereign process that, to be successful, should be nationally owned and led'.[3]

This chapter argues that, although the modes of action of external actors might have changed, they are still very much involved in constitution-making processes. This study's analytical framework, the development enterprise, reveals that the transnational dimension of constitution-making is underpinned by the paradigm of liberal legalism. The chapter is informed by a comment from Tom Ginsburg, that 'constitution-making . . . is part of a much broader movement that has occurred over the last three decades, sometimes called the "rule-of-law" movement or the "law and development" movement'.[4] Despite the diversity of external actors, the lens of the development enterprise highlights that they largely share a background of common sense: namely, liberal legalism. What also comes into focus is the continuity of actors' ideological roots that they share, consciously or not, despite the different modalities of their involvement.

The central argument of this chapter is that external actors conceive of liberal constitutions as a legal tool to accelerate social change, based on the 'modernisation rationale'. This is the idea that Third World territories should replicate the economic and political systems of the West in order to achieve a similar level of development. Legal reforms are seen as an accelerator to

DOI: 10.4324/9781003386186-7

reach liberal democracy, which involves importing the modern law that allowed Western countries to develop economically and politically. Translated into constitutional terms, liberal constitutional democracy became a global standard, with constitution-making as the means of fulfilling that goal. The 'correct' constitutional framework is understood as facilitating social and political goals, including peace and development. This conception of constitution-making was articulated within the realm of decolonisation and became the implicit paradigm in the post-Cold War era, which over time became the background of 'common sense' shared by external actors. As David Kennedy notes, 'background ideas about the world – often experienced as "facts" rather than "ideas" – shape the world before people set to work on the problems they see with the knowledge they have'.[5]

This chapter provides a critical history and holistic analysis of external actor involvement in constitution-making, drawing on scholarship from TWAIL, postcolonial legal theory, peace-building, history and political science. While addressed by these other fields, this is a topic that has received only marginal attention from comparative constitutional scholars. Particularly useful here is the work of international scholar Vijayashri Sripati, who in her 2020 book *Constitution-Making under UN Auspices* examined UN involvement in constitution-making through a detailed historical analysis.[6] This chapter also relies on testimonies from actors involved in constitution-making processes.

In line with the overall scope of this investigation, this analysis is limited to formal constitutions. As such, discussion of former French colonies is excluded as the French Empire used international treaties to legally frame the path to independence; these treaties contained provisions that were constitutional from a material perspective but were not formal constitutions.[7] Second, while this chapter is devoted to external actor involvement during decolonisation and post-Cold War, many of the constitutions adopted during these periods have been substantially reformed. For instance, most of the constitutions adopted during decolonisation have since undergone substantial modifications, or entirely new constitutions have been adopted. It remains that external actor involvement left a mark on the constitutional heritage of these countries. Brun-Otto Bryde writes,

> In most states, the law introduced by the colonial power was not just retained after independence, but the Westernisation of law was even strengthened because the new elites were often more hostile to traditional law than colonial administrators who wanted to keep the natives native.[8]

Despite subsequent modification of these constitutions, the involvement of external actors remains significant as it frames the model in which these constitutional frameworks operate.[9] As Upendra Baxi notes: 'Postcolonial constitutions thus inevitably carry their birthmarks'.[10] Third, while this chapter centres on the role of external actors during constitution-making, the role of domestic actors is significant but outside the scope of this book.[11]

Finally, the discussion of this chapter deals with the discourse of external actors. There are implicit principles and aims concealed behind more explicit, public-facing discourse. In this regard, the concern from metropoles that their colonies had reached a certain degree of 'self-government' is a public-facing discourse. Implicitly, this allowed the metropole to keep close ties with its colonies and to maintain economic relations, which allowed for trade. Sripati has shown how 'powerful Western states create within developing states constitutional regimes that have the effect of throwing open the latter's resources for the transnational capitalist class'.[12]

This chapter offers several key contributions related to the book's research questions. First, by broadening the scope of analysis beyond the mere adoption of the constitution, the development enterprise framework allows for the examination of certain actors – such as UNDP, International IDEA, the Organisation Internationale de la Francophonie (OIF), and other INGOs – that have hitherto been ignored by the literature.[13] Constitutional scholarship has largely focused on the Venice Commission.[14] Second, the lens of the development enterprise reveals the colonial lineage of the transnational dimension of constitution-making; despite their diversity, external actors rely on the paradigm of liberal legalism. This chapter discusses the rebranding in apolitical terms of the rationale of the 'civilising mission', by equating 'democracy' with '(Western) liberal democracy'.

Building upon the discussion in the previous chapters, the development enterprise framework is useful to examine the transnational dimension of constitution-making as it shows the inadequacy of the concept of constituent power. Constitution-making in the context of democratic transition is characterised by the presence of external actors to such an extent that the notion of constituent power is not only unable to offer a comprehensive understanding of the process but fundamentally obfuscates the fact that the bulk of transnational involvement in constitution-making occurs during the drafting phase.

The first section fleshes out the instrumentalist understanding of the law that characterises liberal legalism, revealing how external actors consider constitutions to be a tool to achieve social change; the *legalist* side of liberal legalism is explored here. The second section examines the *liberal* side, highlighting how the logic of modernisation underpins external actor involvement, where only a particular type of constitution is advocated: the liberal constitution.

Constitution-making as a tool to achieve political change

A first manifestation of liberal legalism appears through the instrumentalist understanding external actors hold with regard to constitution-making.

External actors conceive of constitution-making as an optimal legal tool to achieve desired social change during decolonisation and in the post-Cold War period. The prominent external actor during decolonisation, which ranges from the early twentieth century to the aftermath of World War II, is the metropolitan state and, to a lesser extent, the UN. Following the end of the Cold War, external actors diversified and encompassed different international governmental organisations and international non-governmental organisations (INGOs) in the post-Cold War period. The lens of the development enterprise highlights a continuity in external actor involvement over time: their instrumentalist understanding of constitution-making is explicit throughout constitution-making in the context of decolonisation and appears implicitly in post-Cold War constitution-making.

The constitution factory: from Whitehall to the White House

During constitution-making in the context of decolonisation, metropoles relied explicitly on the paradigm of liberal legalism, where making a constitution was conceived as a necessary step towards achieving the sufficient degree of political development that would make Third World territories worthy of self-government. Indeed, despite the vastly different geopolitical contexts, metropoles held a shared understanding that a territory was deemed 'civilised' or politically developed when it finally possessed a written constitution.[15] Following the idea of the rationalisation of the law, the governance of the state must be enshrined in written fundamental law. Having a constitution also carried another function, as it created sovereignty at the international level.[16] For instance, ahead of the negotiations of the Berlin Conference, where European leaders met to negotiate territorial claims on the African continent, Leopold II of Belgium requested Travers Twiss, a British lawyer, to draft a constitution for the *Afrique Equatoriale*, since a written constitution enabled Leopold II to claim sovereignty over that territory.[17] While this dimension of the role constitutions can play is worth keeping in mind, this section focuses on the role that constitution-making played for external actors who sought to achieve political development, highlighting a few paradigmatic cases of constitution-making in the context of decolonisation that reveal the instrumentalist understanding of two external actors during decolonisation: metropoles and the UN.

Whitehall constitutions as transitory tools

Sir Kenneth Roberts-Wray labelled the Colonial Office, where he was a legal advisor, a 'constitutional factory'.[18] The British Empire, which did not have a written constitution, paradoxically ended up being the architect of a substantial number of written constitutions across the world.[19] The constitution was the legal vessel used by the British Empire to grant internal autonomy to its colonies, where political development was signalled by adopting constitutional democracy.[20] The phrase 'self-government when fit for it' was the standard line from British authorities regarding colonies having the aspiration to gain greater autonomy and independence.[21]

Constitutions made in the context of decolonisation were drafted by metropolitan states and enshrined in their respective legal framework. As Issa Shivji points out, law: 'to a large extent, exhibited its instrumental character. It was there to achieve very definite aims and interests of the colonial state'.[22] In the British Empire, constitutions of the British Empire's colonies were drafted by British authorities and adopted within the British legal framework. Constitutions of colonies were 'made law by Order in Council',[23] which involved 'government orders of a legislative character made by the Crown and members of the Privy Council'.[24] Second, the constitutions of the British colonies were ultimately drafted by British authorities and came to be labelled as 'Whitehall constitutions', in reference to the headquarters of the Colonial office.[25] At an institutional level, the Colonial office was responsible for managing British colonial dependencies, and among these tasks was constitutional planning, which was addressed by the legal division of the Colonial Office. From 1946–1953, constitution-making was one of many 'general subjects' dealt with by the Colonial Office.[26] From 1953 onwards, a dedicated 'constitutional department' was established to address 'general questions regarding future policy, co-ordination of constitutional developments, including related aspects of national legislative programme'.[27]

While several consultative constitutional conferences were organised, gathering different domestic representatives under the auspices of the Colonial office,[28] the final word lay in the hands of the British government.[29] The representatives of the different territories were merely consulted and the legislature of the new state was informed once the constitution had been adopted by the Colonial offices.[30] Sir Ivor Jennings, who was heavily involved in Ceylon's [Sri Lanka] constitutional drafting, recalls the back-and-forth dynamic that existed between the local elites as well as the Secretary of State:

> The procedure was as follows. D.S. had a complete brief on each question. He noted on it whether Sir Robert and Sir Barclay had agreed, disagreed or reserved a question. He then came back to the bungalow and gave me the full story, which I promptly wrote out and sent to Sir Oliver by air. Sir Oliver's job was to see that an agreed change was not altered and to argue any point which the Officers of State had refused to concede. Actually, the Secretary of State and his advisers were much readier to concede changes than the Officers of State, and indeed he had a wide discretion. Sir Oliver was thus able considerably to improve the draft.[31]

The instrumental understanding of constitution-making by the British Empire, which acted as an external actor, is revealed by the temporality of constitution-making with regard to independence in the decolonisation context. A written constitution was a condition sine qua non to be granted independence.[32] Despite the British 'piecemeal approach' to decolonisation, a pattern in terms of temporality can be outlined. The constitution of the independent country to be adopted was stamped with the final London approval, in order to be granted independence. Constitutions were adopted in most cases before the adoption of the Independence Act by the British Parliament.[33] For instance, the Constitution of Ceylon was adopted through an Order in Council, in May 1946, following the work of the Soulbury Commission sent by the British government in 1944 to examine the constitutional draft prepared by the Ceylonese government. The independence of Ceylon was granted on 10 December 1947. Similarly, the Nigeria Constitution was adopted through an Order in Council on 30 September 1960,[34] and Nigeria became independent one month later, on 1 October 1960.[35]

Over the span of 20 years (1947–1968), the independence of 21 countries was approved by an act of the British Parliament, the Independence Act;[36] this act included a provision preventing further amendment of the constitution that had been drafted by British authorities. For instance, in the 1957 Ghana Independence Act, referring to the 1954–1956 Gold Coast Constitution Order in Council, it stated that: 'Notwithstanding anything in the foregoing provisions of this Schedule, the constitutional provisions shall not be repealed, amended or modified otherwise than in such manner as may be specified in those provisions'.[37] Similar provisions relating to their respective constitutions were present in the Independence Acts of Barbados,[38] Nigeria,[39] Tanganyika,[40] and Jamaica.[41] The instrumentalist understanding of constitution-making is further revealed by the fact that before the final constitution was stamped with the approval of British authorities, a series of successive constitutions were adopted, incrementally increasing the 'self-government' of the given colony. Before reaching independence, several versions of the constitution were drafted before the country was deemed to be sufficiently civilised to reach independence. William Dale, who worked at the Colonial Office and participated in the drafting of many constitutions, summarises how constitutions were used by the British Empire:

> On independence there was a new emperor, but his suit of clothes was far from new. The weavers in the Colonial Office had begun work on the cloth, and taken out their tailoring shears, long before. *The final constitution was the last of a series* providing for increasingly responsible government, so much so that at the end the tailoring was often largely a matter of scissors and paste.[42]

The adoption of successive different constitutions was used to develop self-government incrementally within the colony, before allowing them to be fully independent. It would allow the colony to develop sufficient knowledge of parliamentary institutions and prevent the territory from falling into chaos or dictatorship.[43] The metropole would thus renounce its 'responsibilities' as soon as it believed the territory was 'mature' enough to govern itself.[44]

Constitutions were seen as transitional tools, and the various steps of devolution towards 'self-government' can be found in the several constitutions that were adopted.[45] Between 1944 and 1961, 92 constitutions were adopted, increasing the self-government of these territories incrementally.[46] For instance, Nigeria was granted six constitutions by the Crown through Order in Council. In the 1914 Constitution, the Council of the Lagos colony was merely advisory, while the 1922 Constitution[47] expanded the membership of the Council and integrated other territories of the colony. A 1946 Constitution was adopted following claims calling for independence, and a 1951 Constitution was made following a process of consultation.[48] The final 1954 Constitution granted autonomy to regional governments.[49]

As this brief sketch reveals, constitutions drafted in the context of decolonisation were used by the metropole before a colonial territory was granted independence, illustrating the idea that in order to be independent, the right legal framework is necessary to signal political maturity, without the tutelage of the metropole. Here we see the inadequacy of the notion of constituent power to examine the transnational dimension of constitution-making, as from an institutional standpoint, with a few exceptions, these constitutions were not drafted by a constituent assembly.[50] Even in the few cases where the constitution was adopted by a constituent assembly, the content of the constitution still had to be approved by the British Empire. For instance, in the case of Pakistan, even if independence had been granted before the adoption of the constitution, the formal approval of the British Governor-General was still necessary.[51] The people's participation in the making of the constitution was extremely limited.[52] Constitutions were typically negotiated between the colonial power and a local political group, which in most cases did not represent the 'people'. As Yash Ghai notes:

> To begin with, it was to be a negotiated agreement between the colonial power and local political groups, not the people directly. The constitution was to prescribe a democratic order with a Bill of Rights and an independent judiciary, similar to that in the metropolitan state.[53]

The vast number of constitutions made during decolonisation are difficult to apprehend via the lens of constituent power, thus revealing the poverty of the concept.

Constitution-making in the Belgian and United States Empires

The instrumentalist understanding of constitution-making in the process of colonisation also characterised other colonial empires, including Belgium and the United States. In Belgium, the constitution was seen as a transitional tool for Belgian authorities to use to support colonies to reach independence. As in the case of the British Empire, it was the metropole, which was entrusted in drafting the constitution of the soon-to-be independent Congo. On 30 July 1958, Belgian authorities entrusted the Belgian Chamber and Senate to draft a report regarding Congo's independence.[54] Consultations were organised and heard 212 Africans and 250 Europeans, and in 1959 the Parliament drafted a report that contained 'the Belgian master-plan for structuring the Congo state'.[55] Popular upheavals taking place in Leopoldville (Congo) in January 1959 forced Belgian authorities to negotiate the terms of independence with the Congolese delegation during a roundtable conference that took place between January and February 1960 in Brussels.[56] The result of these negotiations was a transitory Congolese constitution that set up the framework for the adoption of another constitution that would be adopted within two years.[57] In this regard, the independence of Congo from Belgium followed a similar trajectory to former British colonies. The Congolese constitution was enshrined in legislation on 19 May 1960,[58] with independence granted on 30 June 1960.[59]

The United States' Empire also shared an instrumentalist understanding of constitution-making as exemplified by the Constitution of the Philippines.[60] Following the Spanish-American War, the territory of the Philippines was ceded to the United States in the Treaty of Paris of 1898. From a legal standpoint, the conditions under which the Philippines would be granted independence were enshrined in a US statute. The 1934 Tydings – McDuffie Act stated that the Philippines could become independent following a ten-year period as well as a series of conditions, including the fact that the new constitution should adopt a republican form – a Bill of rights – and that future Philippine citizens should pay allegiance to the US.[61] The draft constitution crafted by the Philippine legislature had to be submitted for approval to the United States President, which would then be submitted to the Filipino People for approval or rejection. Section 3 of the Tydings – McDuffie Act stated:

> Upon the drafting and approval of the constitution by the constitutional convention in the Philippine Islands, the constitution shall be submitted within two years after the enactment of this Act to the President of the United States, who shall determine whether or not it conforms with the provisions of this Act.[62]

The Constitution of the Commonwealth of the Philippines was certified by Franklin Roosevelt on 23 March 1935, where Roosevelt wrote: 'I am happy to state that the Constitution submitted to me on behalf of the Philippine Constitutional Convention for Certification under the Tydings – McDuffie Independence Act conforms with the provisions of the Act'.[63] The Constitution was ratified by the Filipino people on 14 May 1935.

Both of these examples from Belgium and the United States highlight the instrumentalist rationale that underpinned constitution-making. In both cases, the constitution was treated as a transitory tool to reach the threshold of 'self-government' deemed necessary by metropoles to grant independence; importantly, the constitution also *signalled* that the territories had reached this important stage.

The birth of UN involvement in constitution-making

The UN's involvement in constitution-making marks an important shift when examining the transnational dimension of constitution-making. It is the first time that a multilateral international organisation was involved and not a separate metropole. The UN, established in the aftermath of World War II, was initially only marginally involved in constitution-making. Most of the decolonisation process that took place before the 1960s occurred without UN involvement. As Ruppert Emerson explains, 'at least until after 1960 it was really only the stickier situations which brought the UN into the picture'.[64] Entire territories from the British Empire – such as Malaysia, Ghana, Nigeria, Sri Lanka, India, Philippines – and sub-Saharan territories under French control all achieved independence without the UN.[65]

The UN came to be involved in several processes related to territories within the trusteeship system established in 1945;[66] Chapter XII of the UN Charter noted that the objective of the trusteeship system was to 'promote the political economic, social and educational advancement of the inhabitants of the trust territories, and their progressive development towards self-government or independence'.[67] The trusteeship activities resulted in the 1994 independence of Palau.[68]

The UN's initial involvement in constitution-making occurred in Libya,[69] between 1949 and 1952. Following the end of the Second World War, Italy had to cede its colonies to the Western allies, who decided in 1949, that Eritrea, Italian Somaliland, and Libya's process of decolonisation would be led by the UN.[70] At that time, Libya lay within the competing interests of Italy, the United Kingdom, and the United States, yet it fell upon the United Nations General Assembly (UNGA)[71] to address Libya's independence, where Adrian Pelt, a Dutch diplomat, was appointed High Commissioner for Libya to 'assist the Libyans to determine and enact a constitution'.[72] As U Thant, former Secretary-General of the United Nations, noted: 'I would say that Mr. Pelt, advising the representatives of the people of Libya, played a major role in successfully implementing the General Assembly's decision to make the former Italian colony of Libya an independent State'.[73] The Libyan National Assembly promulgated the Constitution on 7 October 1951, after only one month of discussions.[74] The UNGA resolution called for the constitution to be adopted before independence.[75]

The end of decolonisation led to a period where transnational involvement in constitution-making came under severe criticism.[76] In the 1960s, several former colonies, alongside the Soviet Union, pushed for the adoption of resolutions within the UNGA, including the soft law instrument, the 'Declaration on the Granting of Independence to Colonial Countries and Peoples'. This was adopted by the UNGA on 14 December 1960 and declared the right of all people to self-determination.[77] Following the rush to independence of former African colonies, a UN committee was created to implement this declaration.[78] Ten years later, the 1970 'Declaration on Principles of International Law concerning Friendly Relations and Cooperation among States' reiterates the principle of equal rights and self-determination of peoples, in order to 'bring a speedy end to colonialism, having due regard to the freely expressed will of the peoples concerned' and outlining the inalienable right of the state to 'choose its political, economic, social and cultural systems, without interference in any form by another State'.[79] Three years later, the UNGA declared that the

> continuation of colonialism in all its forms . . . is a crime and that colonial peoples have the inherent right to struggle by all necessary means at their disposal against colonial Powers and alien domination in exercise of their right of self-determination.[80]

During this period, the ICCPR was adopted in 1966, but only entered into force in 1976. This legally binding Covenant enshrines the principles in its Article 1 (1) stating that, 'all peoples have the right of self-determination', while the third paragraph outlines the obligations for metropoles to 'promote the realisation of the right of self-determination, and shall respect that right'.[81] By enshrining the principle of self-determination, the ICCPR can be understood as prohibiting the type of foreign involvement in constitution-making that took place during decolonisation.

From that moment onwards, UN involvement in constitution-making occurred in sovereign Third World countries, as political colonialism had largely disappeared.[82] The first instance of UN involvement was in the making of a constitution for Congo in 1960.[83] Following Belgian independence, Patrice Lumumba and Joseph Kasa-Vubu requested UN assistance to protect Congo against Belgium's aggression.[84] The United Nations Security Council (UNSC) mandated a peace operation in July 1960, the UN Operation in Congo (ONUC): 'The initial mandate of ONUC was to ensure the withdrawal of Belgian forces from the Republic of the Congo, to assist the Government in maintaining law and order and to provide technical assistance'.[85]

As Vijayashri Sripati notes, ONUC involved the 'largest programme of technical assistance for any country in the history of the world organization'.[86] Among other things, ONUC was involved in constitution-making:

> The Principal Legal Adviser and two other United Nations experts attached to the Ministry of Justice advised the Government on general problems of organization of the judiciary and . . . a complete revision of the legal code was undertaken, and assistance was given in the drawing up of *a new Constitution* to replace the *Loi fondamentale* in 1964.[87]

Despite the varying historical and political context, when it comes to transnational involvement during decolonisation, constitution-making was explicitly characterised by the paradigm of liberal legalism: written constitutions were seen as the legal tool to achieve the desired social change (i.e., political development), which is acknowledged through being granted independence. This rationale continued to pervade, albeit implicitly, throughout the post-Cold War era.

Post-cold war constitution-making as a tool for peace-building and democratic governance

External actors, despite their multiplication and diversification, share an instrumentalist understanding of constitutions as a tool to achieve a desired set of social goals: democracy, peace, and development. The paradigm of liberal legalism served to shape the decolonisation era and persisted throughout the post-Cold War period, albeit in a more implicit manner, largely because external actors became involved in constitution-making of sovereign countries.

The fall of the Soviet Union led to an eruption of constitution-making processes, accompanied by a proliferation of external actors that became involved in the process. The UN and its different agencies were a prominent actors, with involvement in 41 sovereign states since 1989.[88] Throughout this period, constitution-making was conceived of as a *passage obligé* to transition from an authoritarian regime to a democracy. Venice Commission, an advisory consultative body of the Council of Europe, was created for this exact purpose, providing constitutional assistance to Eastern and Central European countries undergoing a democratic transition.[89] Antonio Pergola, President of the Venice Commission from 1990–2007, expresses this mission:

> the [Venice] Commission was set up within the Council of Europe to provide a collective service of assistance on constitutional matters for the democracies which would be arising from the ashes of the Soviet bloc . . . the thrust of our initial commitment was, to be sure, participating in the constituent season of the emerging democracies.[90]

The Venice Commission was set up in May 1990 for an initial two-year period, following the 'Conference for the Commission for Democracy through Law', which was held in January 1990 and gathered Member States of the Council of Europe as well as several Eastern and Central European countries that were invited as observers.[91] In 1992, it was decided to maintain the Venice Commission through a partial agreement, and by 2001 all Member States of the Council of Europe were members of the Venice Commission.[92] In 2011, the Venice Commission allowed for states outside of the Council of Europe to become members.[93]

In addition to this, the post-Cold War period saw the creation of another specialised international organisation, the International IDEA. Finally, this period also saw the involvement of INGOs, such as the Max Planck Foundation for International Peace and the Rule of Law (Max Planck Foundation), which is examined in this section. Overall, given the prohibition existing in international law, states largely stopped being directly involved in foreign constitution-making. Notable exception include New Zealand's involvement in Palau, Nauru, and Fiji or the United States involvement in the 2005 Iraqi Constitution.[94]

Before examining how the constitution is understood as a legal tool to achieve social change, a caveat is in order. While the social goals examined in this chapter are presented in a separate fashion, in practice they are intertwined. For instance, 'peace' is considered to be a precondition of 'development', and these goals are also conceived holistically by external actors themselves. The 2020 Guidance Note adopted by the Secretary-General in September 2020 similarly conveys an instrumentalist understanding of constitution-making for peace and development:

> A constitution is a state's foundational legal instrument establishing rights, institutions and processes that guide how the state functions and power and resources are shared. As such, constitution making is a central aspect of state building, conflict prevention and resolution, *peacebuilding* and the promotion of human rights, the rule of law and *sustainable human development*.[95]

Beginning in the immediate aftermath of the Cold War, this section proceeds with a close examination of how constitutions are conceived by external actors, at least implicitly, as a transitional tool to achieve two specific social goals: peace and development.

Constitutions for peace

One way that external actors conceive of constitution-making is as a tool to achieve a particular social goal: peace.[96] The end of the Cold War marked a turning point in global peace-building, with a vast increase in the number of operations authorised by the UNSC. Between 1945 and 1989, there was approximately a new mission every four years, while from 1989 onwards, a new mission emerged every six months.[97] This rise in operations also resulted in constitution-making integrated within the peace-building framework. In general, more constitutions are adopted *within* the context of peace-building than any other environment. This has a legal implication with regard to external actors, as it means that transnational involvement in constitution-making is framed within international law.[98] Pursuant to Chapter VII of the UN Charter, the UNSC can approve UN involvement in peace-building constitution-making by demanding constitutional reforms, which are deemed necessary to bring peace.

Because of this context, many traditional peace-building actors were brought into the realm of constitution-making. In 1996, the UN published 'An Agenda for Democratization', where then-Secretary-General, Boutros Boutros-Ghali, notes that constitution-making is part of the peace-keeping mission entrusted to the UN: 'United Nations departments, agencies and programmes have been called upon to help states draft constitutions'.[99] In 2005, further reference is made to this idea in the 'Report of the Secretary-General on the Work of the Organization': 'peacekeepers deployed to conflict zones in record numbers and in complex multidimensional operations working not only to provide security, but also . . . write *constitutions*'.[100]

Constitutions are treated as a tool to prevent current and future conflicts.[101] Hallie Ludsin notes that peace-building aims to 'consolidate peace in the short term; and, in the long term, increase the likelihood that future conflicts are resolved without violence'.[102] The 2001 UN Report of the Secretary-General notes that 'a *carefully crafted constitution* can provide a society with the tools to manage and resolve disputes peacefully, while a flawed constitution can exacerbate existing problems'.[103] In a similar vein, the 2020 Guidance Note states:

> Conflict is frequently linked to disputes about the exercise of state power, the allocation of resources and identity – matters to which the constitution is inextricably linked. In these circumstances, engaging with constitutional matters can be part of a conflict prevention, resolution or peacebuilding strategy.[104]

External actors who engage in constitution-making within the context of peace-building understand constitutions as appropriate legal vessels to enshrine peace-agreements – legal tools to translate political agreement into law. This understanding is shared by the scientific literature, which sees an intrinsic potential for constitutions to be tools to achieve peace.[105]

The relationship between constitutions and peace-agreements can unfold in a variety of forms. Constitutions can be included in peace agreements that are international treaties. One of the paradigmatic cases is the Constitution of Bosnia and Herzegovina, which is contained in Annex No. 4 of the Dayton Agreements signed in 1995 among the Republic of Bosnia and Herzegovina, the Republic of Croatia, and the Federal Republic of Yugoslavia.[106] Further, political negotiations carried out during peace-building processes can be enshrined in the new constitution to come.[107] Kirsti Samuels specifies that constitutions can simultaneously 'be partly a peace agreement and partly a framework setting up the rules by which the new democracy will operate'.[108] Thus, peace-agreements can have significant constitutional implications.[109] Certain peace-agreement international treaties include a framework that details the adoption of the new constitution or a series of guiding principles that the constitution must include. For example, the 2005 Constitution of Burundi adopted following the guidelines of the 2000 Arusha Peace and Reconciliation Agreement for Burundi (Arusha Agreement) contained rules regarding human rights, the structure of government, and future amendments.[110] Specifically, the Arusha Agreement details the political structure of bicameralism in its Article 6 (1),[111] and the same structure was contained in the 2005 Burundi Constitution.[112] Similarly, the rules of amendment laid down in the Arusha Agreement were carried over into the constitution.[113]

The inclusion of peace-agreement features in constitutions is further illustrated in two types of provisions, eternity clauses and sunset clauses. Eternity clauses allow for enshrining political pacts, while sunset clauses are provisions that establish a rigidity for a limited time until expiration or when some conditions have been fulfilled.[114] In the 2009 Guidance Note, then-Secretary General Ban Ki-moon noted that the 'UN is also requested to facilitate peace processes with possible constitutional implications and to assist national actors in addressing constitutional limitations so as to *implement* peace agreements'[115] and that 'UN engagement in and assistance to constitution-making increasingly is a core component of the organization's peace-building and state-building strategy'.[116] Similar wording appears in the 2020 Guidance Note: 'UN engagement in, and assistance to, constitution making is increasingly a core component of its peace, state-building and sustainable human development strategies'.[117] A 2022 report written for UNDPPA by Sumit Bisarya, Head of Constitution-Building Processes at International IDEA notes:

> Constitution-making processes have an 'obvious link' to peace processes, notably because constitutional issues – such as access to public power and resources, autonomy for ethnic groups and the struggle against authoritarian rule – are often root causes of conflict. As a result, constitutional issues tend to surface during peace negotiations, such that constitutional assistance has become an increasingly important part of conflict mediation.[118]

These examples show that constitutions can be understood by external actors as an effective legal vessel to facilitate peace.[119]

Understanding constitutions within peace-building leads to the inclusion of a broad range of actors. Vijayashri Sripati provides an exhaustive inventory of how UN involvement in constitution-making in the context of peace-building unfolds.[120] She focuses in particular on UNSC-mandated assistance, which covers a broad range of cases: Burundi, Namibia, Rwanda, Somalia, Sudan, South Sudan, Afghanistan, Cambodia, East Timor, Nepal, Kosovo, Iraq, and Libya.[121] As Sripati notes, it is not the UNSC itself that is involved in constitution-making but other organs of the UN, such as the United Nations Department of Political and Peacebuilding Affairs (UNDPPA) through its Mediation Support Unit – or UNDP, which has been involved in constitution-making following being granted a mandate by UNSC.[122] Indeed, UNDP has been involved in an ad hoc basis in constitution-making through its Bureau for Crisis Prevention and Recovery (BCPR) created in 2001, which has the aim of 'strengthen[ing] the contribution of UNDP to the conflict prevention and peace-building efforts of the United Nations system'.[123] Surveying the annual reports of BCPR, the first reference to involvement in constitution-making was in 2003, regarding the Afghan constitution: 'In post-crisis reconstruction, opportunities exist for a new constitution, new institutions and new laws to protect women's rights'.[124] Two years later, the report titled 'Constitutional Assistance in Post-Conflict Countries: The UN Experience: Cambodia, East Timor & Afghanistan' conveyed a similar idea.[125] In 2003, UNDP published a report on 'Constitution-Making and Peace Building: Lessons Learned from the Constitution-making Processes of Post-Conflict Societies'.[126] This report clearly highlighted the causal link between constitution-making and peace-building highlighting how 'constitution-making has the potential of contributing both to the short-term goal of conflict resolution and peace-making and to the long-term goal of peace-building and strengthening of the state institutions'.[127] In 2005, UNDP published a report regarding 'Constitutional Assistance in Post-Conflict Countries', which discussed how to best deliver constitutional support in Cambodia, East Timor, and Afghanistan.[128] Three years later, UNDP launched the 'Global Programme on Strengthening the Rule of Law in Conflict and Post-Conflict Situations';[129] through this programme, UNDP became involved in Sudan by providing constitutional capacity development to rule of law institutions, including the Ministry of Legal Affairs and Constitutional Development.[130] Other instances of UNDP involvement in constitution-making include Nepal in 2010,[131] Kenya in 2011, where UNDP 'worked with national partners on reaching consensus on the draft Constitution',[132] and Kyrgyzstan in 2012, where UNDP 'assisted in drafting a new Constitution guiding a peaceful transfer of power'.[133]

Outside of a specific UNSC mandate, other external actors have also been involved in constitution-making in the context of peace-building. International IDEA, even prior to the creation of its dedicated constitution-building programme in 2007,[134] had been involved in constitution-making processes tied to peace-building.[135] For International IDEA, 'constitutional reform' is included under the umbrella goal of 'democratic building and conflict management',[136] which comprises 'developing the process for building consensus, setting priorities, designing political institutions and constitutions, enabling dialogue, and promoting reconciliation and inclusive democracy'.[137] International IDEA first became involved in constitution-making via peace-building in 2004. Its 2005 report, titled 'Ten Years of Supporting Democracy Worldwide', notes 'how constitution-making processes and institutional choices can contribute to conflict management', including Afghanistan, Guatemala, Nigeria, and Kenya.[138] As the report notes, in 2004 a new project aimed to: 'evaluate how constitution-making processes and institutional choices can contribute to conflict management'.[139] From 2007 onwards, International IDEA has been involved in Afghanistan,[140] East Timor,[141] Kosovo,[142] Libya,[143] Myanmar,[144] Nepal,[145] Ukraine,[146] Yemen,[147] and Sudan.[148] In Nepal, following the signing of the 2006 Peace Agreement, International IDEA has supported 'national actors in the process of constitution building by providing knowledge resources and promoting public participation'.[149] In particular, International IDEA was heavily involved in Yemen in 2014, providing 'research support and day-to-day advice to the Yemen Constitution Drafting Committee'.[150] Like UNDP, International IDEA treats constitution-making as an essential tool to manage conflicts, which arise in their majority within state boundaries.[151] Peace-building is defined as an 'important process for generating a wider range of alternatives for building political institutions and processes that enhance democracy and managing conflict', as it 'can catalyze the transition from conflict to peace by stabilizing political competition', as well as 'support the development of governance frameworks that regulate access to power and resources, thereby addressing conditions that may have contributed to long running conflict'.[152] Power-sharing often relates to what a constitution-making process entails. Indeed, International IDEA is explicit about its view of constitution-making: 'Constitutions are the foundations of many democracies, but poorly designed constitutions can increase discord and conflict'.[153]

Another international organisation that it is important to mention is the OIF, created in 1970 and today including 54 members states around the world.[154] The ancestor of the OIF was the Agency of Cultural and Technical Cooperation [*Agence de Cooperation Culturelle et Technique*], which was established at the initiative of leaders of the decolonisation movement in the French Empire (Léopold Senghor or Habib Bourguiba). Its founding statutes state that the OIF: 'operates with absolute respect for the sovereignty of states, languages and cultures, and observes the strictest neutrality in matters of ideology and politics'.[155] The OIF has been involved in constitution-making processes as it 'supports states and national institutions in their efforts for the reform of constitutional texts, as well as laws'.[156] This support has manifested so far within the context of peace-building.[157] The OIF accompanies states in post-conflict settings,[158] where its constitutional assistance consists of 'support for *drafting texts (in the context of setting up constitutional committees)*; support for disseminating texts and best practices; support for managing constitutional and electoral litigation'.[159] It has been involved in the constitution-making process in the Comoros, where it detailed that 'the adoption of the constitution shows how resorting to constitutional engineering allowed for the solving of political difficulties'.[160] The involvement of the OIF is framed by two political declarations adopted in Bamako (2000) and Saint-Boniface (2006), which create mechanisms of early warnings for conflict preventions and democratic backsliding.[161] In its ten-year report following the Bamako Declaration, it states that, 'this return to democracy is symbolised, in some cases, by the adoption of a new constitution or the revision of existing one'.[162] The 2023 reports notes how the OIF supports states in matters relating to constitution-making by 'mobilising French-speaking expertise, at the request of States, from the earliest stages of the constituent process'.[163]

Finally, the Max Planck Foundation is another external actor that has been significantly involved in constitution-making in the context of peacebuilding. The Max Planck Foundation's first foray into constitution-making was its substantial involvement in the drafting of the Sudan Interim National Constitution of 2005 (at this time, the Max Planck Foundation was called the Max Planck Institute for Comparative Public Law and International Law).[164] It has since been involved in Somalia, Yemen, and Libya.[165] The UNDP, International IDEA, and the Max Planck Foundation all conceive of constitutions as a legal tool for peace. In the peace-building context, peace is not only desirable in itself but is a precondition for economic and political development.

Constitutions for development

From the mid-2000s onwards, the involvement of external actors within the realm of democratic governance implicitly relies upon an understanding of the constitution as a legal tool useful to achieve greater democratic governance, outside of a peace-building context.

Constitution-making appears relatively recently within the broader framework of 'democratic governance', as it sets up the principles allowing for the implementation of other policy areas: from fighting corruption to having an independent judiciary in order to attract foreign investment. Democratic governance is a poorly defined concept, which emerged in the early 1990s, defined by UNDP as a 'set of values and principles that underpin state-society relations, allowing people – in particular, the poor and marginalized – to have a say in how they are governed'.[166] While the democratic governance framework is broader and encompasses other legal norms than constitutions, it rests on the idea that a direct link exists between democracy and development, understood as political and economic development. As UNDP states it in its 2011 Annual Report:

> In inclusive societies, all citizens can pursue opportunities and realize their potential. They fully participate in democratic governance, and can depend on well-functioning public institutions and fair justice. Social stability takes root; *development is sustained*.[167]

Democratic governance is understood as necessary for development, as UNDP expressed in its 2006 Annual Report: 'building a strong democracy requires institutions that function. Institutions cannot be developed overnight and need to be built into each country's development strategy'.[168] Indeed, democratic governance is one of UNDP's six areas of expertise and involvement,[169] and it is one of its most significant: it accounted for 47% of the overall UNDP budget in 2006[170] and approximately 25% in 2011.[171]

The first explicit reference to constitution-making within the scope of democratic governance appeared in UNDP's 2008 Annual Report:

> Governing democratically means getting the law right and making sure it is upheld, while ensuring that people know they can resolve disputes impartially and equitably. For countries coming out of conflict, this can mean starting from scratch – *writing a constitution*, recruiting judges, training prison officers and the police.[172]

In 2015, on the topic of UNDP's Democratic Governance Thematic Trust Fund (DGTTF), involvement in constitution-making is explicitly stated: 'Initiatives have backed freer, fairer elections, and *new constitutions* firmly grounded in international norms'.[173] The strategic output of the DGTTF includes supporting, 'parliaments, *constitution-making bodies* and electoral institutions enabled to perform core functions for improved accountability, participation and representation, including for peaceful transitions'.[174] This particular statement illustrates how directly constitutions connect to democratic governance in UNDP's work. UNDP treats constitution-making as an essential part of democratic governance. As noted in its 2015 Annual Report:

> At the heart of a robust social contract between the state and society are systems and processes of democratic governance that enhance accountability of decision-makers, and participation and representation of various groups in the community. In a variety of political settlements, *constitutional debates* provide a great opportunity to shape the content of the social contract.[175]

Democratic governance can also take place within peace-building, as was the case in Nepal in 2008, through the UNDP project 'Support to constitution-building process project'.[176] Recently, UNDP has been involved in Libya under the DGTTF, helping to

> bring members of the Constitutional Drafting Assembly together, including those who initially boycotted the process, and representatives of minorities. They have worked on resolving pending issues in a consultative process aimed at establishing a future political structure that upholds the peaceful transfer of power and guarantees human rights.[177]

Involvement in constitution-making as a specific practice under democratic governance, yet outside the realm of peace-building, is a separate but related area and includes the case of Tunisia.[178]

Prior to explicitly referencing constitution-making, UNDP was involved in the topic on an ad hoc basis, largely through its work in supporting political institutions and elections, which continues today. Election assistance and parliamentary development have been important aspects of UNDP's advisory work, in some cases related to constitutional reform.[179] Elections are either the starting point of a constitution-making process, where the National Constituent Assembly is elected or the end point, when a constitution is ratified through a referendum or new elections. In 2011, UNDP stated in its Annual Report that it supported 'one election every two weeks' around the world.[180] This election support is also related to constitution-making, as was the case in Bhutan (2007),[181] Tunisia, Egypt, and Yemen (2011);[182] in Kenya (2013), in Timor Leste,[183] and in Grenada (2016), where UNDP supported the referendum on constitutional reform.[184]

In most cases, parliaments are where constitutions are drafted, discussed, and ultimately adopted, and parliamentary assistance is another core function of UNDP; parliaments are seen as 'critical to the establishment and consolidation of democracy since they empower ordinary people to participate in the policies that shape their lives'.[185] As noted in a 2007 Annual Report, UNDP supports 'one in four parliaments' around the world.[186] This support manifests in helping to 'train Members of Parliament from both houses, as well as parliamentary staff, on writing and initiating laws, carrying out research and ensuring that new laws adhered to the Constitution'.[187] Again, as constitution-making generally occurs within a parliamentary setting, here UNDP is indirectly involved in constitution-making.

Finally, the 2020 Guidance Note situates constitution-making as central with regard to the achievement of development goals:

> Constitutions and constitution-making processes are also central to the 2030 Agenda, realization of the Sustainable Development Goals (SDGs), and the 'Decade of Action's' prioritisation of solutions that catalyse simultaneous progress on multiple SDGs. Constitutions frame the approach of states to social and economic development and poverty reduction (SDGs

1–4, 7–11), gender equality and women's empowerment (SDG 5), reducing inequality (SDG 10), environmental protection (SDGs 6, 12–15) and fostering peaceful, just and inclusive societies (SDG 16).[188]

Other external actors have been involved in constitution-making within the scope of democratic governance, although none as explicitly as UNDP. Constitutions are treated as a precondition to achieving democracy, with the idea being that good institutions, enshrined in a constitution, will lead to the promotion of the rule of law and democracy, which are indeed the goals of the Venice Commission.[189] The explicit objectives of the Venice Commission include 'examining the problems raised by the working of democratic institutions and their reinforcement and development'.[190] More specifically, priority is given to the '*constitutional*, legislative and administrative principles and techniques which serve the efficiency of democratic institutions and their strengthening, as well as the principle of the rule of law'.[191] Despite constitutional assistance being at the core of the Venice Commission's mission, it is not specifically mentioned as such in the Status.[192] The involvement of the Venice Commission, as an external actor in the constitution-making process, has primarily occurred during the stage of constitutional drafting, through the provision of constitutional assistance to local actors making a new constitution during a transition to democracy.[193]

During its first decade of existence, the Venice Commission centred its work on former Soviet states,[194] where it supported in 'draft[ing] new constitutions in compliance with the European heritage'.[195] In 1990, the Venice Commission was involved in the constitution-making process of Poland, where a constitutional task force composed of 12 representatives of member states of the Council of Europe[196] proceeded to examine the first chapter of the Polish Constitution, focusing on human rights, freedoms, and obligations.[197] That same year, the Venice Commission reviewed a draft of the Constitution of Romania, as well as developing contacts within the Bulgarian National Assembly, in order to support the drafting of the country's new constitution.[198]

From 2005, the Venice Commission has relaxed its admission criteria to extend its reach beyond Europe, expanding its membership and turning 'to more potential "clients": the so-called established democracies and non-European States'.[199] Today, its membership includes the members of the Council of Europe and fifteen other countries across Latin America, Asia, and Africa.[200] Further, it has several observer states as well as international organisations and all participate in its plenary sessions.[201] To date, the Venice Commission has been involved in the constitution-making processes of Albania, Bulgaria, Chile, Czechoslovak Republic, Georgia, Iceland, Kosovo, Kyrgyzstan, Lithuania, Moldova, Montenegro, Poland, Romania, Russia, Serbia, Serbia and Montenegro, Ukraine, Tunisia, and Venezuela.[202]

International IDEA is another organisation that has been involved in constitution-making outside of peace-building contexts. In 2006, International IDEA included constitution-making in their strategy as a 'key component of democratization and conflict management in divided societies'.[203] International IDEA has been involved, in cases of constitution-making in Bolivia and Ecuador[204] and more recently in Tunisia.[205] In Bolivia, in 2007, it provided technical assistance to the constituent assembly as well as 'support with the development and analysis of commission reports on various aspects of constitutional reform'.[206] In its 2023 report, International IDEA develops a syllogism pointing to how constitution-making can foster democratic governance:

> if constitution-makers increase their knowledge and skills on constitution-building and apply these competencies to design a well-informed inclusive constitution-making process; . . . and promote public participation in the process; then responsive, inclusive, participatory and representative decision making (SDG16.7) is ensured in the constitution-building process. And then the likelihood of overall success and legitimacy of the constitutional reforms increases.[207]

Despite the diversification of external actors in the post-Cold War era, external actors share the same rationale that underpins transnational constitution-making, liberal legalism. Constitutions are considered to be a legal tool to achieve social change, be it civilisation, political independence, peace, or economic development. But not just any constitution: the liberal constitution.

Liberal constitutions to achieve political development

This section focuses on the *liberal* dimension of liberal legalism. External actors – in particular UNDP, the Venice Commission, and International IDEA – have been actively involved in constitution-making in the name of promoting peace and/or democracy. It is not just any constitution that is being recommended: it is the liberal constitution. In this chapter, liberal constitution refers to Western constitutions based on the European/Anglo-American liberal tradition. Given the history of the development enterprise, it is only certain types of liberal constitutions that are recommended, at the expense of other liberal constitutional models such as Latin American constitutionalism.[208] This follows from the 'modernisation rationale', which as discussed in the previous chapter, refers to the idea that mimicking the legal framework of Western Europe and North America will help a 'developing' country reach political development faster and that the right constitutional framework can bring about this desired social change.

By starting the inquiry during the decolonisation era, the lens of the development enterprise reveals the 'background of common sense' that external actors involved in constitution-making share, albeit to different extents. This builds on a remark from Sarah Kendall regarding constitution-making as a tool of civility manifesting in the 'efforts of former colonial powers to translate their own constitutional values to nascent independent states', which continues today when constitutions are conceived 'as a means to social and political stability through instantiating a break from the past'.[209]

Pinpointing the specific political model that external actors are advocating for is difficult, especially in the post-Cold War era. As this section will show, while the liberal constitution was advanced by external actors in decolonisation contexts, today this model is implicitly and tacitly defended by external actors.

Liberal constitutions as a signifier of 'civilisation'

Colonial empires were the messengers of political liberalism – promoting this through literature, education and art – but also through constitutions.[210] During decolonisation, external actors believed that the right law to foster economic and political development in the colonies was written and 'rational' law. Translated to the constitutional realm, this meant not only possessing a written constitution but that external actors also advocated for a liberal constitution, as exists in the West.[211] This belief is the translation of the modernisation rationale, which underpinned legal reform in Third World territories, to the constitutional legal framework. Following this creed, metropoles developed economically and politically due to modern, written (understood as 'rational' and 'civilised') law. At the level of the state, this law takes the shape of the liberal constitution, which is thought to be a prerequisite for political development, and since political development is necessary for economic development, colonies ought to have a written constitution that mimics those in Western Europe and North America.

The liberal constitution as a universal model of 'civilisation'

To understand why external actors held – and continue to hold – the liberal constitution as the single model capable of producing political development, it is necessary to look back to the intricate relationship between the (Western) liberal constitution and the colonial enterprise. Historians have long demonstrated the paradox of modern liberal constitutions' colonial lineage: while purporting to embrace the ideals of universality and equality, this political theory was built on a mandate to civilise those who had not yet achieved those standards.[212] Upendra Baxi notes how 'principles of constitutionalism were perfected in Europe at the very historic moment when colonialism flourished'.[213] Indeed, contrary to the theoretical accounts of the beginning of liberal constitutions in a historical vacuum, James Tully argues that European constitutional states emerged within a context of global colonial empire.[214] As Tully has shown, behind 'constitutional democracy' lies 'its historical particularity and makes it appear universal'. In fact, there have also existed 'non-western "customary" legal and political orders of constitutional forms and constituent powers'.[215] Tully's thesis is that the colonial origin of liberal constitutions meant that it carried on the 'mission' of civilising non-European people, as they were considered to be rationally and scientifically inferior. As he writes:

> Non-Western civilizations, many of which are older and more complex than the aggressive Western states, were scientifically classified at various stages of historical backwardness or underdevelopment relative to the "civilized" imperial states, and subjected to calibrated techniques of civilization and modernization.[216]

Tully points out that the 'right of the self-proclaimed civilised imperial powers to extend colonial and international modern constitutional regimes around the world correlated with a "sacred duty to civilize" the indigenous peoples under their rule'.[217] It follows that liberal constitutionalism was spread throughout the colonies by external actors who understood it to be a universal model to reach civilisation.

The liberal written constitution has its origins in Western Europe and North America at the end of the eighteenth century and quickly became the dominant model throughout the world due to colonial conquest.[218] An aspect of the civilising mission lay in the belief that law was a tool to rationalise the political realm and achieve civilisation. Sripati has shown how the constitution became a key 'civilised standard' in international law. A 'civilised standard' refers to the assumptions that distinguish civilised and uncivilised communities.[219] In the development enterprise, it is not only that constitution-making is seen as a tool to achieve social change but that the social change is related to a particular political system: possessing a *liberal* constitution meant a state was worthy of being sovereign. Through the alleged goal of their civilising mission, metropoles engaged in constitution-making as a tool to make those territories achieve civilisation.[220]

The entitlement that came from conceiving liberal constitutions as the standard of civilisation is illustrated in the fact that some countries, without being coerced directly, adopted a liberal constitution to reduce the threat of foreign intervention. The adoption of the 1861 Tunisian Constitution, the first constitution of the Arab world, is illustrative.[221] It was imposed on the Bey of Tunis, Muhammad III as-Sadiq, by British and French diplomats, largely due to the geopolitical importance of Tunisia from the slave and gold trade.[222] The Bey had a monopoly on these resources and trading benefits, which were entirely forbidden to foreigners.[223] Under the threat of British General Consul Richard Wood, who stated unequivocally 'we will interrupt our relations with you, and if necessary we will blockade your ports', the Bey adopted the 1857 Fundamental Pact.[224] The 1861 Tunisian Constitution was adopted due to explicit pressure from the British and French Empires.[225] The Bey presented the constitution to Napoleon III for approval during a meeting in Algiers in 1860.[226]

The benchmark of civilisation is revealed in the involvement of metropoles in colonies through the figure of the 'Mandate' that was created within the League of Nations. As Cooper summarised it: 'the League, in the end, underscored the normality of colonial empire even while suggesting that there were international standards which colonial powers should meet'.[227] Within the League of Nations, metropoles acted as Mandatory powers imposing constitutions on the territories they were entrusted with.[228] The League of Nations had divided territories, depending on their level of civilisation and entrusted 'advanced nations', acting on behalf of the League,[229] to bring territories to civilisation that were 'not yet able to stand by themselves under the strenuous conditions of the modern world'.[230] For instance, France had a mandate on the territories of Syria and Lebanon and was tasked with guiding these territories towards independence, in agreement with domestic authorities. Lebanon's constitution was drafted by the Representative Council of the Great Lebanon and promulgated by the Representative of France on 23 May 1926. In Syria, which was constituted as a federation of autonomous states, the constitution was adopted by a National Constituent Assembly in 1928 and promulgated by the French High Commissioner in 1930.[231] However, a closer look reveals that these constitutions were adopted following the approval of French authorities. Similarly, the British Empire was involved within the League of Nations framework in, for instance, the making of the Constitution of Iraq or Palestine.[232]

'A political system like our own'

In contexts of decolonisation, it was again clear and explicit that the model that should be adopted by colonies was the liberal constitution. The transfer of institutions existing in the constitutional framework of the metropole towards one of the future independent colonies is illustrative of another feature of liberal legalism: by mimicking constitutional legal structures, the colonies would achieve political development.

In the British Empire, this translated to adopting the 'Westminster model' in the colonies; the model covers a set of features including more than one political party or a legislature elected through a secret ballot.[233] Even if until the aegis of the decolonisation era British officials considered this model to be a 'wholly inappropriate export',[234] it remained that liberal constitutions were held up as a paragon of civilisation and political development. Indeed, for most of the early twentieth century, British authorities believed colonies not to be ready and it was only in the mid-twentieth century that it was considered appropriate to export British parliamentary institutions. For instance, in India, the 1930 Simon Commission considered that the British parliamentary system, 'has been fitted like a well-worn garment to the figure of the wearer, but it does not follow that it will suit everybody'.[235] British authorities came to consider it in light of the coming decolonisation, it was 'a brief uncharacteristic lapse in the mid-twentieth century'.[236] Constitutional developments in Ceylon are illustrative of this shift. In its 1928 report, the Donoughmore Commission noted that it would not be possible to transplant the 'Westminster model' given that some prerequisites such as a balanced political party system, 'the establishment of a purely parliamentary system of government on the existing British model is not suited to conditions in Ceylon'.[237] The Donoughmore Commission report warns against 'slavishly [to] follow[ing] the forms and practices of the British model'.[238] By 1945, the Donoughmore Commissioner acknowledged that while the 'prospect of transplanting British institutions with success may appear remote . . . we think that Ceylon is well qualified for a Constitution framed on the British model'.[239]

In Belgium and the United States, a similar logic followed. The 1959 report on Congo drafted by the Belgian Parliament included the idea that, 'Belgium proposes to establish in the Belgian Congo an autonomous state, benefitting from a democratic regime, within the respect of human rights and African values'.[240] In the same vein, the United States framed its involvement in the Philippines within the terms of its civilising missions. United States President William McKinley insisted that, 'the Philippines are ours not to exploit but to develop, to civilize, to educate, to train in the science of self-government'.[241]

Another instance of the explicit mention of the necessity to mimic liberal constitutions is in the institutional transfers that took place during decolonisation.[242] Crawford Young commenting on the Congolese case notes how the Belgian regime implanted 'a system modelled upon the democratic values and their structural embodiment which are cherished at home'.[243] Similarly, he points to the demand of the Congolese people who asked to be 'bequeathed a constitution which is a replica of the metropolitan format'.[244] By transferring institutions, the idea was that using certain institutional designs could work as a stabiliser or as an accelerator of development.

The use of federalism by metropoles to stabilise and achieve development is particularly salient with regard to the instrumentalist understanding of the constitution to achieve political development. In particular, the British Empire saw federalism as a useful model for the colonies. For instance, in 1948 in Malaya, the British authorities introduced a federal system in the Constitution.[245] Similarly, in the Caribbean, the short-lived West Indies Federation is another example of a British colony where federalism was imposed.[246] Nigeria was also built as a federation,[247] as well as the territories of Northern and Southern Rhodesia and Nyasaland.[248] In the Belgian Empire, the constitutional system adopted as a result of the negotiation that took place in Brussels in January–February 1960 was a 'parliamentary regime, copied with very few alterations from the Belgian blueprint'.[249] This is exemplified in a speech from Raymond Scheyven, the minister in charge of economic and financial affairs for the Belgian Congo, who stated 'We have presented to the Congo a political system like our own', detailing that 'there are communes, provincial assemblies, a bicameral system, a political system where the Chief of State is not responsible before Parliament'.[250] Finally, the United States also attempted to replicate its own system in the Philippines, as enshrined in the 1934 Tydings – McDuffie Act, which outlined that to become independent, the Philippines would have to adopt a series of institutional features characteristic of the US. Section 2 (a) of the Tydings – McDuffie Act states that the constitution should 'be republican in form, shall contain a bill of rights'.[251] The Constitution of the Commonwealth of the Philippines, adopted in 1935, included all of these features, even going beyond the Tydings – McDuffie Act to set up a Supreme Court and US-specific impeachment provisions.[252]

In sum, during decolonisation, metropoles were explicit that the model necessary to achieve political development, and thus the minimum standard needed to grant independence, was the liberal constitution. In the post-Cold War period, this idea continued but only implicitly.

The end of history and the liberal constitution

External actor involvement in constitution-making in the post-Cold War era was motivated by the same idea that underpinned constitution-making in the context of decolonisation; however, instead of explicitly stating their intentions, actors were more implicit with their goals. Here again, constitution-making was conceived of as a tool to achieve social and political goals (i.e. peace, development, and democracy), and specifically, *liberal* constitutions were embraced. In contrast with the 'civilisation mission', the rationale of liberal legalism is implicit and less apparent. The rationale of liberal legalism is further concealed behind the fact that only one possible set of options to choose from exists. While no primary evidence exists of actors explicitly stating this preference, it is revealed through the selection of the constitutional model. Indeed, external actors rely on a similar model, the liberal constitution, which can take different institutional shapes. Different facets of the constitution can be chosen: presidential or parliamentary, flexible or rigid, unitary or federal, and in all cases external actors chose the kind of constitution within the liberal democratic model, as opposed to the 'Moscow model', which after the fall of the Berlin Wall had almost entirely disappeared.[253]

The 'Moscow model' refers to the defining features of socialist public law and the respective ideological underpinning, which stood in stark contrast to European and Anglo-American political liberalism. Indeed, the East/West divide has underpinned comparative constitutional law since its emergence as an academic discipline. As Michel Rosenfeld and András Sajó remind us: 'foreign constitutional systems were often studied as part of Soviet legal studies, and, respectively studies on Western bourgeois state law. Comparative law was understood as the study of sovereign systems, with a heavy ideological accent'.[254] The dissolution of the Soviet Union led to the Moscow model losing its influence and to countries quickly abandoning it in favour of the liberal democratic model. Jaakko Husa, for instance, notes that: 'From the end of the 1980s the old socialist legal family has diminished dramatically. As a result, socialist law has almost disappeared or at least shrunk significantly'.[255] Liberal constitutional democracy became the only model available to build new constitutions. This led IGOs to advance liberal democracy in its own right and also to advance it as the right legal framework to address the desired social goals of peace and development.

Advancing liberal democracy in its own right

The end of the Cold War triggered a paradigmatic shift among international organisations, as liberal democracy became a goal in its own right, free from the colonial scaffolding of 'civilisation'. While the UN had refrained from embracing a particular kind of political system, a shift occurred in then Secretary-General Boutros Boutros-Ghali's 1996 report, 'An Agenda for Democratization', which states that 'ample evidence suggesting that, over the long term, democracy is an ingredient for both sustainable development and lasting peace'[256] and that 'a culture of democracy, marked by communication, dialogue and openness to the ideas and activities of the world, helps to foster a culture of development'.[257] Fostering democracy around the world became a core goal of the UN.[258]

In this context, a variety of international organisations emerged, with the explicit mission of promoting democracy. The Venice Commission was specifically created to promote the rule of law and democracy,[259] with former President Antonio Pergola claiming, 'I have always held that the Venice Commission should be enabled to enrich its mission by promoting and spreading the values of the Council of Europe among non-European lawyers willing and ready to espouse them'.[260] As Gianni Buquicchio, another former president of the Venice Commission, noted: 'While being respectful of the States' margin of appreciation, the Commission has nevertheless at times *encouraged developments in a liberal direction*'.[261]

Further, the embrace of the liberal democratic model can be illustrated in the standards upon which the Venice Commission grounds its mission. Even though, as its 2007 Annual report states, 'the Commission does not put forward models of the ideal constitution or law',[262] the Venice Commission does advocate 'the adoption of constitutions that conform to the *standards of Europe's constitutional heritage*'.[263] These 'common standards' are comprised of 'respect for fundamental rights', 'democracy' and 'the rule of law'.[264] Involvement in constitutional assistance is thus justified as providing compatibility with European and international standards, as well as the feasibility of certain constitutional options, 'largely based on common European experience in this sphere'.[265] In terms of hard law, the Venice Commission bases its activities on the European Convention on Human Rights and the jurisprudence of the European Court of Human Rights.[266] Specifically relating to constitution-making, the Venice Commission treats constitutions as a vessel to achieve 'common European heritage', as stated in its 2003 Annual Report:

> One of the functions of a Constitution is to define and reflect the core values of the respective country. The Venice Commission as the Council of Europe body dealing with constitutional law, therefore, has the task of ensuring that the values affirmed by the national constitutions of the member states *correspond to the values* of the Council of Europe.[267]

The values of the Council of Europe are tied to liberal constitutional democracy as they refer to 'human rights, democracy and the rule of law'.[268] In its 2023 report, the Venice Commission reiterated that its assistance aims: 'to provide a complete, precise, and objective analysis of the compatibility of laws and constitutional provisions with European and international standards'.[269]

Another important international organisation that explicitly promotes democracy is International IDEA, which was created in 1995 by 14 member states, with an overall mandate involving the 'promotion and advancement of sustainable democracy worldwide'[270] and 'strengthen[ing] and support[ing] national capacity to develop the full range of democratic instruments'.[271] This mission is explicitly stated in its founding document: 'Democracy must be advanced in its own right. There is also a wider recognition of the link between democracy, peace and development'.[272] Boutros Boutros Ghali supported the creation of this international organisation, as he participated at the founding conference in 1995 where he declared: 'Democracy supports peace, by leading to responsible government. It fosters development, by promoting the free flow of ideas which prevent stagnation and decay'.[273] As democratic building is 'as yet a relatively young thematic area, consisting of a fragmented community of rapidly multiplying player', International IDEA seeks to advance 'democracy as a normative agenda'.[274] In its 2007 Report, International IDEA notes how constitutions are, 'a meeting point between democracy building, development and conflict resolution. Why? Because a constitution is essentially a compact about the shape of a society and the power structures within it'.[275]

Finally, it is worth pointing out the particularity of the OIF. It is currently governed by the Francophonie Charter, where the commitment to democracy is enshrined in its Statute; the Francophonie Charter holds among its objectives 'the establishment and development of democracy'.[276] However, its ancestor, the Niamey Convention, signed in 1970 by leaders of decolonisation movements in the French Empire, such as Léopold Senghor or Habib Bourguiba, stated in its Article 1 that the OIF's activities are carried out 'in the absolute respect of national sovereignty, language and cultures, and observes the strictest neutrality in political or ideological considerations'.[277] In contrast, the political declaration guiding the action of the OIF, the 2000 Bamako Declaration, clearly states that

> democracy, as the political framework for the rule of law and the protection of human rights, is the system of government that best promotes long-term stability and legal security; thanks to the climate of freedom that it creates, democracy also establishes the conditions for freely accepted mobilization on the part of the people to achieve development; *democracy and development cannot be dissociated: these are the factors promoting a lasting peace*.[278]

Within this framework of democracy promotion, particularly through conflict prevention, the OIF has developed 'the reinforcement of constitutional and institutional engineering as part of the support of making and/or reform of fundamental texts'.[279]

The holy trinity: liberal constitutions for peace, development, and democracy

The reason why liberal constitutional democracy should be advanced, according to its proponents, is that it is understood as offering the right legal framework to achieve two other goals: peace and development. Balakrishnan Rajagopal discusses how in the post-Cold War era, the three ideas of 'development, peace, and democracy', which previously were considered to be independent from each other, began to converge as a 'holy trinity'.[280] Rajagopal summarises this convergence:

> *Peace* is essential for the functioning of the basic mechanisms of *democracy* as well as *development*, whereas a culture of democracy is likely to lead to peace, both intra-nationally by defusing discontent and tensions, and internationally by enabling democratic states to trust each other more, due to their openness.[281]

The 'holy trinity' also motivates many external actors involved in constitution-making. The role that constitutions play to ensure peace – and thus development towards democracy – is stated by UNDP.[282] In the UNDP's 2003 Annual Report, the perspective is forwarded that 'development cannot take root when people are fleeing to a refugee camp, or fearing that a trip to the market might mean death from a landmine or the blast of a car bomb'.[283] More recently, the link among peace, development, and constitution-making was illustrated in the UN's Sustainable Development Goals, with constitution-making appearing in the background of SDG 16, 'Peace, justice and strong institutions',[284] which recognises that 'peace and security are fundamental for sustainable development, and that sustainable development is critical for sustaining peace'.[285] Peace is a 'critical enabler for delivering sustainable development through ensuring responsive, inclusive, participatory and representative decision-making at all levels'.[286] Finally, the relationship between peace and development was made clear by UN Secretary-General, António Guterres, who claimed that 'address[ing] the root causes of conflict, helps to reinforce national capacities and infrastructures for peace, and integrates sustainable development, peace, and human rights in a holistic way'.[287] Finally, the 2020 Guidance-Note of the Secretary General on United Nations Constitutional assistance also explicitly links those three goals as it states that 'constitution making is a central aspect of conflict prevention, peacebuilding and promoting human rights, the rule of law and sustainable human development'.[288]

International NGOs also share this conception. For instance, the Max Planck Foundation highlights in a recent report how 'by working with state and non-state actors from across the political spectrum, the project underlines the importance of the rule of law, democratic values and the respect of fundamental rights in designing new constitutional frameworks'.[289]

Aside from the recent integration of constitution as tools for peacebuilding or democratic governance, they have also been integrated within the broader strategy of development advocated by development-oriented international organisations. Sripati has shown through her work that the constitution is embedded within the development agenda, inserted through different mechanisms of the Bretton Woods Institutions (the World Bank and the IMF).[290] Constitutions were integrated within the rule of law and poverty reduction agenda, used as the legal vessel to achieve other targeted political aims linked with economic development, such as having a market economy. A 2003 report by the World Bank titled 'Legal and Judicial Reform: Strategic Directions' states that: 'The rule of law requires a set of basic laws that frame the governance of the state and its people. These basic laws include the *constitution*, civil code and civil procedure and criminal code'.[291] A 2011 UN Conference on the Least Developed Countries stated that: 'LDCs have accepted good governance as a necessity for development. . . . Meaningful progress has been made in adopting democratic *constitutions*, drafting new legislation, and setting up legal frameworks against corruption'.[292] Sripati argues that because the World Bank and the IMF prescribe a constitution to ensure a market economy, 'the BWIs [Bretton Woods Institutions] in effect, prescribed *Western liberal market constitutional democracy* as a means of promoting such growth or reducing poverty'.[293] She further points out how international financial institutions have been involved in UN constitutional assistance.[294] While assistance in constitutional drafting is mainly the task of the UNDP or the UN mission sent in the context of peace-building, international financial institutions lie in the background, often playing an advisory role, further evidencing the place constitutions occupy within the broader development agenda. For example, in Nepal in 2006,[295] UN mediation resulted in the adoption of a Comprehensive Peace Agreement, which included among other things to 'restructure the state along the lines of good governance, through first, an *interim constitution*'.[296] This demand had previously been included in the IMF's Poverty Reduction and Growth Facility, approved in 2003 and 2007, which Nepal was compelled to implement.[297] During the adoption of the constitution, following the UNSC resolution,[298] the UN Mission in Nepal joined the UN Office of the United Nations High Commissioner for Human Rights (OHCHR) 'in drafting and auditing the constitution'.[299] The World Bank also assisted the Nepalese Constituent Assembly through 'providing advice and analytical work on fiscal federalism, building on the work on public financial management and global knowledge'.[300] Sripati demonstrates that the liberal constitution is advocated for by the World Bank and the IMF because it ensures a certain legal, political, and economic model favourable to 'economic development'.[301]

In the post-Cold War period, implicit constitution equates to liberal constitutions. In that sense, it is not as much that the model from specific Western countries that is pushed forward as it could be the case in the decolonisation era – where the British Empire promoted the Westminster model – but a blueprint, embedded in (Western) liberal constitutional democracy. External actors have indeed developed guidebooks or toolboxes on constitution-making, which include different options regarding the system of government, human rights, and independent institutions.[302] What is striking is that external actors do not push for a certain institutional system based on a particular jurisdiction as was the case during decolonisation but rather a blueprint of liberal constitutional democracy. For instance, International IDEA's 'A Practical Guide to Constitution Building' (2011) contains different options for designing the executive branch or the legislature citing examples not only from the West.[303] It cites the South African example with regard to the substantive power of legislature.[304]

Conclusion

This chapter has applied the lens of the development enterprise to examine the transnational dimension of constitution-making and has illustrated the implicit rationale shared by external actors: liberal legalism. External actors use the constitution as a means of reaching 'civilisation' or, in more contemporary terminology, to reach 'political development' embodied in liberal constitutional democracy. Constitutions are at the heart of this project, as they are understood as the legal tool necessary to achieve these goals. However, as this chapter has argued, not just any kind of constitution is advocated: the liberal constitution is understood as the model capable of providing the legal framework necessary to achieve the social goals of civilisation, peace, and political development.

It is important to highlight that while this chapter shows external actors were involved both in constitution-making processes that took place within contexts of decolonisation and post-Cold War, how much constitution-makers have listened to them might have varied according to the context. The question of the impact of transnational involvement is beyond the scope of this research that has deliberately chosen to focus on the process rather than the outcome. With that said, the background of common sense shared by external actors has important implications regarding the potential impact their involvement *could* have.

This chapter has shown that constitution-making is a multifaceted process, where external actors play a significant role throughout the different stages. While the scope of their involvement may have been greater during the colonial era and through decolonisation – where external actors were the primary actors involved in constitution-making – they were still actively involved in the post-Cold War period, although their involvement was mostly restricted to the stage of constitutional drafting. Following decolonisation, not only were external actors involved in constitution-making in *sovereign* countries, but practices that were common during decolonisation came to be framed by a series of international norms. As this chapter has discussed, several declarations adopted by the UNGA in the 1960s and 1970s highlighted the inalienable rights of states to choose their political system, without interference from other states. In the same vein, Article 1 of the ICCPR recognises the right to self-determination of states, which led to the de jure prohibition of the involvement of external states in constitution-making processes. Following these prohibitions, external actors restricted their involvement to the drafting stage of the constitution-making process.

This chapter has shed light on implicit assumptions regarding external actor involvement in constitution-making, highlighting the continuity of the liberal legalist rationale. Despite the variety of historical and political contexts, transnational constitution-making is united through the paradigm of liberal legalism. External actors share the *legalist* side of liberal legalism, which is an instrumentalist understanding of constitutions as legal tools to achieve a desired set of social goals. During decolonisation, written constitutions were seen as the legal tool par excellence to achieve a desired social change (i.e. political development), which was acknowledged through being granted independence. This rationale continued to pervade, albeit implicitly, throughout the post-Cold War era, where the social goals changed shape to become the 'holy trinity' of democracy, peace, and development.

Grounded in institutional documentation, this chapter has sketched the active involvement of UNDP, International IDEA, the Max Planck Foundation, the Venice Commission, and the OIF in constitution-making, as part of their shared project to advance these social goals. External actors hold a similar understanding with regard to the *liberal* side of liberal legalism, as the paradigm does not advocate for any constitution but the *liberal constitution*. It is here that the historical analysis proves useful, given how implicit and vague this dimension has become in the post-Cold War era. During decolonisation, metropoles explicitly stated that the model necessary to achieve political development – and thus the minimum standard needed to gain independence – was the liberal constitution. In the post-Cold War period, this idea persisted but only implicitly; with the fall of the Soviet Union, external actors did not need to advocate for one model or another, as suddenly no alternative existed; the liberal constitutional model was the last one standing.

The lens of the development enterprise allows for a more comprehensive examination of the transnational dimension during the drafting process, revealing important external actors that the framework of constituent power is unable to grasp. Constitution-making in the context of democratic transition is characterised by the presence of external actors to such an extent that the notion of constituent power is not only unable to offer a complete understanding of the process but fundamentally obfuscates the fact that the bulk of transnational involvement occurs during the constitutional drafting phase. This chapter has shown that the participation of 'the people' in the making of a constitution has been extremely limited throughout constitutional history; it is only recently that participation has become a condition of the democratic legitimacy of a constitution. During decolonisation, constitutions were typically negotiated between the colonial power and a local political group, which in most cases did not represent 'the people'. Examining the involvement of British, Belgian, or United States officials in constitution-making processes during decolonisation reveals how limiting the framework of constituent power is to understand the legal phenomenon; it fails descriptively. Because the development enterprise is grounded on an anti-foundationalist conception of constitution-making, it allows for a wider range of external actors to be examined. Broadening the scope of analysis beyond the mere adoption of the constitution, the development enterprise offers a more comprehensive picture of external actor involvement, locating the transnational dimension of constitution-making in the drafting phase.

By tracing the evolution of the different external actors involved in constitution-making – ranging from metropoles to a diverse set of governmental and non-governmental organisations – this chapter has shown how the process has evolved but also how it has remained, at its core, a development enterprise. To achieve the social and political goals associated with liberal democracy and because constitution-making is a complicated legal activity, the key actor channelling the paradigm of liberal legalism is the 'expert'. This dimension of the development enterprise is examined in the following chapter.

Notes

1 Sumit Bisarya, *Advice on Applying Mediation Fundamentals in UN Constitutional Assistance* (UNDPPA November 2022) 15.
2 Kenneth Roberts-Wray, 'The Legal Machinery for the Transition from Dependence to Independence' in James Anderson (ed), *Changing Law in Developing Countries* (Allen & Unwin 1963) 60.
3 UNSG, *Guidance Note of the Secretary-General on United Nations Constitutional Assistance* (UNSG 2020) 3.
4 Tom Ginsburg, 'Constitutional Advice and Transnational Legal Order' in Gregory Shaffer, Terence C. Halliday and Tom Ginsburg (eds), *Constitution-Making and Transnational Legal Order* (CUP 2019) 125.
5 David Kennedy, *A World of Struggle: How Power, Law, and Expertise Shape Global Political Economy* (Princeton UP 2018) 89.
6 Vijayashri Sripati, *Constitution-Making Under UN Auspices: Fostering Dependency in Sovereign Lands* (OUP 2020).
7 Georges Fischer, 'La décolonisation et le rôle des traités et des constitutions' (1962) 8 Annuaire français de droit international 805, 829.
8 Brun-Otto Bryde, 'North and South in Comparative Constitutional Law – from Colonial Imposition Towards a Transnational Constitutionalist Dialogue' in Wolfgang Benedek, Hubert Isak and Renate Kicker (eds), *Development and Developing International and European Law Essays in Honour of Konrad Ginther on the Occasion of His 65th Birthday* (Peter Lang 1999) 699.
9 Other non-legal related aspects have been pointed out as having substantially impacted constitution-making during this period, such as the role of religion or socialist ideology. See Julian Go, 'Modeling the State: Postcolonial Constituitions in Asia and Africa' (2002) 39 Southeast Asian Studies 558, 565, 570.
10 Upendra Baxi, 'Postcolonial Legality' in Henry Schwarz and Sangeeta Ray (eds), *A Companion to Postcolonial Studies* (Blackwell Publishing 2000) 542.
11 Amelia Odida has unpacked the colonial lineage in the UN's rhetoric with regard to constitution-making by analysing its involvement in Libya and Eritrea and discussed resistance from domestic actors. Amelia Odida, 'Making Policy, Problems, and Constitutions: Decolonising the UN Policy of Constitutional Assistance' (UCL, University College London 2022) 13.
12 Sripati (n 6) 8.
13 See Ginsburg (n 4); Sara Kendall, '"Constitutional Technicity": Displacing Politics Through Expert Knowledge' (2015) 11 Law, Culture and the Humanities 363. On UNDP see Christina Murray and Cindy Wittke, 'International Institutions, Constitution-Making and Gender' in Helen Irving (ed), *Constitutions and Gender* (Edward Elgar Publishing 2017).
14 This literature is mostly descriptive, consisting of accounts from Venice Commission members and commentary on its reports. Maartje De Visser, 'A Critical Assessment of the Role of the Venice Commission in Processes of Domestic Constitutional Reform' (2015) 63 The American Journal of Comparative Law 963–64.
15 Dietmar Rothermund, 'Constitution Making and Decolonization' (2006) 53 Diogenes 9, 12.
16 See Sripati (n 6) 99–151.
17 Andrew Fitzmaurice, 'The Justification of King Leopold II's Congo Enterprise by Sir Travers Twiss' in Shaunnagh Dorsett and Ian Hunter (eds), *Law and Politics in British Colinal Thought* (Palgrave Macmillan 2011) 118, 125; Sripati (n 6) 108.
18 Roberts-Wray (n 2) 60–61.
19 Fischer (n 7) 822.

20 The process was accelerated, despite British officials doubts regarding the capacity of their African colonies; the turmoil in these territories led to a 'wind of change' and several colonies were granted independence. Frederick Cooper, 'Decolonization in Tropical Africa' in Martin Thomas and Andrew Thompson (eds), *The Oxford Handbook of the Ends of Empire* (Oxford Univeristy Press 2018) 325; Fischer (n 7) 806.
21 Cyril Lionel Robert James, *The Life of Captain Cipriani: An Account of British Government in the West Indies* (Duke UP 2014) 39; Harshan Kumarasingham, 'Written Differently: A Survey of Commonwealth Constitutional History in the Age of Decolonisation' (2018) 46 The Journal of Imperial and Commonwealth History 874, 877.
22 Issa Gulamhussein Shivji, 'Law in Independent Africa: Some Reflections on the Role of Legal Ideology' (1985) 46 Ohio State Law Journal 689–90.
23 William Dale, 'The Making and Remaking of Commonwealth Constitutions' (1993) 42 International & Comparative Law Quarterly 67; Fischer (n 7) 825.
24 See Jonathan Law, *A Dictionary of Law* (OUP 2015) 436.
25 Dale (n 23) 69.
26 Anne Thurston Pugh, *Records of the Colonial Office, Dominions Office, Commonwealth Relations Office, and Commonwealth Office* (Her Majesty's Stationery Office 1995) 331.
27 ibid 325, 335, 338, 354, 337.
28 Dale (n 23) 68.
29 Fischer (n 7) 825.
30 ibid.
31 Harshan Kumarasingham (ed), *Constitution-Maker: Selected Writings of Sir Ivor Jennings* (CUP 2015) 23.
32 In some cases, the British Empire also resorted to international treaties, generally for countries not entering into the Commonwealth. Cyprus is one of these instances, where its constitution was the result of conferences gathering representatives of the Greek and Turkish Cypriots with the government of the United Kingdom first in Zurich, then in London. Despite having the legal shape of a treaty, it contained material constitutional provisions shaping the basic constitutional structure of the Cypriot constitution laid down in the 1959 Zurich Agreement, which could not be amended. Fernando Mendez and Vasiliki Triga, 'Constitution-Making, Constitutional Conventions and Conflict Resolution: Lesson Drawing for Cyprus' (2009) 11 Journal of Balkan and Near Eastern Studies 363.
33 Rothermund (n 15) 245.
34 Nigeria, Nigeria (Constitution) Order in Council (30 September 1960), Federation of Nigeria Official Gazette 221–393.
35 United Kingdom, Nigeria Independence Act (29 July 1960) HM Stationery Office.
36 These include (ordered chronologically) Ceylon, United Kingdom, Ceylon Independence Act (10 December 1947), HM Stationery Office; India, United Kingdom, India Independence Act (8 July 1947), HM Stationery Office; Ghana, United Kingdom, Ghana Independence Act (7 February 1957), HM Stationery Office; Malaysia, United Kingdom, Malaya Independence Act (31 July 1957), HM Stationery Office; Nigeria, United Kingdom (n 35); Tanganyika, United Kingdom, Tanganyika Independence Act (22 November 1961), HM Stationery Office; Sierra Leone, United Kingdom, Sierra Leone Independence Act (28 March 1961), HM Stationery Office; Jamaica, United Kingdom, Jamaica Independence Act (19 July 1962), HM Stationery Office; Trinidad and Tobago, United Kingdom, Trinidad Independence Act (11 August 1962), HM Stationery Office; Uganda, United Kingdom, Uganda Independence Act (1 August 1962), HM Stationery Office; Kenya,

United Kingdom, Kenya Independence Act (3 December 1963), HM Stationery Office; Malawi, United Kingdom, Malawi Independence Act (10 June 1964), HM Stationery Office; Zambia, United Kingdom, Zambia Independence Act (31 July 1964), HM Stationery Office; Malta, United Kingdom, Malta Independence Act (31 July 1964), HM Stationery Office; Gambia, United Kingdom, Gambia Independence Act (17 December 1964), HM Stationery Office; Guyana, United Kingdom, Guyana Independence Act (12 May 1966), HM Stationery Office; Botswana, United Kingdom, Botswana Independence Act (3 August 1966), HM Stationery Office; Lesotho, United Kingdom, Lesotho Independence Act (3 August 1966), HM Stationery Office; Barbados, United Kingdom, Barbados Independence Act (17 November 1966), HM Stationery Office; Mauritius, United Kingdom, Mauritius Independence Act (29 February 1968), HM Stationery Office; Swaziland, United Kingdom, Swaziland Independence Act (26 July 1968), HM Stationery Office.

37 United Kingdom, Ghana Independence Act (n 36). First Schedule, §6.
38 United Kingdom, Barbados Independence Act (n 36).
39 United Kingdom, Nigeria Independence Act (n 35).
40 United Kingdom, Tanganyika Independence Act (n 36).
41 United Kingdom, Jamaica Independence Act (n 36).
42 Dale (n 23) 68. [Emphasis added].
43 Fischer (n 7) 824.
44 ibid 823.
45 Rothermund (n 15) 9.
46 James McPetrie, 'Survey of Constitutions Drafted at the Colonial Office since 1944' in James Anderson (ed), *Changing Law in Developing Countries* (George Allen & Unwin LTD 1963) 32–41.
47 Monsuru Muritala, 'Modern Political Experience: Constitutional Development in Nigeria, 1960–2020' in Aderemi Suleiman Ajala and Samuel Oluwole Ogundele (eds), *Nigerian Cultural History and Challenges of Postcolonial Development* (Cambridge Scholars Publishing 2023) 188. The 1922 was called the Clifford Constitution.
48 ibid 189. Also called Macpherson Constitution.
49 ibid 190. Also called Lyttleton Constitution.
50 Burma constitutes an exception to the overall trend and its constitution was adopted in September 1947 by constituent assembly designated according to the Government of Burma Act of 1935. Fischer (n 7) 825–26.
51 Viktor Mayer-Schonberger, 'Into the Heart of the State: Intervention Through Constitution-Making' (1994) 8 Temple International and Comparative Law Journal 315, 323.
52 Except for British Cameroon and Togoland, where there was a formal constitution through a plebiscite, or Malta through a referendum. See Rupert Emerson, 'Colonialism, Political Development, and the UN' (1965) 19 International Organization 484, 492. See Dale (n 23) 71.
53 Yash Ghai and Jill Cottrell, 'The State and Constitutionalism in Postcolonial Societies in Africa' in Abdul Paliwala, Christopher McCrudden and Upendra Baxi (eds), *Law's Ethical, Global and Theoretical Contexts: Essays in Honour of William Twining* (CUP 2015) 175.
54 Chambre des représentants, *Rapport du groupe de travail pour l'étude du problème politique au Congo du 20 janvier 1959* (Chambre des représentants 1958–1959).
55 Crawford Young, *Politics in Congo: Decolonization and Independence* (Princeton UP 1965) 162.

56 Jacques Brassinne de La Buissière and Georges-Henri Dumont, 'Les autorités belges et la décolonisation du Congo' [2010] Courrier hebdomadaire du CRISP 9, 39.
57 Young (n 55) 173–74.
58 Loi fondamentale du 19 mai 1960 relative aux structures du Congo, *Moniteur belge*. The Belgian colony, the *Congo Free State*, which had been acquired by King Leopold II (which achieved international recognition in 1885) before being bought off by the Belgian State, it then became the *Belgian Congo* in 1908. It was regulated until then by the 1908 Colonial Charter. See David Van Reybrouck, *Congo. Une histoire* (Actes Sud 2012) 77; H. Kabwe Sabwa, *Droit minier en République Démocratique du Congo* (Bruylant 2019) 27–33.
59 Belgium, Loi fondamentale du 19 mai 1960 relative aux structures du Congo (19 May 1960), Moniteur belge.
60 On the United States as a colonial empire see Julian Go, 'The Provinciality of American Empire: "Liberal Exceptionalism" and US Colonial Rule, 1898–1912' (2007) 49 Comparative Studies in Society and History 74; Julian Go, 'American Colonial Empire: The Limit of Power's Reach' [2005] Lessons of Empire 201.
61 United States of America, The Philippines Independence Act. Tydings McDuffie Act (24 March 1934), United States Statutes at Large 48 Stat. 456 Section 2, a.
62 ibid Section 3.
63 FDR Presidential Library, 'March 1935' <www.fdrlibrary.marist.edu/daybyday/resource/march-1935-15/> accessed July 2020.
64 Emerson (n 52) 491.
65 ibid.
66 Sripati (n 6) 116.
67 UN, *UN Charter* (26 June 1945) United Nations 1 UNTS XVI art 76, b.
68 Eric De Brabandere, *Post-Conflict Administrations in International Law: International Territorial Administration, Transitional Authority and Foreign Occupation in Theory and Practice* (Martinus Nijhoff Publishers 2009) 57. The UN was involved in the drafting of the constitutions of West Samoa or Nauru. See Sripati (n 6) 118, 171.
69 Sripati (n 6) 161.
70 Odida (n 11) 10.
71 Sripati (n 6) 163.
72 ibid.
73 Adrian Pelt, *Libyan Independence and the United Nations: A Case of Planned Decolonization* (Yale UP 1970) xi.
74 UNGA, *Second Annual Report of the United Nations Commissioner in Libya. Prepared in Consultation with the Council for Libya* (UNGA 1951) 61–71.
75 UNGA, *Resolution No 289: Question of the Disposal of the Former Italian Colonies* (21 November 1949) GAOR, 4th sess, A/RES/289 §3.
76 Sripati (n 6) 167–69.
77 UNGA, *Declaration on the Granting of Independence to Colonial Countries and Peoples* (14 December 1960) GAOR, 15th sess, Suppl no 16 A/RES/1514(XV) §2, §5.
78 Emerson (n 52) 490.
79 UNGA, *Declaration on Principles of International Law Concerning Friendly Relations and Co-operation among States in Accordance with the Charter of the United Nations* (24 October 1970) GAOR, 25th sess, Suppl no 28 Res 2625.
80 UNGA, *Basic Principles of the Legal Status of the Combatants Struggling Against Colonial and Alien Domination and Racist Regimes* (12 December 1973) GAOR, 28th sess, Suppl no 30 Res 3103.

81 UN General Assembly, *International Covenant on Civil and Political Rights* (16 December 1966) 999 United Nations, Treaty Series 171.
82 Exceptions are the Puerto Rico, Palestine and West Sahara territories. Sripati (n 6) 172.
83 ibid 173.
84 Vijayashri Sripati, 'Hammarskjöld and International Executive Rule: A Third World Perspective on International Law' in Henning Melber and Carsten Stahn (eds), *Peace Diplomacy, Global Justice and International Agency: Rethinking Human Security and Ethics in the Spirit of Dag Hammarskjöld* (CUP 2013) 486.
85 Sripati (n 6) 175.
86 ibid 177.
87 UN, *Yearbook of the United Nations, 1963* (UN 1965) 11. [Emphasis added].
88 Sripati (n 6) 225.
89 See Venice Commission, *Resolution (90) 6 on a Partial Agreement Establishing the European Commission for Democracy through Law* (10 May 1990) Venice Commission [CM]/Res(90)6E; Venice Commission, *Resolution Adopting the Revised Statute of the European Commission for Democracy through Law* (27 February 2002) Venice Commission CDL (2002) 2027 art 8 (3); Stefanie Schmahl and Marten Breuer, *The Council of Europe: Its Law and Policies* (OUP 2017) 3203.
90 Venice Commission, *Annual Report of Activities 1999* (Venice Commission 1 April 2000) 4.
91 Venice Commission, *Annual Report of Activities 1990* (Venice Commission 22 February 1991) 2. Resolution adopted by the Conference for the constitution of a Commission for democracy through Law (Venice, 19–20 January 1990); Venice Commission, *Resolution (90) 6 on a Partial Agreement Establishing the European Commission for Democracy through Law* (n 89).
92 Venice Commission, *Annual Report of Activities 2001* (Venice Commission 9 March 2002) 5; Simona Granata-Menghini, 'La Commission de Venise du Conseil de l'Europe: méthodes et perspectives de l'assistance constitutionnelle en Europe' [2017] Les Nouveaux Cahiers du Conseil constitutionnel 69–70.
93 Venice Commission, *Resolution Adopting the Revised Statute of the European Commission for Democracy through Law* (n 89) 27.
94 See Guy Powles, 'Constitution Making in Western Samoa' (1961) 22 The Indian Journal of Political Science 179; Alison Quentin-Baxter, 'Making Constitutions, From the Perspective of Constitutional Adviser' (2002) 33 Victoria University Wellington Law Review 239. Elisabeth Perham ongoing doctoral research discusses on external constitutional advisors in constitution-making processes, with a geographic focus on small island states in Oceania.
95 UNSG (n 3) 3. [Emphasis added].
96 Bisarya (n 1) 1.
97 James Dobbins, 'Europe's Role in Nation Building' (2008) 50 Survival 83, 110.
98 Catherine Turner and Ruth Houghton, 'Constitution Making and Post-Conflict Reconstruction' in *International Law and Post-Conflict Reconstruction Policy* (Routledge 2015) 154.
99 Boutros Boutros-Ghali, *An Agenda for Democratization* (UN Department of Public Information 20 December 1996) 2.
100 UNSG, *Report of the Secretary-General on the Work of the Organization* (2005) GAOR, 60th sess, Suppl no 1 A/60/1 §10.
101 Hallie Ludsin, 'Peacemaking and Constitution-Drafting: A Dysfunctional Marriage' (2011) 33 University of Pennsylvania Journal of International Law 239, 243.

102 ibid 242.
103 UNSG, *Report of the Secretary-General on the Prevention of Armed Conflict. A/55/985 – S/2001/574* (UNSG 7 June 2001) 16. [Emphasis my own].
104 UNSG (n 3) 2.
105 See Kirsti Samuels, 'Post-Conflict Peace-Building and Constitution-Making' (2005) 6 Chicago Journal of International Law 663, 681; Donald Horowitz, 'Conciliatory Institutions and Constitutional Processes in Post-Conflict States' (2007–2008) 49 William & Mary Law Review 1213, 1232; Jennifer Widner, 'Constitution Writing in Post-Conflict Settings: An Overview' (2007) 49 William & Mary Law Review 1513, 1515. See Emmanuel De Groof, *State Renaissance for Peace: Transitional Governance Under International Law* (CUP 2020).
106 The General Framework Agreement for Peace in Bosnia and Herzegovina [Initiated in Dayton on 21 November 1995 and signed in Paris on 14 December 1995] OSCE Annex No 4.
107 Christine Bell, 'Peace Agreements: Their Nature and Legal Status' (2006) 100 American Journal of International Law 373, 392.
108 Samuels (n 105) 664.
109 Christina Murray and others, *Constitutions and Peace Processes a Primer* (UNDPPA – Berghof Foundation 2020) 11: 'Such was the case, for example, in Angola (1994, 2002), Tajikistan (1997), Côte d'Ivoire (2003), Chad (2007), Kenya (2008), Zimbabwe (2008), Madagascar (2009), Kyrgyzstan (2010), Yemen (2011) and South Sudan (2015, 2020)'.
110 Burundi, Arusha Peace and Reconciliation Agreement for Burundi (28 August 2000), UN Peacemaker Protocol II.
111 ibid.
112 Burundi, Constitution of Burundi (2005), Constitute Project art 147, al 141.
113 Burundi (n 110). The Protocol II states 'The Constitution may not be amended except with the support of a four-fifths majority in the National Assembly and a two-thirds majority in the Senate'. Article 300 of the 2005 Constitution of Burundi states 'the bill or the proposal of amendment of the Constitution is adopted with a majority of four-fifths of the members of the National Assembly and two-thirds of the members of the Senate'.
114 Silvia Suteu, *Eternity Clauses in Democratic Constitutionalism* (OUP 2021).
115 UNSG, *Guidance Note of the Secretary-General Regarding United Nations Assistance to Constitution-Making Processes* (UNSG 2009) 3. [Emphasis my own].
116 ibid.
117 UNSG (n 3) 3.
118 Bisarya (n 1) 1.
119 See for instance, Nicole Töpperwien, *From Armed Intra-State Conflict to a Functioning Constitutional Order Reconciling Principles of Third-Party Support – A Reflection* (Berghof Foundation 2019) 11.
120 Vijayashri Sripati, 'UN Constitutional Assistance Projects in Comprehensive Peace Missions: An Inventory 1989–2011' (2012) 19 International Peacekeeping 93, 225–337.
121 ibid 112. See for an inventory of all UNSC resolutions, ibid 225–337.
122 Vijayashri Sripati, 'United Nations Constitutional Assistance in Statebuilding' in *Routledge Handbook of International Statebuilding* (Routledge 2013) 146.
123 UNDP, *Annual Report of the Administrator for 2001* (UNDP 6 May 2002) 4; UNDP, *Annual Report of the Administrator for 2002* (UNDP 17 April 2003) 12.
124 UNDP, *Annual Report of the Administrator for 2002* (n 123) 9.
125 Michele Brandt, *Constitutional Assistance in Post-Conflict Countries: The UN Experience: Cambodia, East Timor & Afghanistan* (UNDP June 2005).

126 Jamal Benomar, *Constitution-Making and Peace Building: Lessons Learned From the Constitution-Making Processes of Postconflict Countries* (United Nations Development Programme 2003).
127 ibid 3.
128 Brandt (n 125) 1.
129 UNDP, *2009 Annual Report* (UNDP June 2009) 20; UNDP, *2010 Annual Report. Global Programme on Strengthening the Rule of Law in Conflict and Post-Conflict Situations* (UNDP 2011) 4.
130 UNDP *2010 Annual Report* (n 129) 98.
131 ibid 86.
132 UNDP, *Annual Report 2010/2011* (UNDP May 2011) 24.
133 UNDP, *Annual Report 2011/2012* (UNDP June 2012) 15.
134 International IDEA, *Annual Results Report 2007* (International IDEA 2008) 14.
135 International IDEA, *Annual Results Report 2005* (International IDEA 2006) 5.
136 International IDEA, *Annual Results Report 2003* (International IDEA 2004) 10; International IDEA (n 135) 3.
137 International IDEA, *Annual Results Report 2003* (n 136) 43.
138 International IDEA, *Ten Years of Supporting Democracy Worldwide* (International IDEA 2005) 142.
139 ibid.
140 International IDEA, *A Record of Actions 2015* (International IDEA 2016) 54.
141 International IDEA (n 138) 92.
142 International IDEA, *Annual Results Report 1999* (International IDEA 2000) 30; International IDEA (n 138) 92.
143 International IDEA, *A Record of Actions 2012* (International IDEA 2013) 21; International IDEA (n 140) 54.
144 International IDEA, *A Record of Actions 2013* (International IDEA 2014) 21; International IDEA, *A Record of Actions 2014* (International IDEA 2015) 40; International IDEA, *A Record of Actions 2018* (International IDEA 2019) 28; International IDEA, *Annual Results Report 2019* (International IDEA 2020).
145 International IDEA (n 134) 29; International IDEA, *Annual Results Report 2008* (International IDEA 2009) 34; International IDEA (n 143) 23; International IDEA, *A Record of Actions 2013* (n 144) 17; International IDEA (n 140) 53; International IDEA, *A Record of Actions 2016* (International IDEA 2017) 2016; International IDEA, *International IDEA. Supporting Democracy Worldwide a Retropsective Report on our Work 2012–17* (International IDEA 2018) 37.
146 International IDEA (n 140) 54; International IDEA, *A Record of Actions 2018* (n 144) 32.
147 International IDEA, *A Record of Actions 2014* (n 144) 40; International IDEA, *Annual Results Report 2019* (n 144) 36.
148 Max Planck Foundation, *Annual Report 2021* (Max Planck Foundation 2022) 67.
149 International IDEA, *Annual Results Report 2008* (n 145) 26.
150 International IDEA, *A Record of Actions 2014* (n 144) 40.
151 International IDEA, *Annual Results Report 2008* (n 145) 33.
152 ibid.
153 International IDEA, 'What We Do – Constitution-Building' <www.idea.int/our-Work/what-we-do/Constitution-building> accessed October 2021.
154 It counts 54 Members States; 7 associated members; 27 observers. OIF, 'L'Organisation internationale de la Francophonie' <www.francophonie.org/lorganisation-internationale-de-la-francophonie-81> accessed April 2019. See

'Charte de la Francophonie' (23 November 2005) <www.axl.cefan.ulaval.ca/francophonie/francophonie_charte.htm>.

155 Convention relative à l'agence de coopération culturelle et technique (ACCT) [20 March 1970] OIF. [My own translation].

156 OIF, *Rapport du Secrétaire Général de la Francophonie 2012–2014* (OIF 2014) 89. [My own translation].

157 The OIF has dealt with constitution-making more broadly, but the actual involvement in the constitutional drafting has, according to the data available, been taking place within peace-building contexts. On general constitution-making considerations see OIF, *Rapport sur l'état des pratiques de la démocratie, des droits et des libertés dans l'espace francophone – 2018* (OIF 2018) 6–17.

158 OIF, *Rapport sur l'état des pratiques de la démocratie, des droits et des libertés dans l'espace francophone. 2000–2010* (OIF 2010) 10.

159 OIF, *Rapport sur l'état des pratiques de la démocratie, des droits et des libertés dans l'espace francophone – 2014* (OIF 2014) 40. [My own translation; Emphasis my own].

160 OIF, *Rapport sur l'état des pratiques de la démocratie, des droits et des libertés dans l'espace francophone. 2000–2010* (OIF 2000–2010) 14. [My own translation].

161 See measures contained in Chapter V of the Bamako Declaration that allows the Secretary-General to take a series of measures in case of 'of a breakdown of democracy, or massive human rights violations'. See Chapter V of the OIF, 'Déclaration de Bamako' (3 November 2000).

162 OIF (n 160) 12. [My own translation].

163 OIF, *Rapport sur l'état des pratiques de la démocratie, des droits et des libertés dans l'espace francophone – 2022* (OIF 2023) 46.

164 Rüdiger Wolfrum, Daniel Gruss and Tilmann Röder, *Ten Years of Global Knowledge Transfer 2002–2012* (Max Planck Institute 2012) 5.

165 Rüdiger Wolfrum, Daniel Gruss and Tilmann Röder, *Global Knowledge Transfer Working Group – Ten Years of Global Knowledge Transfer Projects and Research 2002–2012* (Max Planck Foundation) 61, 86, 102.

166 UNDP, *Democratic Governance and Diverging Pathways to More Inclusive Societies* (UNDP 2014) 6.

167 UNDP (n 133) 10. [Emphasis added].

168 UNDP, *2007 Annual Report* (UNDP June 2007) 20.

169 UNDP, *2003 Annual Report* (UNDP June 2003) 12; UNDP, *Annual Report of the Administrator for 2001* (n 123) 13.

170 UNDP, *2006 Annual Report* (UNDP June 2006) 4; UNDP (n 132) 6.

171 In 2011 – roughly a quarter of UNDP budget was devoted to Democracy governance (1.183534 of total budget of 4756524). In 2001, it created the Democratic Governance Thematic Trust Fund (DGTTF). UNDP, *Evaluation of the Democratic Governance Trust Fund. Consolidated Report* (UNDP May 2008) iii.

172 UNDP, *2008 Annual Report* (UNDP June 2008) 22. [Emphasis added].

173 UNDP, *UNDP Thematic Trust Funds Annual Report 2015* (UNDP 2015) 38. [Emphasis added].

174 ibid. [Emphasis added].

175 ibid 39. [Emphasis added].

176 UNDP, *Annual Progress Report Nepal – 2008* (UNDP 2008) 2. See also UNDP, *Annual Progress Report Nepal – 2007* (UNDP 2007).

177 UNDP (n 173) 40.

178 UNDP, *Annual Report 2013/2014* (UNDP June 2013) 14.

179 In Afghanistan, see UNDP, *Multi-Year Funding Framework Report on UNDP Performance and Results for 2004: Executive Board of UNDP and UNFPA* (UNDP 12 May 2005) 47. Democratic Republic of the Congo – UNDP (n 168) 20; Bangladesh – UNDP, *Annual Report of the Administrator 2003* (UNDP 12 May 2004) 13–14. Grenada – UNDP, *Annual Report 2016. UNDP Thematic Trust Funds 2016. Crisis Prevention and Recovery, Democratic Governance, Environment* (UNDP June 2016) 20; UNDP (n 173) 40. Kenya – UNDP (n 133) 11. Sierra Leone – UNDP (n 172) 19. Bhutan. ibid 20; UNDP, *2005 Annual Report* (UNDP June 2005) 15. Benin – UNDP (n 169) 14.
180 UNDP (n 132) 14.
181 UNDP (n 172) 20.
182 UNDP (n 133) 10.
183 ibid 11.
184 UNDP (n 179) 20.
185 UNDP (n 172) 21.
186 UNDP (n 168) 23.
187 UNDP (n 170) 5–6.
188 UNSG (n 3) 3.
189 Venice Commission (n 89) art 1(1).
190 ibid.
191 ibid art 2 (2) a. [Emphasis added].
192 Its 2002 status did not specify its range of action *ratione loci*; the Venice Commission has been involved in constitutional assistance of countries that were not yet members. For instance, in 2000, regarding Armenia it states 'quite independently from the accession procedure, the Armenian authorities had already asked us to assist their country in reforming its constitution'. Venice Commission, *Annual Report of Activities 2000* (Venice Commission 10 March 2001) 2.
193 Granata-Menghini (n 92) 71.
194 Venice Commission (n 91) 11.
195 Helmut Steinberger, 'Venice Commission' in *Max Planck Encyclopedia of Public International Law* (OUP May 2007) §8.
196 Venice Commission (n 91) 12.
197 ibid 3, 12.
198 ibid 3.
199 Visser (n 14) 970.
200 Venice Commission, 'For Democracy Through Law' <www.venice.coe.int/WebForms/pages/?p=01_Presentation&lang=EN> accessed April 2020.
201 ibid.
202 Albania – Venice Commission, *Annual Report of Activities 1991* (Venice Commission 14 February 1992) 2; Venice Commission, *Annual Report of Activities 1993* (Venice Commission 24 February 1994) 3. Bulgaria – Venice Commission (n 91) 3; Venice Commission (n 202) 2; Chile – Venice Commission, *Annual Report of Activities 2022* (Venice Commission August 2023) 11; Czechoslovak Republic – Venice Commission, *Annual Report of Activities 1992* (Venice Commission 10 February 1993) 2. Georgia – Venice Commission, *Annual Report of Activities 1993* ibid 4. Iceland – Venice Commission, *Annual Report of Activities 2012* (Venice Commission August 2013) 69; Venice Commission, *Annual Report of Activities 2013* (Venice Commission September 2014) 10. Kosovo – Venice Commission (n 92) 6; Venice Commission, *Annual Report of Activities 2007* (Venice Commission 2008) 28. Kyrgyzstan – Venice Commission, *Annual Report of Activities 1992* ibid 2. Lithuania. ibid 3. Moldova – Venice Commission, *Annual Report of Activities 1993* ibid 3; Venice Commission, *Annual*

Report of Activities 2003 (Venice Commission 13 March 2004) 7. Montenegro – Venice Commission, *Annual Report of Activities 2004* (Venice Commission 12 March 2005) 9; Venice Commission, *Annual Report of Activities 2006* (Venice Commission 2007) 28. Poland – Venice Commission, *Annual Report of Activities 1990* (n 91) 3; Venice Commission, *Annual Report of Activities 1991* ibid 3. Romania – Venice Commission, *Annual Report of Activities 1990* (n 91) 3; Venice Commission, *Annual Report of Activities 1991* ibid 4. Russia – Venice Commission, *Annual Report of Activities 1992* ibid 3. Serbia – Venice Commission, *Annual Report of Activities 2007* ibid 26. Serbia and Montenegro – Venice Commission, *Annual Report of Activities 2002* (Venice Commission 15 March 2003) 4. Ukraine – Venice Commission, *Annual Report of Activities 2005* (Venice Commission 2006) 6; Venice Commission, *Annual Report of Activities 2008* (Venice Commission 2009) 7. Tunisia – Venice Commission, *Annual Report of Activities 2011* (Venice Commission August 2012). Venezuela – Venice Commission, *Annual Report of Activities 2017* (Venice Commission August 2018) 15.

203 International IDEA (n 135) 15. It has been involved in constitutional reform in Lebanon. See International IDEA, *Annual Results Report 2019* (n 144) 40; International IDEA, *A Record of Actions 2018* (n 144) 30; Chile International IDEA, *A Record of Actions 2014* (n 144) 40; International IDEA, *A Record of Actions 2015* (n 140) 54.

204 International IDEA (n 134) 26–27; International IDEA, *Annual Results Report 2008* (n 145) 37–38.

205 International IDEA, *A Record of Actions 2013* (n 144) 17; International IDEA, *A Record of Actions 2014* (n 144) 40.

206 International IDEA, *Annual Results Report 2007* (n 134) 26.

207 International IDEA, *Annual Results Report 2022* (International IDEA 2023) 16.

208 See Roberto Gargarella, *Latin American Constitutionalism, 1810–2010: The Engine Room of the Constitution* (OUP 2013).

209 Kendall (n 13) 365.

210 Harshan Kumarasingham, 'Liberal Ideals and the Politics of Decolonisation' (2018) 46 The Journal of Imperial and Commonwealth History 815–16.

211 When referring to the liberal constitution in this chapter, it refers Western liberal constitutional democratic constitution.

212 The colonial lineage of constitutional democracy, while little discussed in mainstream constitutional scholarship, has been well acknowledged through the work of historians and critical legal scholars. See Upendra Baxi, 'Constitutionalism as a Site of State Formative Practices' (1999) 21 Cardozo Law Review 1183; John McLaren, 'The Uses of the Rule of Law in British Colonial Societies in the Nineteenth Century' in Shaunnagh Dorsett and Ian Hunter (eds), *Law and Politics in British Colonial Thought* (Palgrave Macmillan 2010); David Armitage and Armitage David, *The Ideological Origins of the British Empire* (CUP 2000). Quoted in Sripati (n 6) 95.

213 Baxi (n 10) 540.

214 James Tully, 'The Imperialism of Modern Constitutional Democracy' in Martin Loughlin and Neil Walker (eds), *The Paradox of Constitutionalism: Constituent Power and Constitutional Form* (OUP 2007) 319.

215 ibid 317. See James Tully, *Strange Multiplicity: Constitutionalism in an Age of Diversity* (CUP 1995). See Baxi, 'Constitutionalism as a Site of State Formative Practices' (n 212).

216 Tully, 'The Imperialism of Modern Constitutional Democracy' (n 214) 331.

217 ibid.

218 Patrick Glenn, *The Cosmopolitan State* (OUP 2013) 69 in Sripati (n 6) 83.

219 Sripati (n 6) 91.
220 ibid 94. Metropoles were also driven by political and economic interests as it has been shown in the work of Vijayashri Sripati.
221 Nathan Brown, *Constitutions in a Nonconstitutional World: Arab Basic Laws and the Prospects for Accountable Government* (SUNY Press 2012) 16.
222 Theresa Liane Womble, 'Early Constitutionalism in Tunisia, 1857–1864: Reform and Revolt' (PhD dissertation, Princeton University 1997) 27.
223 Mezri Bdira, *Relations internationales et sous-développement. La Tunisie 1857–1864* (Acta Universitatis Upsaliensis 1978) 27–28.
224 Andre Raymond, 'British Policy towards Tunis (1830–1881)' (PhD dissertation, University of Oxford October 1953) 256.
225 Elie Fitoussi and Aristide Bénszet, *L'Etat tunisien et le protectorat français: Histoire et organisation (1525 à 1881)(1881 à 1931)* (Rousseau & Cie 1931) 62; Womble (n 222) 80.
226 Fitoussi and Bénszet (n 225) 68.
227 Cooper (n 20) 318. See also Simon Chesterman, *You, the People: The United Nations, Transitional Administration, and State-Building* (OUP 2005) 11–25.
228 Sripati (n 6) 138.
229 Covenant of the League of Nations [28 June 1919] League of Nations art 22 (21).
230 ibid.
231 Pierre-François Gonidec, *Droit d'outre-mer. Tome I. De l'empire Colonial de la France à la Communauté* (Editions Montchrestien 1959) 199.
232 See Michael Hennessy Picard, 'Le constitutionnalisme d'occupation en Iraq' (PhD dissertation, Université du Québec à Montréal 2017); Sripati (n 6) 111–12.
233 Dale (n 23) 72–73. See Andrew Harding, 'The "Westminster Model" Constitution Overseas: Transplantation, Adaptation and Development in Commonwealth States' (2004) 4 Oxford University Commonwealth Law Journal 143.
234 AF Madden, 'Constitution-Making and Nationhood: The British Experience – An Overview' (1988) 26 Journal of Commonwealth & Comparative Politics 123–24.
235 Indian Statutory Commission, *Report of the Indian Statutory Commission. Volume II – Recommendations* (Indian Statutory Commission 1930) 6. Madden reports similar views of the Donoughmore Commissioners in Ceylon. Madden (n 234) 125.
236 Madden (n 234) 124.
237 Walter John Hely-Hutchinson, *Ceylon: Report of the Special Commission on the Constitution* (H. M. Stationery Office 1928) 44.
238 ibid.
239 Colonial Office, *Ceylon. Report of the Commission on Constitutional Reform* (Colonial Office 1945) 109.
240 Chambre des représentants (n 54) 18. [My own translation].
241 United States Senate, *Hearings Before the Committee on the Philipines* (Government Printing Office 1915) 193.
242 Fischer (n 7) 822.
243 Young (n 55) 176.
244 ibid.
245 Rothermund (n 15) 14.
246 ibid 15.
247 ibid.
248 Cooper (n 20) 325.
249 Young (n 55) 176.

250 ibid quoting Jules Gérard-Libois and Benoît Verhaegen, *Congo 1960* (Centre de Recherche et d'Information Socio-Politiques 1961) 106–7.
251 United States of America (n 61).
252 Philippines, Constitution of the Philippines (1935).
253 See, Harding (n 233) 144; Heinz Klug, 'Postcolonial Collages: Distributions of Power and Constitutional Models: With Special Reference to South Africa' (2003) 18 International Sociology 114–15.
254 Michel Rosenfeld and András Sajó, 'Introduction' in Michel Rosenfeld and András Sajó (eds), *The Oxford Handbook of Comparative Constitutional Law* (OUP 2012) 6.
255 Jaakko Husa, 'Classification of Legal Families Today – Is It Time for Memorial Hymn?' (2004) 56 Revue internationale de droit comparé 15–16.
256 Boutros-Ghali (n 99) 9.
257 ibid.
258 Balakrishnan Rajagopal, *International Law From Below: Development, Social Movements and Third World Resistance* (CUP 2003) 143.
259 Venice Commission, *Resolution Adopting the Revised Statute of the European Commission for Democracy through Law* (n 89) art 1(1).
260 Venice Commission, *Annual Report of Activities 2002* (n 202) 3.
261 Gianni Buquicchio and Simona Granata-Menghini, 'The Venice Commission Twenty Years On, Challenges Met, but Challenges Ahead' in Marjolein Roosmalen and others (eds), *Fundamental Rights and Principles Liber Amicorum Pieter Van Dijk* (Intersentia 2013) 245. [Emphasis my own].
262 Venice Commission, *Annual Report of Activities 2007* (n 202) 10.
263 Venice Commission, *Annual Report of Activities 2006* (n 202) 15. [Emphasis my own].
264 Venice Commission, *Annual Report of Activities 2007* (n 202) 10.
265 ibid.
266 Paul Craig, 'Transnational Constitution-Making: The Contribution of the Venice Commission on Law and Democracy' (2017) 2 UC Irvine Journal of International, Transnational, and Comparative Law 57, 77.
267 Venice Commission, *Annual Report of Activities 2003* (n 202) 2. [Emphasis my own].
268 ibid.
269 Venice Commission, *Annual Report of Activities 2022* (n 202) 7.
270 Declaration, International Institute for Democracy and Electoral Assistance [27–28 February 1995] International IDEA 4.
271 The International Institute for Democracy and Electoral Assistance Statutes [21 November 2008] International IDEA art 2 (1) d.
272 Declaration (n 270) 3.
273 ibid 11.
274 International IDEA (n 138) 11.
275 International IDEA, *Annual Results Report 2007* (n 134) 14.
276 'Charte de la Francophonie' (n 154) art 1.
277 Convention relative à l'agence de coopération culturelle et technique (ACCT) [20 March 1970]. 'Charte de la Francophonie' (n 154) art 1.
278 OIF, 'Déclaration de Bamako' (n 161). [Translation from the OHCHR see OHCHR, 'Bamako Declaration' <https://www2.ohchr.org/english/law/compilation_democracy/oif.htm> accessed April 2021. [Emphasis my own].
279 OIF, *Rapport sur l'état des pratiques de la démocratie, des droits et des libertés dans l'espace francophone – 2012* (OIF 2012) 36. [My own translation]; OIF (n 163) 20.

280 Rajagopal (n 258) 143.
281 ibid. [Emphasis my own].
282 UNDP has become through diverse programmes the locus to operationalise conflict prevention, that has become a key objective of the UN system as a whole. UNDP, *Annual Report 2013/2014* (n 178) 18.
283 UNDP, *2004 Annual Report* (UNDP June 2004) 7.
284 UNDP, 'Goal 16: Peace, Justice and Strong Institutions' <www.UNDP.org/content/UNDP/en/home/sustainable-Development-goals/goal-16-peace-justice-and-strong-institutions.html> accessed August 2019. They succeed to the Millennium Development Goals which included democratic governance as well as support crisis prevention. UNDP, *Annual Report of the Administrator 2003* (n 179) 4.
285 UNDP-DPA, *Joint UNDP-DPA Annual Report 2015* (UNDP-DPA 2016) 1.
286 UNDP, *Annual Report 2016. UNDP Thematic Trust Funds 2016. Crisis Prevention and Recovery, Democratic Governance, Environment* (n 179) 19.
287 UNDP-DPA, *Joint UNDP-DPA Programme on Building National Capacities for Conflict Prevention Annual Report 2016* (UNDP-DPA 2017) 1.
288 UNSG (n 3) 1.
289 Max Planck Foundation, *Annual Report 2021* (n 148) 37.
290 Sripati (n 6) 216.
291 World Bank, *Legal and Judicial Reform: Strategic Directions* (World Bank 2003) 37 cited in Sripati (n 6) 197. [Emphasis added].
292 UNSG, *Ten-Year Appraisal and Review of the Implementation of the Brussels Programme of Action for the Least Developed Countries for the Decade 2001–2010* (7 February 2011) §46 in Sripati (n 6) 200. [Emphasis my own].
293 Sripati (n 6) 206. [Emphasis my own].
294 ibid 225–337.
295 Nepal' example has been drawn from ibid 249–50.
296 See Comprehensive Peace Accord signed between Nepal Government and the Communist Party of Nepal (Maoist) [22 November 2006] UN Peacemaker §3 and 7 <https://peacemaker.un.org/sites/peacemaker.un.org/files/NP_061122_Comprehensive%20Peace%20Agreement%20between%20the%20Government%20and%20the%20CPN%20%28Maoist%29.pdf>; Nepal, Interim Constitution of Nepal (2007), Constitute Project art 33 (c).
297 Sripati (n 6) 249 quoting Nepal: *Letter of Intent* to the IMF, 31 October 2007.
298 UNSC, Resolution 1740 (23 January 2007).
299 See UNGA, *Report of the OHCHR on the Human Rights Situation and the Activities of her Office, Including Technical Cooperation, in Nepal* (5 February 2010) UNGA UN Doc A/HRC/13/73.
300 World Bank, *Interim Strategy for Nepal for the Period FY 2010–2011* (World Bank 2009) §36.
301 See Sripati (n 6).
302 See more in-depth discussion in the next chapter.
303 Markus Böckenförde, Nora Hedling and Wahiu Wahiu, *A Practical Guide to Constitution Building* (International IDEA 2011).
304 ibid 211.

Chapter 5

The expert as a key actor in transnational constitution-making

'Officially, I did not exist'.[1] With these words, Sir Ivor Jennings summarised his involvement in the 1948 Ceylonese (Sri Lankan) Constitution. Several decades later, this sentiment still rings true with regard to contemporary constitution-making processes. Tom Ginsburg reflects that he has advised 'more than two dozen countries engaged in the constitution-making process, ranging from simply engaging with civil society actors to submitting memos to a drafting committee to working with them on repeated constitutional drafts'.[2] Officially, Ginsburg did not exist as a participant in these processes, and neither do any of the multitude of other external experts who are involved in constitution-making. Indeed, the presence of foreign experts rarely appears in the Rules of Procedures of constitution-making bodies or in the general norms framing the process.[3] Often, the provision of expertise lies at the discretion of the body tasked with drafting the constitution. For instance, in the Rules of Procedure governing the drafting of the 2014 Tunisian Constitution, the constituent commissions of the National Constituent Assembly could seek expertise through hearings or written reports.[4]

This chapter argues that the involvement of experts is a central feature of transnational constitution-making. Building upon the conceptual discussion of Chapter 3, it examines a particular actor, the expert, who plays an important role in constitution-making processes. Bringing expertise to accelerate social goals is the raison d'être of the development enterprise and by examining the figure of the expert within constitution-making, a particular stage of the process calls for further attention: constitutional drafting. From the drafting of constitutions of future independent colonies to contemporary contexts of democratic transition, the provision of expertise has been a key element of the development enterprise.

Despite widespread practice, scholarly attention on the figure of the expert in constitution-making has been sparse and often limited to constitutional experts' recollection of their own experiences.[5] The issues discussed by the literature often relate to the biases constitutional experts may carry, such as focusing on their own jurisdictions. In contrast, experts' 'background of common sense', identified in Chapter 2 as liberal legalism, has received little

DOI: 10.4324/9781003386186-8

critical attention. While some studies have touched upon the political dimension of constitutional advice, the overall assumption is that expert involvement is merely 'technical'.[6] Jurgen de Poorter in a special volume dedicated to constitutional advice notes that 'while political, economic or social factors undoubtedly shape the design and operation of constitutional law, the advice that takes centre stage in this volume is firmly grounded in the law'.[7]

Cases of 'excessive' political involvement are frowned upon and treated as poor examples of transnational constitution-making.[8] Criticism regarding experts' self-interest when providing constitutional advice has been voiced. One clear illustration of this criticism is the case of Peter Galbraith, an American diplomat who participated in the drafting of the 2005 Iraqi Constitution, representing the Iraqi Kurds. Galbraith had been a forceful advocate for Kurdish autonomy of natural resources, although it turned out that he had a personal stake in the constitutional design he advocated for.[9] A *New York Times* investigation revealed that he would earn over $100 million from a Norwegian oil company thanks to shares he acquired in an oil field in the Iraqi Kurdish region.[10]

Scholars across the social sciences have been interested in the provision of expertise in the context of legal reform, with international relations studies centring on practices that lead to framing certain issues as apolitical.[11] There has to date been very little scholarship specifically devoted to the topic of legal expertise – a key contribution here is the work of David Kennedy who has examined the role of 'expertise' in the global political economy.[12]

To examine this aspect of the development enterprise, this chapter draws on primary sources that include testimonies from constitutional experts and constitution-makers and on institutional documentation from external actors.[13] It draws on secondary sources that include work from historians who have studied the role of constitutional scholars in constitution-making in contexts of decolonisation and development.

As usual, several caveats must be outlined before beginning the chapter proper. First, 'expert' here refers to foreign experts; the study of domestic experts is beyond the scope of this inquiry but certainly deserves further attention. While the presence of foreign experts is the focus of this work, this chapter does not aim to erase the role played by domestic actors.[14] Particularly in the case of constitution-making in context of decolonisation, certain domestic leaders were educated in the metropolitan system, which blurs the line between foreign and local expertise.[15] As Madden explains, 'some African leaders educated in the British system were conditioned to think British was best and were resentful of being denied it'.[16] Second, as in the previous chapter, the goal is not to exhaustively document all foreign experts present in constitution-making processes but to show that the expert is a legal actor that deserves closer examination if the transnational dimension of constitution-making is to be better understood. Third, another layer of difficulty is added due to the fact that the content and depth of expertise provided is context-specific. Various drafting situations exist. For instance, there are cases of constitution-making where a constitution was drafted within a post-conflict context, which then became part of a peace deal involving the UN. In other cases, countries engaged in a constitution-making process following popular demand, as was the case in Chile.[17] It is also important to note that transnational involvement can occur formally and/or informally. Some external actors sign a Memorandum of Understanding with the constitution-making body, whereas others are only ever involved through informal channels. For example, International IDEA and the Max Planck Foundation formalised their support to Chile's Constitutional Convention through a cooperation agreement and a Memorandum of Understanding respectively.[18] A decade earlier, UNDP had signed a Memorandum of Understanding with the Tunisian National Constituent Assembly.[19] In this chapter, all external actors providing expertise are included, regardless of the terms framing the involvement.

Fourth, as this chapter aims to demonstrate the continuity that exists between the decolonisation and post-Cold War periods, it acknowledges that the political and legal contexts in which these experts were involved have changed significantly. For example, contemporary external actors tend to insist on the necessity of 'ownership' of the constitutional text by 'the people' to ensure democratic legitimacy and thus constitutional success; this dimension was less prevalent in constitution-making that occurred in the context of decolonisation. While the chapter does not equate this type of expertise with contemporary expertise, it argues that pervading similarities can still be found. Finally, this chapter focuses on the role of experts in the *process* rather than the *outcome* of the constitution, beginning from the premise that the process affects the outcome to varying degrees depending on the specific context.[20]

The lens of the development enterprise highlights the extent of expert involvement, a dynamic that tends to be side-lined in comparative constitutional scholarship but is in fact central to constitution-making. The antifoundationalist framework reveals that a multiplicity of actors are involved in the process, each bringing their own political assumptions. 'Political' is understood here in its broadest sense. Marieke Louis and Lucile Maertens offer a useful definition of politics in this context as 'the activities which eventually have an impact on the daily lives of a broader collectivity because they involve considerations on the legitimacy of detaining power, exercising authority and delivering adequate policies'.[21] This is particularly relevant as the provision of foreign expertise tends to be very loosely, if at all, regulated by national actors. Treating constitutional expertise as political contradicts the discourse of both practitioners and constitutional scholars, who understand expertise as 'technical' and 'apolitical'. For instance, in the constitution-making process in Kenya, the Review Act established the Committee of Experts as an apolitical and technical body.[22] Local constitution-makers accept that expertise provided by national actors can be politically motivated, but even the most critical constitution-makers tend to assume that expertise from international organisations is technical rather than political. Mabrouka M'Barek, who was a member of the Tunisian National Constituent Assembly, criticised the colonial roots of foreign influence yet still considered that the Venice Commission 'was consulted for its technical advice'.[23] The fact that foreign expertise is considered apolitical has deeply political consequences, as it sets the horizon of possibilities for the new constitutional order; this involves the rights of individuals and how political power is distributed.

This chapter approaches the figure of the expert through their involvement in constitution-making and discusses how experts and external actors position themselves as political outsiders during constitution-making processes that took place during decolonisation and in the post-Cold War period. It then moves on to unpack how external actors conceive themselves as neutral providers of expertise.

Involvement of constitutional experts in constitution-making processes

Despite differences between constitution-making undertaken in the context of decolonisation and post-Cold War constitution-making, experts involved in constitution-making processes undertake similar types of tasks. The involvement of external actors in constitution-making processes occurs by providing constitutional advice to constitution-makers. Constitutional advice can be understood as 'encompassing the seeking and rendering of advice on constitutional topics, including the study of the processes and institutions that enable and contextualise such advice'.[24] Ginsburg defines it as 'a subsidy of information and ideas on a constitutional topic'.[25] It oscillates, depending on the context, between raising awareness, that is, bringing to the attention of their interlocutor the necessity to include certain rights or certain institutional frameworks – and commenting on constitutional drafts.[26] This section describes the involvement of constitutional experts in constitution-making processes undertaken within decolonisation processes in the British Empire, the emergence of United States constitutional expertise in the development decades, and how the provision of expertise changed in the post-Cold War era.

Drafting constitutions in the context of decolonisation

The drafting of constitutions in context of decolonisation within the British Empire offers significant insight concerning the figure of the constitutional expert, simply due to the volume of constitutions that were drafted during this period. The figure of the expert is inextricable from constitution-making undertaken in the context of decolonisation. On the one hand, metropoles relied on experts to draft the constitutions in the Colonial Office or in constitutional committees; on the other hand, the governments of the colonies worked with British constitutional scholars to draft constitutions and provide advice during negotiations with the metropole. Regardless of their institutional affiliation, constitutional experts were characterised by holding a certain specialised knowledge related to self-government.

In constitution-making processes undertaken in the context of decolonisation, experts were involved in at least three capacities. First, there were the lawyers working in the Colonial Office; as Sir Ivor Jennings, a prominent figure in such processes, wrote, 'the development of the British dependencies towards independence led to the rise of the constitution-makers. The legal advisers at the Colonial Office did most of the work'.[27] Second, legal scholars served on constitutional committees that were established during the drafting of constitutions. These committees would gather political representatives of the colony and members of the Colonial Office, including: Arthur Berriedale Keith, a constitutional scholar and historian who served the Colonial Office from 1901–1914 and was involved in Nigeria, Natal, and the Caribbean.[28] William Dale, legal advisor to the Commonwealth Office from 1935–1966, was a first-hand witness to several constitution-making processes of Whitehall lawyers drafting at least 33 complete constitutions 'to say nothing of a deluge of intermediate instruments'[29] and observed that 'the drafting of the constitutions was in London, done in the Colonial Office'.[30] Stanley Alexander Smith, a London School of Economics and Cambridge law professor, was another legal expert whose 1964 work *The New Commonwealth and its Constitutions* remains influential.[31] He served as a constitutional commissioner in Mauritius for many years[32] and in 1954 became Secretary of the Buganda Constitutional Committee [territory of the Uganda protectorate] and led the Namirembe Conference.[33]

Finally, independent constitutional scholars, who acted as advisors to governments of the colony, were also involved. While a wide range of experts collaborated during the drafting of constitutions undertaken in the context of decolonisation, a major figure that dominated the transnational transfers was Sir Ivor Jennings, the constitution-maker par excellence from the 1940s until his death in 1965.[34] Jennings' journey as a constitutional advisor began in Ceylon, where he was the founding Vice-Chancellor and eventually became a central architect of Ceylon's independence.[35] He then moved on to advise neighbouring countries, including Pakistan, British Malaya,[36] the Maldives, and Nepal.[37] As Harshan Kumarasingham outlines, 'Jennings was a major "constitution-maker" working as a constitutional advisor and constitutional commission member from Singapore to Sudan'.[38] Ceylon is an illustrative case of Jennings' involvement in constitutional drafting. He advised D.S. Senanayake, a leader of the independence movement who became the first Prime Minister of Ceylon, as well as other leading Ceylonese political figures, his involvement proceeding in a largely unofficial manner.[39] Despite the lack of formality, Jennings was closely involved in the drafting of the new constitution. On the topic of the drafting process, Jennings recalls the many back-and-forths between Ceylonese authorities and the Colonial Office:

> D.S. insisted that he and I should see it. We started out with no less than 88 suggestions. Sir Barclay and I went to Temple Trees and dealt with all but the more important amendments, and then D.S. came in to discuss the substantial points of difference. Sir Henry Moore, who was in Nuwara Eliya, was anxious to take part in the discussions, and D.S. agreed: indeed he may have suggested it. . . . Sir Henry, again supported by D.S., was anxious to have me present, so as to have legal opinion on both sides.[40]

Similarly, Sir Benegal Rau, an Indian-born Cambridge-educated scholar, was appointed as a constitutional advisor to the India National Constituent in July 1946 and was also involved in the drafting of the Burmese Constitution in 1947.[41] In Malaysia, the constitutional draft was carved out by a group of experts coming from several Commonwealth countries.[42] The figure of the expert is thus significant in the context of constitution-making during decolonisation in the British Empire.

Development decades and the rise of US constitutional experts

The development decades (i.e. 1960–1970s) saw a huge growth in the number of US constitutional experts sent abroad. Examples of US professors advising other territories before this period exist. In territories under US control, experts were involved in the drafting of new constitutions.[43] The most obvious case is Liberia, which was largely founded by the American Colonization Society in 1821.[44] The 1847 Liberian Constitution was also drafted by Harvard professor of law Simon Greenleaf.[45] Other examples of US constitutional advising include Columbia professor Frank Goodnow, who provided input to the 1912 Provisional Constitution of the Republic of China[46] and professors Carl Friedrich and James Pollock, who served as special advisors to the US military government in Germany after WWII and were involved in the 1949 German Constitution.[47] Further, in Japan, it is well documented that the staff of General Douglas MacArthur drafted 1947 Japanese Constitution in seven days.[48] US Supreme Court Justices and constitutional law professors were consulted by Sir B.N. Rau, constitutional advisor to the Indian Constituent Assembly, who was responsible for the overall structure of the 1946 Indian Constitution.[49] Finally, US Supreme Court Justice Thurgood Marshall contributed a substantial portion of the drafting of the 1962 Kenyan Constitution.[50]

Two US constitutional law professors deserve a closer examination, simply due to the sheer number of constitutions they provided advice for: Albert

Blaustein and Dick Howard. Together, the two men advised constitution-making processes in at least 25 countries, across Asia, Africa, Latin-America, and Europe. Albert Blaustein was a law professor at Rutgers University and started his constitutional advising career as a consultant funded by the Ford Foundation. He was involved 'on behalf of the United States' in the drafting of the 1967 Constitution of South Vietnam.[51] He was then involved in the following constitution-making processes: Bangladesh (1972), Cambodia (1974), Zimbabwe (1978–1980), Peru (1979), Liberia (1982–1983), Niger (1983–1988), Brazil (1985–1988), Namibia (1987), Uganda (1988–1989), Mozambique (1988–1989), and Fiji (1989).[52] In the early 1990s, Blaustein was also involved in the democratisation that occurred in Central and Eastern Europe following the disbanding of the Soviet Union, consulting on the constitutions of Croatia, Lithuania, Romania, Slovenia, and the Russian Federation.[53] Some concrete examples of Blaustein's constitutional advice can be found in his own writing:

> Neither in drafting the 1979 Constitution of Zimbabwe nor in revising the 1990 Constitution of Fiji could I eliminate the redundant phrase that peppers virtually all the constitutions of the former British colonies: 'that is to say'. Then there are those legalese favorites, 'whereas' and 'wherein'. I was instrumental in deleting those words from the first draft of the 1972 Bangladesh Constitution.[54]

Dick Howard, a law professor at the University of Virginia, was involved in fewer constitution-making processes than Blaustein but was still involved in Brazil, Hong Kong, the Philippines, Malawi, Albania, Outer Mongolia, Hungary, Poland, Czechoslovakia, Romania, and South Africa.[55]

The institutionalisation of transnational constitutional expertise

In the post-Cold War period, foreign experts became institutionalised through organisations such as International IDEA, the Venice Commission, as well as other private actors such as INGOs, which are composed of experts. The Venice Commission is a paradigmatic example of an external actor exclusively composed of experts. Indeed, it was created to provide 'constitutional first-aid'[56] through 'independent expert analysis of the constitutional and legal situation in a given country to the international community'.[57] As Antonio La Pergola, whose vision launched the Venice Commission, expressed in 2001:

> The Venice Commission has been fulfilling its appointed tasks ever since the eve of that turning point in history which was the breakdown of the hideous divide of Europe into two opposite camps. Our reputation as a *highly qualified team of legal experts* has been firmly established.[58]

The institution itself is composed of two members – one effective and one substitute – from each member state, for a renewable four-year term, but Venice Commission members act in their individual capacity.[59] The Venice Commission's Statute defines its experts as those 'who have achieved eminence through their experience in democratic institutions or by their contribution to the enhancement of law and political science',[60] and they must act in an 'independent, impartial, and objective' manner.[61] Experts include constitutional and international law professors, constitutional court judges, ombudsmen, as well as members of various parliaments.[62]

International IDEA is another international organisation composed of experts. Alongside its Council, which is composed of representatives from member states,[63] there is a Board of Advisors of up to 15 members, serving in their personal capacities, 'who shall be eminent personalities or experts from a wide variety of backgrounds', selected 'on the basis of their accomplishments and experience, whether professional or academic, in areas of importance for the activities of the Institute'.[64] Several influential legal scholars served on the Board of Advisors, including, Christine Bell and Cheryl Saunders.[65]

Similarly, for UNDP, within its peace-building and democratic governance capacity, the provision of expertise is a key activity.[66] The joint UNDP and UNDPPA Programme on Building National Capacities for Conflict Prevention was set up in 2004,[67] with a mission to 'draw on the complementary capacities of each partner for expertise across the conflict prevention and peace-building spectrum'.[68] Associated with the programme are Peace and Development Advisors who provide expertise in contexts of peace-building to 'national partners in dialogue processes, the development of national infrastructures and mechanisms for peace, and other initiatives to build national capacities for conflict prevention'.[69]

UNDP defines itself as 'one of the world's leading providers of services to bolster democratic governance',[70] noting that it 'devotes the biggest share of its resources, 40 per cent of its programme expenditure, to democratic governance [$1.5 billion each year]' which makes it the 'largest providers of democratic governance technical cooperation globally'.[71] In 2005, UNDP mapped its network of democratic governance expertise, which included '1,200 practitioners and 380 registered expert practitioners'.[72] For instance, in the Nepalese constitution-making process in 2008, UNDP was involved in 'build[ing] the capacity of the Constituent Assembly and its secretariat through technical support';[73] further UNDP noted that 'delegates and technical advisors (subject to the CA's[Constitutional Assembly] request) will be developed to assist in the preparation and approval of a new Nepali constitution'.[74] Indeed, one of its goals was to set up a 'constitutional advisory support unit'.[75] The 2020 Guidance Note refers to the creation of an inter-agency Constitutions Working Group, where 'members track constitutional assistance efforts within their agencies and departments, document the experiences of their respective department or agency to build institutional capacity, record lessons learned and provide constitutional advice to their colleague'.[76] Finally, INGOs such as DRI have their work 'carried out by an international network of experienced associates, each of whom have worked in democratic governance and human rights for ten to 20 years, often in senior positions'.[77] The Max Planck Foundation is similarly composed of legal experts.[78] Not only do external actors (both governmental and non-governmental organisations) institutionalise expertise related to constitution-making, they also position themselves as apolitical experts who only engage in technical, not political, questions.

Justifying involvement with specific knowledge

The role of experts is significant in the development enterprise as they provide specialised knowledge to constitution-makers. Sent from the metropoles to draft constitutions in Third World territories, the experts' specialised knowledge stems from their training in modern law and, more importantly, their elite status from a country that has achieved 'civilisation' and political development. In post-Cold War constitution-making, the role of experts is equally significant, with external actors presenting themselves as technicians of democracy, able to provide the knowledge necessary for constitution-making, aimed at implementing liberal constitutional democracy.

Constitutional experts in the British Empire

Unlike the waves of engineers and academics sent to the colonies and then independent states in the early- to mid-twentieth century, who relied on a specific scientific discipline to ground their expertise, constitution-making was not perceived as a scholarly field but as a political practice; the field of constitution-making within the academic discipline of comparative constitutional law did not exist until the early 1990s. Prior to this, the issues surrounding constitution-making were circumscribed to practitioners and were not conceived of as legal issues. Constitutional manuals illustrate how constitution-making processes are related to historical descriptions of how the constitutions of other countries have been adopted. One of the first books written on how to adopt and revise modern constitutions is illustrative of this trend. In 1893, Charles Borgeaud published *Etablissement et révision des constitutions en Amérique et en Europe* [Establishment and revision of constitutions in America and Europe]. In this study, he outlines the importance of understanding how a constitution has been adopted in order to understand its institutional framework. It did not contain a comparison of different constitutional structures; that was to that point discussed in political science.[79]

The experts sent by metropoles, while drafting the constitutions of the soon-to-be independent territories, conceived of themselves as providing technical expertise, through their institutions and professors working on their behalf, on the science of self-government. Regardless of their institutional affiliations – ranging from the Colonial Office to the constitutional commissions; from academia to the governments of the colony – these experts were granted this title because of their knowledge of rational law. In the framework of the British Empire, it meant transposing the Westminster model to territories seeking independence, which originated from a shift in British Government regarding whether or not the colonies could be worthy of liberal institutions. To bring about liberal institutions and the Westminster model in its colonies was a relatively late development in the history of the British Empire. In first instance, British officials believed the Westminster model could not be implanted.[80] The metropolitan constitutional architecture was the key reference point for their expertise. For example, Vincent Harlow, a historian of the British Empire, was involved in the Sudanese constitutional commission, advocating for a Bill of rights framework in the MENA region, inspired by the influential British constitutional theorist Albert Dicey.[81]

To devise the constitutional framework of the would-be independent territory, the experts relied on their legal education, mainly limited to their jurisdiction. As Brun-Otto Bryde outlines, 'they draw the own respective model of the foreign adviser as the best road to development without due regard to the conditions of the receiving country (or even other models in other parts of the world)'.[82] Metropolitan institutional frameworks were internalised by constitutional scholars, who then worked to circulate these legal ideas. M.G. de Winton, legal advisor to the United Kingdom, who participated in constitution-making processes, noted that 'constitution-writing often took place under extreme conditions, which meant that constitution-makers did not always have the luxury of time to seriously consider other options'.[83] Jennings observed that the core constitutional features of the metropole were routinely implanted in the colonial constitutions. Regarding the essential concepts grounding the Westminster model in the Commonwealth, he notes:

> How far has all this been exported? The answer is, I think, nearly all of it. . . . The technique of parliamentary drafting by government draftsmen is everywhere the same. Sir [Thomas] Erskine May's Parliamentary Practice is on the table of every legislature from Victoria, B.C., to Nairobi, and from Dar-es-Salaam to Hong Kong or Wellington, New Zealand. In every legislature there are lawyers who speak the language of Magna Carta.[84]

Despite the different adaptations made to the Westminster system in each colony, the core of the model is shared. As Jennings writes in his memoirs, the Westminster model would be adapted by working with a local lawyer, trained in Britain. To explain the dynamics of constitutional advising, he refers to an invented 'draftsman' named Wilkins who has been tasked to draft the constitution of an imaginary land Arcadia because 'one must not tell the secrets of the conference, the Cabinet, or the party'.[85]

> Among those who met Wilkins at the Arcady airport was a lawyer whom we will call Henrico. He had been assigned to help Wilkins as 'junior'. Wilkins welcomed him with open arms . . . Henrico's job was not merely to help Wilkins but also to *give him local colour*. He knew a good deal about his own people; he knew the local laws; he had worked with the politicians and knew their foibles. What is more, he would be able to criticise Wilkins' drafts. When two lawyers work together their job is to disagree until they agree. That is to say, they argue with each other until they convince themselves. What they then decide is probably right, for the decision has been examined from all angles.[86]

Before delving into an examination of post-Cold War constitution-making, it is worth pointing out that early UN involvement in constitution-making was aimed at providing advice. For instance, in Libya, the UN aimed to 'advise the Libyan people without making their decisions for them . . . the best he [the UN Commissioner] could do was to help them in elaborating an appropriate democratic constitution, adapted to the country's particular traditions and needs'.[87] In his memoirs, Adrian Pelt, the UN Commissioner in Libya, explains how the working group tasked with drafting the Constitution called on the expertise of the UN:

> Recognizing its own lack of knowledge on the matter [the distribution of powers], it therefore requested the secretariat of the United Nations Mission in Libya to provide translations into Arabic of the relevant chapters of the Constitutions of Argentina, Australia, Brazil, Burma, Canada, the Federal Republic of Germany, India, Indonesia, Mexico, Switzerland, the United States, and Venezuela, later adding those of the Netherlands and the Union of South Africa.[88]

Pelt claims that Chapter 9 of the Libyan Constitution that deals with federal finance is 'almost entirely based on proposals formulated by UN financial experts collaborating with some of their British professional colleagues on the Provisional Libyan Government staff and in the Tripolitanian Administration'.[89]

In the context of decolonisation, the expert was a common fixture of constitution-making processes. The provision of expertise changed, from taking full responsibility to draft the constitution to offering advice to domestic actors; however, the justification for involvement remained the same: expertise was based on an in-depth knowledge of modern public law, which was deemed rational and politically developed.

After the decolonisation period, the specialised knowledge of the constitutional expert continued to be related to the expert having been trained in a country that had reached political development. Possessing this specialised knowledge justified foreign actors intervening in the sovereign process of constitution-making. Thomas Carothers notes that the US government responded to the democratisation processes of the 1980s and 1990s 'with many constitutional aid projects', which aimed to 'transfer knowledge about the American constitutional experience by sending US experts abroad to advise constitution drafters, hosting conferences on constitution writing, bringing foreign constitution drafters to the United States on study tours'.[90]

The 'technician of democracy' as the expert

Following the end of the Cold War and the wave of democratisation in Central and Eastern Europe, as well as in the African continent, a sudden need to draft constitutions existed so these states could create the necessary institutions to reach liberal democracy. From the early 1990s onward, because constitution-making became a core area of democratisation, there was an increase of experts in constitution-making related-matters.

The underlying idea of constitutional expertise is that constitution-making is such a complex activity, and setting up democratic institutions is so essential, that it is justifiable to bring in foreign actors to advise on the process; in short, foreign experts possess a knowledge that local constitution-makers do not. These external actors position themselves as having expertise concerning both the highly developed democratic institutions of their own country (or the West at large), as well as having comparative knowledge due to their experience in other foreign cases of constitution-making. As Gianni Buquicchio observes, the Venice Commission was in the 'business [of] comparative constitutional engineering, which is a very complex and delicate exercise'.[91] The Venice Commission provides assistance to countries drafting constitutions and/or prepares opinions 'on whether a proposal for a legislative text meets the European standards in a given field and on how to improve the texts on the basis of European experience'.[92] This is illustrated in the criteria used to create the working group that would provide legal opinions on a constitutional draft, normally composed of four to six people,[93] who were selected based on their knowledge of comparative constitutional law, of the particular country and any specifics related to the context and overall personal experience.[94] To form such opinions, experts from the Venice commission travel to the country to discuss these issues with national authorities.[95]

In the same vein, International IDEA positions itself as a 'provider of expertise' on the topic of democratic transition, particularly with regard to constitution-making. International IDEA is meant to play a key role 'by providing comparative knowledge and experience in the field of elections, constitution building, political parties, women's political empowerment and democracy self-assessments'.[96] An aspect of this activity is the production and dissemination of research,[97] as its report states, 'there is still relatively little comparative knowledge available for constitution-makers to rely on'.[98] International IDEA develops this knowledge through its Constitution-Building Programme, created in 2007. Specifically, it has developed expertise in constitution-making, which entails 'supporting inclusive constitution-building processes that respond to national priorities'.[99] Its programme provides 'comparative knowledge resources and the tools for use by the constitution builders, particularly those located in democratizing and post conflict contexts'.[100] International IDEA established its expert profile by publishing reports and working papers from constitutional scholars, in what it refers to as 'Constitution Briefs', which cover topics such as the protection of ethnic minorities, the relationship between constitutions and international law, courts and federalism, and constitutional design in territorially divided societies.[101] As its 2022 Annual Report notes, it provides experience and knowledge that constitution-makers do not have:

> Countries are increasingly using small commissions to consult with the public, conduct research and develop draft constitutions. Almost always, the members of such commissions have never been involved in constitution building before, and International IDEA supports them through providing comparative information and experiences to help them navigate their path through the reform process.[102]

International IDEA provided such comparative knowledge to Chilean constitution-makers.[103]

Expertise can also be based on the network of experts that external actors have access to, as is the case for the OIF, which offers constitutional assistance to countries in peace-building contexts. Among its different actions, the OIF aims to

> strengthen the Francophone support system for states in the drafting and revision of fundamental texts. Upstream, La Francophonie will strengthen its presence in constitutional processes by expanding its range of expertise on essentially constitutional issues before, during and after crisis recovery or peacebuilding processes.[104]

In its 2014 Annual Report, the OIF insists that over the years 'it has developed a recognised legal expertise and a sought-after constitutional assistance', providing 'high-level expertise' when supporting the making or revision of constitutions.[105] The expertise of the OIF lies on the network of francophone constitutional experts it can rely on,[106] as it has done in the Central African Republic for over a decade or in the Comoros.[107]

Expertise can also come from the knowledge gained by external actors in other areas of their work, as is the case of experts within UNDP. In general, UNDP positions itself as a provider of expertise in a wide range of areas – from poverty reduction to environmental protection – including constitution-making.[108] As UNDP notes in its 2014–2017 Strategic Plan, they are 'able to draw on knowledge and expertise gained in all development settings, thus, able to grasp and respond flexibly to common concerns and important differences between countries and regions'.[109] For example, a 2004 UNDP report on the topic of institution building notes that 'during the post-conflict period, a major area of our expertise, we look for ways to help not only defuse tensions by filling immediate gaps, but also to help countries rebuild functioning institutions that can ensure stability'.[110] Similarly, UNDP peace and development advisors aim to combine the different fields of expertise that exist across the UN system[111] by sharing 'best practices' and 'lessons learnt',[112] in order to leverage 'existing capacities and expertise within DPA [Department of Political Affairs] and UNDP, for instance, on constitutional processes'.[113] The 2020 Guidance Note released by the UN Secretary-General points to technical advice on constitution-making as a key area of constitutional assistance,[114] which 'often involves mobilizing and convening a wide range of expertise, from both within and outside the UN system and within and outside the country, to provide access to and understanding of international and comparative good practice'.[115]

In a report for UNDPPA, Sumit Bisarya, currently head of the constitution-building unit of International IDEA, explains how having first-hand knowledge of past experiences is key:

> In terms of personnel and profile, it is helpful to bear a few considerations in mind. First, it is not enough to select 'a lawyer'. Lawyers rarely, if ever, study or practice constitution making or why certain constitutional design choices are made, yet advisers require precisely these areas of knowledge to provide useful input. A legal background may be relevant but not as valuable as an understanding of constitutional design and constitution-making processes, preferably based on extensive experience in constitution making – either as a participant or as an adviser – in multiple relevant contexts.[116]

He also notes how familiarity with a local context or region is also highly relevant to provide useful expertise to constitution-making processes.[117]

International NGOs also position themselves as providers of expertise to countries undergoing democratic transitions. Since 2002, the Max Planck Institute for Comparative Public Law and International Law has provided constitutional assistance to states in a peace-building or post-revolution context,[118] and since 2013, these services have been transferred to the Max Planck Foundation.[119] A key objective of the Max Planck Foundation is to work directly with states undergoing a constitutional transition, providing advice related to the 'development of new constitutions and laws, as well as for the revision of existing ones'.[120] The Max Planck Foundation has been involved in Afghanistan,[121] Iraq, Libya, Somalia, Sudan, South Sudan, and Yemen.[122] In addition to direct practical involvement, the Max Planck Foundation has published several academic reports on the topic, positioning itself as knowledge provider to 'utilize the valuable practical expertise of the Institute in the field of international law and foreign public law and to share it with political decision-makers and interested groups'.[123] In its 2021 report, its focus was stated to be at 50% on constitutional law and 28% on legislative and constitutional drafting.[124] It also notes it provided research papers on an ad-hoc basis to members of the Chilean Convention or its Commission covering rights to education and environments rights.[125]

DRI, a Berlin-based INGO created in 2006,[126] also positions itself as a knowledge provider, with a goal of overcoming a lack of national expertise on the topic of constitution-making: 'Major constitutional reforms do not happen often in any country and national expertise is often limited. In this decisive moment, we support officials and civil society to conduct an inclusive constitution-making process to underpin a democracy'.[127] With regard to constitution-making, DRI considers 'three elements to be equally important: The process of making a constitution, the actual text, and its implementation'.[128] DRI has been involved in constitution-making in Egypt,[129] in Libya, Myanmar, Tunisia, Ukraine, and Yemen.[130] This support often involves 'exploring democratic constitutional design options in one-on-one meetings between DRI experts and constitution-makers'[131] and by producing briefing papers and reports.[132] DRI was involved in the 2013 Myanmar constitutional reform, meeting with the Constitutional Amendment Committee to 'provide comparative information on constitutional reform in political transitions'.[133] In Libya it was involved with members of the Libyan Constitution Drafting Assembly on 'key aspects of drafting a constitution, and as a result, these members started using comparative examples in the debates of the assembly'.[134] It provided one-to-one constitutional to Tunisian constitution-makers.[135]

External actors as 'neutral' providers of constitutional expertise

The second feature of expertise relates to political neutrality. Because external actors hold specialised scientific knowledge, they see themselves as positioned outside of the realm of political action. The broader trend at the end of the Cold War that characterised other areas of legal reform, including constitution-making, was that 'the end of ideologies, and the promotion of democracy seemed to be a mere *technical* process'.[136] External actors began to conceive of themselves as political outsiders, providing apolitical, neutral expertise on constitutional matters.

Outside the political process

During constitution-making processes undertaken within contexts of decolonisation, actors were part of the process and relatively transparent regarding the political ideology they carried out. From a practitioner's perspective, at least discursively, the civilising mission was the north star of these experts, whose explicitly aims was to bring modern institutions that would allow these territories to develop. At an academic level, the scientific study of constitution-making had not yet emerged, and it was conceived as a political practice.

In post-Cold War constitution-making, the political dimension of constitution-making is attributed to the domestic institution tasked with adopting the new constitution, often some kind of national constituent assembly. Louis Aucoin, a constitutional advisor in Rwanda, East Timor, and Cambodia, discusses this point:

> Foreign advisers play a dramatically different role in modern constitution-making than the myth suggests. They provide comparative information about a variety of constitutional models while remaining respectful of the sovereign right of indigenous actors to choose among them.[137]

While it is true that from a purely legal standpoint the constitution is ultimately adopted by a domestic institution, external actors remain actively involved during a particular stage of constitution-making: constitutional drafting. Because external actors are most actively involved during the early phase of constitutional drafting, they can more easily position themselves as political outsiders. Tom Ginsburg, for instance, notes how dangerous it can be for constitutional advisors to be involved in internal politics, suggesting that they should not.[138]

Very few cases exist where foreign expertise has been structured and formalised. In Albania in 1997, the Administrative Center for the Coordination of Assistance and Public Participation was opened under the guidance of the Organization for Security and Co-operation in Europe, where foreign experts were formally involved, and in Eritrea, between 1993–1996, a Foreign Advisory Board, chaired by US legal scholars, provided constitutional expertise through a formal channel.[139] More recently, prior to the adoption of the 2010 Kenya Constitution, the Committee of Experts, tasked with proposing a constitutional draft, was composed of ten experts, including foreign experts from other African countries.[140] Finally, two foreign experts, Yash Pal Ghai (Kenya) and Christina Murray (South Africa), were also appointed to Constitution Commission tasked with proposing a constitutional draft for Fiji in 2012–2013.[141] The Commission was in charge of

> prepar[ing] a draft Constitution and any consequential changes to existing laws as may be necessary or advisable to give full effect to the draft

> Constitution, on the basis outlined in section 3, with an Explanatory Report, and present it to the people of Fiji for their comments.[142]

External actors tend to highlight the non-prescriptive nature of their work. The Venice Commission highlights how 'the Commission does not attempt to impose solutions or abstract models; it prefers to acquire an understanding of the aims pursued by the legal text in question, the surrounding political and legal context and the issues involved'.[143] International IDEA echoes a similar understanding, stating that it works by 'providing non-prescriptive comparative knowledge and options and by facilitating processes that help stakeholders to explore solutions that suit their context'.[144] International IDEA details how it supported Chile's Constitutional Convention where 'constitution-makers learned how to make informed choices regarding constitutional design and process'.[145] The Max Planck Foundation, for instance, notes the apolitical nature of its work by underlining how it informs actors across the political spectrum and 'train[s] the participants to discuss controversial constitutional questions in an academic manner which implies an approach away from politics and individual positions towards a notion of shared, objective interests'.[146] The Max Planck Foundation also highlights how political neutrality was key to deliver advice in Chile:

> The [Max Planck] Foundation was able to forge a trusting relationship based on its political neutrality and commitment to academic excellence with the Constitutional Convention in Chile. Through this, the Foundation contributed comparative approaches to key questions of constitution-drafting, constitutional and international law and thus, assisted to enhance the quality of debate and drafting in the Constitutional Convention.[147]

Sumit Bisarya discusses how impartiality with regard to the different parties of the constitution-making process is 'the most important':

> If one or more parties or groups feel that the adviser is favouring another side, the integrity of the provided assistance may be damaged. Rather than counselling one group or another on how to gain an advantage in negotiations, a UN adviser's role is to maintain impartiality by helping all parties to reach an informed, deliberative and inclusive consensus on a constitutional framework.[148]

He notes that an important qualification for constitutional advisors is impartiality: 'those fluent in the language of only one party may be perceived as closer to that side of a conflict, for example. In such situations, a support team may be necessary to provide the required balance'.[149] In addition to positioning themselves outside of the political process, external actors conceive the advice provided as technical.

The discursive turn towards 'technicity'

Constitution-making came to be understood as a technical solution to a social problem. As Sara Kendall notes, 'overall, a turn towards "constitutional technicity" can be observed . . . cast[ing] constitution-drafting practice as a domain of technical expertise inhabited by neutral and politically divested actors'.[150] The idea behind this move towards 'technicity' was to distance themselves from the political endeavour that constitutions inherently carry because of their object. Indeed, following the wave of decolonisation and the prohibition by international legal norms to interfere in sovereign processes, conceiving their involvement in constitution-making as 'technical' made it compliant with international law. Further, the involvement in constitutional drafting often happens informally. Indeed, it is the domestic body tasked with constitution-making (i.e. a National Constituent Assembly) that adopts the constitution. Conceiving of constitution-making as technical rather than political allows external actors to position themselves outside the realm of domestic and international politics.

To understand how constitution-making, an inherently political endeavour, ended up being conceived as a technical matter, one has to go back further in time to understand how 'governance' in general became a technical issue. Quentin Deforge has fleshed out the building of international expertise in governance-related matters and how this has circumvented the prohibition to intervene in domestic political affairs of States.[151] It is in 1991 that a policy paper drafted by the World Bank '*juriste en chef*' points out that the organisation can work on 'governance' as long as it is enshrined within the goal of economic growth.[152] Then, in 1995 at UNDP the head of the new division of 'Management Development and Governance' managed to create a separate 'governance policy'.[153] Gradually, constitutions become included within the framework of governance.

Current external actors' involvement in constitution-making is justified because they provide constitutional expertise, which is understood as something eminently technical: there lies the legal technical solution to the social issues raised by transitioning to democracy. External actors are not the ones pulling the political trigger, which remains in the hands of the body tasked with adopting the constitution. The language used by external actors to describe the expertise they provide reveals a technical understanding of their involvement. It involves constitutional design choices. Tom Ginsburg, for instance, conceives advice-giving as the subsidy of 'knowledge gathering in ways that can empower local decision-makers'.[154] The knowledge includes providing design choices regarding judicial review or federalism vs unitary systems.[155] The advice in later stages involves 'identify[ing] problems with the proposed text, highlight[ing] internal contradictions, and offer[ing] modifications on points where it does not conform with international norms'.[156] Bisarya notes how the principal role of constitutional advisor is 'to help stakeholders identify and think through questions regarding their own constitution'.[157]

The fact that external actors increasingly see constitution-making as a technical issue is illustrated in the blossoming of 'constitutional toolboxes', which provide a blueprint to be used in processes of democratic transition. In the last decade in particular, external actors have published a series of 'guidebooks' that offer a template to help with various elements of constitution-making (i.e. state structure, human rights, judicial review, state finance, defence and security, women's rights). Such guidebooks include International IDEA's 'A Practical Guide to Constitution Building' (2011),[158] UNDP's 'Guidance Note on Constitution-Making Support' (2014),[159] and the OHCHR's 'Human Rights and Constitution-Making' report (2018).[160] Guides published by INGOs include the Public International Law & Policy Group's 'Post-Conflict Constitution Drafter's Handbook',[161] Interpeace's 'Constitution-Making and Reform: Options for the Process',[162] the Max Planck Foundation's 'Manuals on Constitution building: Structures and Principles of a Constitution',[163] and the Center for Constitutional Transitions' 'Democracy without Political Parties: Constitutional Options'.[164] In these different toolboxes, constitution-making amounts to little more than a Lego set, where essential pieces are provided and there is only a finite range of solutions, with some clearly more effective than others. The detailed and highly technical steps are enumerated, and if followed, choosing the right design would allow a country to implement the appropriate constitutional form to achieve peace and political development.[165] For instance, International IDEA's guide includes a chapter on 'The Design of the Executive Branch', which details a series of 'design options' available to the country undergoing a constitution-making process. These include 'Design for a centralized executive in a democratic setting', 'Options for institutional de-concentration within the executive', 'Institutional checks on the executive', 'Designing the executive's substantive powers'.[166] Similarly, the Max Planck Foundation provides a set of options to ensure the separation of powers based on the particular model of government of the country in transition.[167] Further, external actors also produce tailored research papers for constitution-makers. For instance, the Max Planck Foundation has produced a number of papers covering 'fundamental rights, forms of government, the inclusion of economic models in constitutions, political systems and constitutional drafting techniques'.[168]

Constitution-making is framed as a technical response to the social problem of achieving peace, development, and democracy. Gianni Buquicchio and Simona Granata-Menghini's comment shows how the Venice Commission is considered to hold the necessary technical knowledge to answer social issues:

> Before 'transplanting' any model, its compatibility with the different legal, political and social context needs to be tested. In metaphorical terms, the Venice Commission disposes of the knowledge and methodological tools to identify the donor and to predict the compatibility of the beneficiary.[169]

External actors frame their involvement in constitution-making as apolitical given that they see themselves as *merely* providing technical expertise grounded in the specific scientific knowledge of comparative constitutional law.[170] The content of expertise is considered to be 'technical' and 'scientific', moving away from the colonial language of 'civilised'. Here, the Venice Commission is a prime example of how external actors see themselves as providers of neutral expertise. Its involvement in constitution-making is manifested through 'assistance in the drafting of constitutional texts'[171] and the provision of expertise on constitutional drafts that, in most cases, have not yet been adopted by the body tasked with drafting the constitution.[172] The Venice Commission stresses this idea in its 2001 Annual Report: 'the Commission is not a political body but a *technical* body providing legal advice, the year 2001 confirmed that the *legal* expertise of the Commission can contribute to the solution of *political* disputes'.[173] Former President of the Venice Commission, Gianni Buquicchio, echoes this point: 'The Venice Commission's business is comparative constitutional engineering, which is a very complex and delicate exercise'.[174]

Through different legal opinions made on constitutional drafts adopted in contexts of democratic transition, the Venice Commission's advice is constructed in 'technical' language with apolitical terminology. Buquicchio and Deputy Secretary of the Venice Commission, Simona Granata-Menghini, reflecting on 20 years of work stress that,

> the Commission also needs to be impartial and neutral. The attitude of not taking any side, of not supporting not only any opposing political sides, but also any equally acceptable constitutional and legal options is crucial for the Commission to be accepted as a valid interlocutor by the national authorities.[175]

They continue:

> It also examines the expediency and workability of the constitutional or legal models actually chosen. . . . When there are several options equally in line with the standards, as is often the case, it is not the role of the Commission to express its preference, but only to indicate which option in its view better fits the situation in the country and whether it may function in practice.[176]

The options available are 'carefully examined in particular by those members who come from a legal system where the same solution is in place and functions well'.[177] The selection of institutions to include in a constitution, as well as the particular form it should take, is treated as a technical problem with technical solutions that can be found in the body of comparative constitutional law.

UNDP also understands its mandate as the provision of neutral, technical expertise. This is exemplified in its 2008 Annual Report, where its mission is to 'provide knowledge, policy advice, advocacy, and technical support in four focus areas on the basis of good practice and comparative advantage: poverty reduction, democratic governance, crisis prevention and recovery, and environment and sustainable development',[178] and it explicitly sees itself as '*neutral*, able to act as an *impartial* facilitator of dialogue and cooperation on important development issues'.[179] Within democratic governance, UNDP has positioned itself as a 'leading provider of *technical* advice on the modernisation of state institutions',[180] building 'on its strength of being trusted and *perceived as being neutral*' in election and parliament assistance.[181] Indeed, in its 2018–2021 Strategic Plan, the link between 'neutral expertise' and constitutional assistance is clearly stated:

> given] its reputation as an *impartial partner*, UNDP helps Governments to convene across line ministries and development partners to promote 'whole-of-government' and 'whole-of-society' responses vital for transformational change. . . . This is facilitated by long-standing UNDP partnerships at the highest levels of government, including with ministries of planning and finance; law-making bodies, such as parliaments; and *constitutional authorities*.[182]

Like the Venice Commission, UNDP envisions the building of institutions and the drafting of constitutions as a technical matter. This conception is itself encapsulated in the 2020 Guidance note, which states under 'Technical Advice on Constitutions and constitutional Reforms' the provision of 'constitutional design options, including comparative examples of constitutional good practice'.[183]

Finally, INGOs also insist on their political neutrality. For instance, DRI explicitly states that it is an independent and non-partisan organisation.[184] It provides constitutional support through advice and advocacy, with the ultimate goal of strengthening democratic institutions via 'unbiased expert analysis'; DRI 'conduct[s] comprehensive field research and produce[s] specialist assessments of electoral frameworks, legislatures and constitutional arrangements to support local ways of promoting the right of all citizens to participate in political life'.[185] The Max Planck Institute emphasises that

> *political neutrality* is another fundamental requirement for the successful transfer of knowledge. . . . A key element of the advice and training work is that it is first and foremost based on verified knowledge. This principle has thus far been ensured by incorporating it into the work of the Max Planck Foundation.[186]

For instance, it notes how it provided 'neutral technical legal assistance' in Chile[187] or how it assisted the final committees (Harmonisation, Preamble, and Transitory Norms) through in-person consultation.[188]

It should be noted that unlike other organisations, the OIF insists that its 'legitimacy comes from sharing universal values, humanist principles clearly stated, and a common language', which allows the OIF to 'mobilise mediators, lawyers, constitutional scholars'.[189] At the same time, the organisation refers to constitutional expertise as provided through 'constitutional engineering', distinguishing it from the political dimension of its other activities.[190] In its 2012 report, this is made clear as it exposes the different stages of constitution-making and specifies that:

> The assistance varies according to the stages and includes at least three dimensions: political (negotiation, mediation or facilitation); legal (drafting of constitutional engineering); and capacity development (awareness campaigns and education on text ownership).[191]

The discursive turn towards technicity is what allows external actors to be involved in constitution-making processes. Because the expertise is technical, anchored in scientific knowledge, external actors are positioning themselves as outsiders of the political process.

Conclusion

This chapter has focused on a particular legal actor that an antifoundationalist conception of constitution-making has brought into the light: the foreign legal expert. From the drafting of constitutions of future independent colonies to contemporary constitutional drafting in the context of democratic transition, the provision of expertise has been a key element of the development enterprise and, as such, a defining feature of the transnational dimension of constitution-making. This involvement stems from the idea that the complexity of constitution-making demands the presence of a foreign expert in order to help erect essential democratic institutions. These external actors position themselves both as possessing expertise concerning the highly developed democratic institutions of their own country (or the liberal constitution at large) as well as having comparative knowledge due to their experience in other cases of constitution-making. This chapter has identified the trend towards institutionalising foreign expertise within organisations such as the Venice Commission, International IDEA, or INGOs. The core argument of the chapter is that external actors justify their involvement in the constitution-making processes of sovereign countries by the fact that they are merely providing 'neutral', 'apolitical', and 'technical' expertise.

The chapter calls for more attention to be given to a particular stage of constitution-making, constitutional drafting, given the significant role that external actors play during this phase, largely through the provision of expertise. This is important as the topic of the foreign expert is sparse not only in constitution-making literature but also in the public imagination. There are practical implications for this lacuna: domestic actors who are unaware of the role of experts may not frame this involvement within the Rules of Procedures of the body tasked with making the constitution.

Notes

1 Harshan Kumarasingham (ed), *The Road to Temple Trees: Sir Ivor Jennings and the Constitutional Development of Ceylon: Selected Writings* (Center for Policy Alternatives 2015) 16.

2 Tom Ginsburg, 'Some Advice on Constitutional Advice' in *European Yearbook of Constitutional Law 2021: Constitutional Advice* (Springer 2022) 14.

3 One notable exception is the 2010 Kenya Constitution. See Christina Murray, 'Making and Remaking Kenya's Constitution' in Tom Ginsburg and Sumit Bisarya (eds), *Constitution Makers on Constitution Making: New Cases* (CUP 2022).

4 Tunisia, Rules of Procedure (20 January 2012) Official Gazette of the Republic of Tunisia 0354 Article 59. English translation available at International IDEA, 'Tunisia: Constituent Assembly's Rules of Procedure' <https://constitutionnet.org/vl/item/tunisia-constituent-assemblys-rules-procedure> accessed 13 November 2023.

5 Examples of recollection of expert's own experience include Louis Aucoin, 'The Role of International Experts in Constitution-Making: Myth and Reality' (2004) 5 Georgetown Journal of International Affairs 89; Ginsburg, 'Some Advice on Constitutional Advice' (n 2); Xavier Philippe, 'Le rôle des organisations non gouvernementales dans les processus constituants postconflictuels: expertise ou plaidoyer' in Xavier Philippe and Natasa Danelciuc-Colodrovschi (eds), *Transitions constitutionnelles et constitutions transitionnelles* (Institut Universitaire Varenne 2014). On constitutional experts, see Barbara Perry, 'Constitutional Johnny Appleseeds: American Consultants and the Drafting of Foreign Constitutions' (1992) 55 Albany Law Review 767; Elisabeth Perham, PhD candidate at University of New South Wales is currently working on the involvement of foreign advisors in South-Pacific constitutions.

6 Regarding the political dimension of foreign expertise in constitution-making see Séverin Andzoka-Atsimou, *L'ingénierie constitutionnelle, solution de sortie de crise en Afrique? les exemples de l'Afrique du Sud, de la République démocratique du Congo, du Burundi et du Congo-Brazzaville* (L'Harmattan 2016); Jean Du Bois de Gaudusson, 'Le rôle de l'expertise constitutionnelle dans la transition constitutionnelle' in Xavier Philippe and Natasa Danelciuc-Colodrovschi (eds), *Transitions constitutionnelles et constitutions transitionnelles* (Institut Universitaire Varenne 2014); Sara Kendall, '"Constitutional Technicity": Displacing Politics Through Expert Knowledge' (2015) 11 Law, Culture and the Humanities 363; Muna B Ndulo, 'Constitution Making: The Role of External Actors' (2014) 1 Southern African Journal of Policy and Development; Alicia Pastor y Camarasa, 'Constitution-Making and Transnational Expertise: Lessons from the 2014 Tunisian Constitution' in Robert Howard, Kirk Randazzo and Rebecca Reid (eds), *Research Handbook on Law and Political Systems* (Edward Elgar 2023); Mark Tushnet, 'Some Skepticism about Normative Constitutional Advice' (2007) 49 William and Mary Law Review 1473; Mark Tushnet, 'The Politics of Constitution-Making' in Mark Tushnet and Dimitry Kochenov (eds), *Elgar Handbook on the Politics of Constitutional Law* (Edward Elgar 2023).

7 Jurgen de Poorter and others, 'Introduction: Mapping the Emerging Field of Constitutional Advice' [2022] European Yearbook of Constitutional Law 1–2.
8 See the discussion of the involvement of Yash Ghai in the Fijian context in Ginsburg, 'Some Advice on Constitutional Advice' (n 2) 16.
9 Eidgenössische Technische Hochschule Zürich (Charles Recknagel), 'Iraq Oil Scandal Threatens Former Diplomat' <https://ethz.ch/content/specialinterest/gess/cis/center-for-securities-studies/en/services/digital-library/articles/article.html/108606> accessed October 2023.
10 James Glanz and Walter Gibbs, 'US Adviser to Kurds Stands to Reap Oil Profits' *The New York Times* <www.nytimes.com/2009/11/12/world/middleeast/12galbraith.html>.
11 See the work around the practices of depoliticisation in international organisations from Marieke Louis and Lucile Maertens, *Why International Organizations Hate Politics: Depoliticizing the World* (Routledge 2021) 3.
12 David Kennedy, *A World of Struggle: How Power, Law, and Expertise Shape Global Political Economy* (Princeton UP 2018).
13 See Introduction for a detailed account of data collection.
14 See Amelia Odida, 'Making Policy, Problems, and Constitutions: Decolonising the UN Policy of Constitutional Assistance' (UCL, University College London 2022).
15 Sarah Stockwell, 'Imperial Liberalism and Institution Building at the End of Empire in Africa' (2018) 46 The Journal of Imperial and Commonwealth History 1009.
16 AF Madden, 'Constitution-Making and Nationhood: The British Experience – An Overview' (1988) 26 Journal of Commonwealth & Comparative Politics 123, 131.
17 Ginsburg, 'Some Advice on Constitutional Advice' (n 2) 16.
18 International IDEA, *Annual Results Report 2021* (International IDEA 2022) 36; Max Planck Foundation, *Annual Report 2021* (Max Planck Foundation 2022) 38.
19 Chalev Dimiter, Mazen Shaquoura and Abou Abass, 'Rôle des Nations Unies dans le processus constitutionnel tunisien et résultat en termes de garanties relatives aux droits de l'homme' in *La Constitution de la Tunisie – Processus, principes et perspectives* (United Nations Development Programme 2016) 465.
20 For a study on the impact of external actors involvement see Ilana Rothkopf, *Constituting Peace: Foreign Actors, Constitution-Making, and Armed Conflict* (University of Notre Dame Press 2022).
21 Louis and Maertens (n 11) 4.
22 Kenya, The Constitution of Kenya Review Act (2009), National Council for Law Reporting; Murray (n 3) 50.
23 Mabrouka M'Barek, 'Makers of Our Own History' in Tom Ginsburg and Sumit Bisarya (eds), *Constitution Makers on Constitution Making: New Cases* (CUP 2022) 170–71.
24 de Poorter and others (n 7) 1–2.
25 ibid 3.
26 For a detailed description see Pastor y Camarasa, 'Constitution-Making and Transnational Expertise: Lessons from the 2014 Tunisian Constitution' (n 6).
27 Harshan Kumarasingham (ed), *Constitution-Maker: Selected Writings of Sir Ivor Jennings* (CUP 2015).
28 Harshan Kumarasingham, 'Written Differently: A Survey of Commonwealth Constitutional History in the Age of Decolonisation' (2018) 46 The Journal of Imperial and Commonwealth History 874, 879.

29 William Dale, 'The Making and Remaking of Commonwealth Constitutions' (1993) 42 International & Comparative Law Quarterly 67.
30 ibid.
31 Kumarasingham, 'Written Differently' (n 28) 882–83.
32 David Yale, 'Professor S. A. De Smith' [1974] Cambridge Law Journal 177–78.
33 David Williams, 'Smith, Stanley Alexander De' in *Oxford Dicionary of National Biography* (OUP 23 September 2004).
34 See Harshan Kumarasingham's extensive work on Commonwealth constitution-making. He brought to publication personal documents of Sir Ivor Jennings. Kumarasingham (ed), *Constitution-Maker: Selected Writings of Sir Ivor Jennings* (n 27). Harshan Kumarasingham, 'A Transnational Actor on a Dramatic Stage – Sir Ivor Jennings and the Manipulation of Westminster Style Democracy in Pakistan' in Gregory Shaffer, Terence Halliday and Tom Ginsburg (eds), *Constitution-Making and Transnational Legal Order* (CUP 2019) 57.
35 Stockwell (n 15) 1016.
36 Kumarasingham, 'A Transnational Actor on a Dramatic Stage – Sir Ivor Jennings and the Manipulation of Westminster Style Democracy in Pakistan' (n 34) 62.
37 ibid 55. See Mara Malagodi, 'Constitution Drafting as Cold War Realpolitik: Sir Ivor Jennings and Nepal's 1959 Constitution' in Harshan Kumarasingham (ed), *Constitution-Making in Asia Decolonisation and State-Building in the Aftermath of the British Empire* (Routledge 2016).
38 Kumarasingham, 'Written Differently' (n 28) 882–83.
39 Kumarasingham (ed), *Constitution-Maker: Selected Writings of Sir Ivor Jennings* (n 27) 19; Kumarasingham, 'A Transnational Actor on a Dramatic Stage – Sir Ivor Jennings and the Manipulation of Westminster Style Democracy in Pakistan' (n 34) 57.
40 Kumarasingham (ed), *Constitution-Maker: Selected Writings of Sir Ivor Jennings* (n 27) 22.
41 Oxford Dictionary of National Biography (Sarvepalli Gopal and Katherine Prior), 'Rau, Sir Benegal Narsinga' (2004) <https://doi.org/10.1093/ref:odnb/35681> accessed 13 November 2023.
42 Georges Fischer, 'La décolonisation et le rôle des traités et des constitutions' (1962) 8 Annuaire français de droit international 805, 826.
43 It was not formally a colony. See Julian Go, 'The Provinciality of American Empire: "Liberal Exceptionalism" and US Colonial Rule, 1898–1912' (2007) 49 Comparative Studies in Society and History 74; Julian Go, 'American Colonial Empire: The Limit of Power's Reach' [2005] Lessons of Empire 201.
44 Gerold W Schmidt, 'The New Constitutional Developments in the Republic of Liberia' [1981] Verfassung und Recht in Übersee/Law and Politics in Africa, Asia and Latin America 243.
45 ibid; George Athan Billias, *American Constitutionalism Heard Round the World, 1776–1989: A Global Perspective* (New York UP 2009).
46 Tom Ginsburg, 'Constitutional Advice and Transnational Legal Order' in Gregory Shaffer, Terence C. Halliday and Tom Ginsburg (eds), *Constitution-Making and Transnational Legal Order* (CUP 2019) 107–8.
47 ibid 109. See Charles Friedrich, 'Rebuilding the German Constitution' (1949) 43 The American Political Science Review 461.
48 Perry (n 5) 770.
49 ibid 771.
50 Mary Dudziak, 'Working Toward Democracy: Thurgood Marshall and the Constitution of Kenya' (2006) 56 Duke Law Journal 721. See Perry (n 5) 772.
51 Perry (n 5) 778.

52 ibid 789.
53 ibid 778.
54 Albert Blaustein, 'Constitution Drafting: The Good, the Bad, and the Beautiful' (1991) 2 Scibes Journal of Legal Writing 49, 58.
55 University of Virginia, 'Howard Named Among Greatest 20th-Century Virginians' (2008) <www.Law.virginia.edu/html/news/2007_fall/howard.htm> accessed July 2020.
56 Venice Commission, *Annual Report of Activities 2004* (Venice Commission 12 March 2005) 9; Venice Commission, *Annual Report of Activities 2003* (Venice Commission 13 March 2004) 9; Venice Commission, *Annual Report of Activities 2005* (Venice Commission 2006) 8; Venice Commission, *Annual Report of Activities 2006* (Venice Commission 2007) 15.
57 Gianni Buquicchio and Simona Granata-Menghini, 'The Venice Commission Twenty Years On, Challenges Met, but Challenges Ahead' in Marjolein Roosmalen and others (eds), *Fundamental Rights and Principles Liber Amicorum Pieter Van Dijk* (Intersentia 2013) 251.
58 Venice Commission, *Annual Report of Activities 1999* (Venice Commission 1 April 2000) 4. [Emphasis added].
59 Venice Commission, Rules of Procedure (22 October 2018), Venice Commission CDL-AD(2018)2018 art 1, 2(1); Venice Commission, Resolution Adopting the Revised Statute of the European Commission for Democracy through Law (27 February 2002), Venice Commission CDL (2002) 2027 art 2 (3).
60 Venice Commission (n 59).
61 Venice Commission, Rules of Procedure (n 59) art 3a (1).
62 Simona Granata-Menghini, 'La Commission de Venise du Conseil de l'Europe: méthodes et perspectives de l'assistance constitutionnelle en Europe' [2017] Les Nouveaux Cahiers du Conseil constitutionnel 69, 72; Maartje De Visser, 'A Critical Assessment of the Role of the Venice Commission in Processes of Domestic Constitutional Reform' (2015) 63 The American Journal of Comparative Law 963, 968.
63 The International Institute for Democracy and Electoral Assistance Statutes [21 November 2008] International IDEA art 7.
64 ibid art 8.
65 International IDEA, 'Board of Advisers' <www.idea.int/about-us/board_of_advisers> accessed February 2021.
66 UNDP, *2003 Annual Report* (UNDP June 2003) 12; UNDP, *Annual Report of the Administrator for 2001* (UNDP 6 May 2002) 13. In 2001 a thematic trust fund was created to concentrate the funding. Both areas constitute two of UNDP's mandate pillars alongside with poverty reduction and environmental and sustainable development. UNDP, *Annual Report 2010/2011* (UNDP May 2011) 1.
67 UNDP-DPA, *Joint UNDP-DPA Programme on Building National Capacities for Conflict Prevention Annual Report 2016* (UNDP-DPA 2017) 8.
68 ibid.
69 UNDP-DPA, *Joint UNDP-DPA Annual Report 2015* (UNDP-DPA 2016) 5; UNDP-DPA, *Joint UNDP-DPA Programme on Building National Capacities for Conflict Prevention Annual Report 2017* (UNDP-DPA 2018) 5.
70 UNDP, *2007 Annual Report* (UNDP June 2007) 20.
71 UNDP, *2008 Annual Report* (UNDP June 2008) 19.
72 UNDP, *Multi-Year Funding Framework Report on UNDP Performance and Results for 2004: Executive Board of UNDP and UNFPA* (UNDP 12 May 2005) 48.
73 UNDP, *Annual Progress Report Nepal – 2008* (UNDP 2008) 6.

74 ibid 2.
75 UNDP, *Annual Progress Report Nepal – 2007* (UNDP 2007) 2.
76 UNSG, *Guidance Note of the Secretary-General on United Nations Constitutional Assistance* (UNSG September 2020) 7–8.
77 DRI, 'DRI. Who We Are' <https://Democracy-reporting.org/who-we-are/> accessed August 2019.
78 Max Planck Foundation, 'Staff' <www.mpfpr.de/foundation/staff/> accessed August 2019.
79 Charles Borgeaud, *Établissement et révision des constitutions en Amérique et en Europe* (Thorin et fils 1893) iv–v.
80 Harshan Kumarasingham, 'Liberal Ideals and the Politics of Decolonisation' (2018) 46 The Journal of Imperial and Commonwealth History 815, 817.
81 Charles Parkinson, *Bills of Rights and Decolonization: The Emergence of Domestic Human Rights Instruments in Britain's Overseas Territories* (OUP 2007) 61–63 quoted in Kumarasingham, 'Written Differently' (n 28) 877.
82 Brun-Otto Bryde, 'Constitutional Law in "Old" and "New" Law and Development' (2008) 41 Verfassung und Recht in Übersee/Law and Politics in Africa, Asia and Latin America 10–11.
83 MG Winton, 'Decolonisation and the Westminster Model' in Anthony Kirk-Greene (ed), *Africa in the Colonial Period III The Transfer of Power: The Colonial Administrators in the Age of Decolonization* (OUP 1979) 185 quoted in Julian Go, 'Modeling the State: Postcolonial Constituitions in Asia and Africa' (2002) 39 Southeast Asian Studies 558, 562.
84 Kumarasingham (ed), *Constitution-Maker: Selected Writings of Sir Ivor Jennings* (n 27) 274. See Stockwell (n 15) 1016.
85 Kumarasingham (ed), *Constitution-Maker: Selected Writings of Sir Ivor Jennings* (n 27) 273.
86 ibid 273–74.
87 Adrian Pelt, *Libyan Independence and the United Nations: A Case of Planned Decolonization* (Yale UP 1970) 515.
88 ibid 511.
89 ibid 575.
90 Thomas Carothers, *Aiding Democracy Abroad: The Learning Curve* (Carnegie Endowment 2011) 160.
91 Buquicchio and Granata-Menghini (n 57) 246.
92 Venice Commission, *Annual Report of Activities 2003* (n 56) 3. See also Venice Commission, *Annual Report of Activities 2004* (n 56) 9; Venice Commission, *Annual Report of Activities 2006* (n 56) 15; Venice Commission, *Annual Report of Activities 2007* (Venice Commission 2008) 10.
93 Paul Craig, 'Transnational Constitution-Making: The Contribution of the Venice Commission on Law and Democracy' (2017) 2 UC Irvine Journal of International, Transnational, and Comparative Law 57, 66.
94 Granata-Menghini (n 62) 74.
95 Venice Commission, *Annual Report of Activities 2022* (Venice Commission August 2023) 7.
96 International IDEA, *Annual Results Report 2008* (International IDEA 2009) 6.
97 The International Institute for Democracy and Electoral Assistance Statutes [21 November 2008] art 2 (2) d.
98 International IDEA, 'What We Do – Constitution-Building' <www.idea.int/our-Work/what-we-do/Constitution-building> accessed October 2021.
99 International IDEA, *Annual Results Report 2005* (International IDEA 2006) 5; International IDEA, *Annual Results Report 2007* (International IDEA 2008) 8.

100 International IDEA, *Annual Results Report 2008* (n 96) 33.
101 Sumit Bisarya, *Protecting Ethnic Minorities Within Minorities* (International IDEA 2020); Cheryl Saunders, *Constitutions and International Law* (International IDEA February 2020); Cheryl Saunders, *Courts in Federal Countries* (International IDEA April 2019); Tom Ginsburg, *Constitutional Design for Territorially Divided Societies* (International IDEA August 2018).
102 International IDEA, *Annual Results Report 2022* (International IDEA 2023) 21.
103 International IDEA, *Annual Results Report 2021* (n 18) 36.
104 OIF, *Rapport sur l'état des pratiques de la démocratie, des droits et des libertés dans l'espace francophone – 2014* (OIF 2014) 41. [My own translation].
105 ibid 39. [My own translation]. See also OIF, *Rapport du Secrétaire Général de la Francophonie 2008–2010* (OIF 2010) 35–36.
106 OIF, *Rapport sur l'état des pratiques de la démocratie, des droits et des libertés dans l'espace francophone. 2000–2010* (OIF 2010) 10; OIF, *Rapport sur l'état des pratiques de la démocratie, des droits et des libertés dans l'espace francophone – 2012* (OIF 2012) 37.
107 OIF, *Rapport du Secrétaire Général de la Francophonie 2012–2014* (OIF 2014) 81; OIF, *Rapport du Secrétaire Général de la Francophonie 2014–2016* (OIF 2016) 10; OIF, *Rapport sur l'état des pratiques de la démocratie, des droits et des libertés dans l'espace francophone. 2000–2010* (n 106) 14.
108 UNDP, *Annual Report of the Administrator for 2000* (UNDP 16 May 2001) 6. Despite the changes in name of its different areas of work, democratic governance, and crisis prevention and recovery remains a constant. UNDP, *Annual Report 2010/2011* (n 66) 1.
109 UNDP, *UNDP Strategic Plan: 2014–2017. Changing the World* (UNDP 2013).
110 UNDP, *2004 Annual Report* (UNDP June 2004) 8.
111 UNDP-DPA, *Joint UNDP-DPA Programme on Building National Capacities for Conflict Prevention Annual Report 2016* (n 67) 8.
112 ibid 9.
113 ibid 51.
114 UNSG, *Guidance Note of the Secretary-General on United Nations Constitutional Assistance* (n 76) 7.
115 ibid 4–5.
116 Sumit Bisarya, *Advice on Applying Mediation Fundamentals in UN Constitutional Assistance* (UNDPPA November 2022) 4.
117 ibid.
118 Rüdiger Wolfrum, Daniel Gruss and Tilmann Röder, *Ten Years of Global Knowledge Transfer 2002–2012* (Max Planck Institute 2012) 5.
119 Max Planck Foundation, *Annual Report 2013* (Max Planck Foundation 2014) 3.
120 Wolfrum, Gruss and Röder (n 118) 5.
121 Max Planck Foundation, *Annual Report 2013* (n 119) 34.
122 Wolfrum, Gruss and Röder (n 118) 10, 61, 67, 88, 102; Max Planck Foundation, *Annual Report 2013* (n 119) 14, 18, 28, 32.
123 Wolfrum, Gruss and Röder (n 118) 7.
124 Max Planck Foundation, *Annual Report 2021* (n 18) 5.
125 ibid 38.
126 DRI, 'DRI. Who We Are' (n 77).
127 DRI, 'DRI. Constitutions' <https://Democracy-reporting.org/constitutions/> accessed August 2019.
128 ibid.

129 DRI, *Annual Report 2011* (DRI December 2012) 17; DRI, *Annual Report 2012* (DRI December 2013) 12; DRI, *Annual Report 2013* (DRI December 2014) 17.
130 DRI, *Annual Report 2012* (n 129); DRI, *Annual Report 2013* (n 129) 7; DRI, *Annual Report 2014* (DRI December 2015) 7, 17; DRI, *Annual Report 2015* (DRI December 2016) 12.
131 DRI, 'DRI. Constitutions' (n 127).
132 ibid.
133 DRI, *Annual Report 2012* (n 129) 16; DRI, *Annual Report 2013* (n 129) 20; DRI, *Annual Report 2014* (n 130) 14.
134 DRI, *Annual Report 2014* (n 130) 9. See DRI, *Annual Report 2012* (n 129) 14; DRI, *Annual Report 2017* (DRI December 2018) 18; DRI, *Annual Report 2013* (n 129) 10.
135 Alicia Pastor y Camarasa, 'Demystifying How Constitutions Are Made: External Actors' Modes of Actions in the 2014 Tunisian Constitution' [2022] Michigan Journal of Law & Society 51, 94.
136 Boris Petric and Giorgio Blundo, 'Good Governance and Democracy Promotion: Empirical Perspectives on Transnational Powers' in Boris Petric (ed), *Democracy at Large: NGOs, Political Foundations, Think Tanks and International Organizations* (Springer 2012) 3. [Emphasis added].
137 Aucoin (n 5) 90. He was himself a foreign advisor in several constitution-making processes. United States Institute for Peace, 'Louis Aucoin' <https://bookstore.usip.org/browse/author/7d597673-e9c0-490d-83cf-f9e5a1a04f5d/Aucoin-Louis?page=1> accessed August 2019.
138 Ginsburg, 'Some Advice on Constitutional Advice' (n 2) 22.
139 Aucoin (n 5) 92, 93.
140 Committee of Experts on Constitutional Review, *Report of the Committee of Experts on Constitutional Review Issued on the Submission of the Reviewed Harmonized Draft Constitution to the Parliamentary Select Committee* (Committee of Experts on Constitutional Review 8 January 2010).
141 Fiji, Decree No 57 on Fiji Constitutional Process (Constitution Commission) (18 July 2012), Government of Fiji Gazette 1589 art 6 (3).
142 ibid art 7 (j).
143 Venice Commission, *Annual Report of Activities 2022* (n 95) 7. See Venice Commission, *Annual Report of Activities 2021* (Venice Commission August 2022) 7.
144 International IDEA, *Annual Results Report 2022* (n 102) 15.
145 International IDEA, *Annual Results Report 2021* (n 18) 36.
146 Max Planck Foundation, *Annual Report 2022* (Max Planck Foundation 2023) 30.
147 Max Planck Foundation, *Annual Report 2021* (n 18) 39.
148 Bisarya, *Advice on Applying Mediation Fundamentals in UN Constitutional Assistance* (n 116) 10.
149 ibid 5.
150 Kendall (n 6) 371.
151 Quentin Deforge, 'La fabrique transnationale du politique. Une sociologie historique du champ réformateur de la "gouvernance" (1961–2019)' (PhD dissertation, Université Paris-Dauphine 2019) 41.
152 ibid.
153 ibid.
154 Ginsburg, 'Some Advice on Constitutional Advice' (n 2) 27.
155 ibid 18–19.
156 ibid.

157 Bisarya, *Advice on Applying Mediation Fundamentals in UN Constitutional Assistance* (n 116) 15.
158 Markus Böckenförde, Nora Hedling and Wahiu Wahiu, *A Practical Guide to Constitution Building* (International IDEA 2011).
159 UNDP, *UNDP Guidance Note on Constitution-Making Support* (UNDP 2014).
160 OHCHR, *Human Rights and Constitution-Making* (OHCHR 2018).
161 Paul Williams and others, *Post-Conflict Constitution Drafter's Handbook* (The Public International Law & Policy Group 2007).
162 Michele Brandt and others, *Constitution-Making and Reform: Options for the Process* (Interpeace 2011).
163 Katharina Diehl and others, *Max Planck Manuals on Constitution building: Structures and Principles of a Constitution* (Max Planck Institute 2009).
164 Michael Riegner and Richard Stacey, *Democracy Without Political Parties: Constitutional Options* (Center for Constitutional Transitions June 2014).
165 The author thanks Xavier Philippe for the evocative metaphor. Unlike an IKEA set, which allows you to build the identical furniture as outlined in the catalogue, the Lego metaphor shows the potential for creating something different with the pieces available. See Günter Frankenberg, 'Constitutional Transfer: The IKEA Theory Revisited' (2010) 8 International Journal of Constitutional Law 563, 565.
166 Böckenförde, Hedling and Wahiu (n 158) 160–72.
167 Diehl and others (n 163) 59.
168 Max Planck Foundation, *Annual Report 2021* (n 18) 38.
169 Buquicchio and Granata-Menghini (n 57) 246.
170 Mark Tushnet, 'Comparative Constitutional Law' in Mathias Reimann and Reinhard Zimmermann (eds), *The Oxford Handbook of Comparative Law* (OUP 2017) 1228.
171 Venice Commission, *Annual Report of Activities 2003* (n 56) 3. See also Venice Commission, *Annual Report of Activities 2004* (n 56) 9; Venice Commission, *Annual Report of Activities 2006* (n 56) 15; Venice Commission, *Annual Report of Activities 2007* (n 92) 10.
172 Granata-Menghini (n 62) 74.
173 Venice Commission, *Annual Report of Activities 2001* (Venice Commission 9 March 2002) 9. [Emphasis added].
174 Buquicchio and Granata-Menghini (n 57) 246.
175 ibid 243.
176 ibid 244.
177 ibid 243.
178 UNDP, *UNDP Strategic Plan, 2008–2011 – Accelerating Global Progress on Human Development* (UNDP 2008) 1.
179 UNDP, *UNDP Strategic Plan: 2014–2017. Changing the World* (n 109) 18. [Emphasis added].
180 UNDP, *2006 Annual Report* (UNDP June 2006) 7. [Emphasis added].
181 UNDP, *Multi-Year Funding Framework Report on UNDP Performance and Results for 2004: Executive Board of UNDP and UNFPA* (n 72) 47. [Emphasis added].
182 UNDP, *UNDP Strategic Plan 2018–2021* (UNDP 2017) 11. [Emphasis added].
183 UNSG, *Guidance Note of the Secretary-General on United Nations Constitutional Assistance* (n 76) 5.
184 DRI, 'DRI. Who We Are' (n 77).
185 DRI, *Annual Report 2011* (n 129) 6. DRI, 'What We Do' <https://Democracy-reporting.org/what-we-do/> accessed August 2019; DRI, 'Where We Work' <https://Democracy-reporting.org/where-we-Work/> accessed August 2019.

186 Wolfrum, Gruss and Röder (n 118) 8. [Emphasis added].
187 Max Planck Foundation, *Annual Report 2022* (n 146) 22.
188 ibid.
189 OIF, *Rapport du Secrétaire Général de la Francophonie 2014–2016* (n 107) 7. [My own translation].
190 OIF, *Rapport sur l'état des pratiques de la démocratie, des droits et des libertés dans l'espace francophone. 2000–2010* (n 106) 202.
191 OIF, *Rapport sur l'état des pratiques de la démocratie, des droits et des libertés dans l'espace francophone – 2012* (n 106) 36. [Emphasis my own. My own translation].

Conclusion

Towards a new theory of constitution-making

Beginning with the observation that constitutional legal orders are increasingly characterised by their porosity and embeddedness within a wider transnational legal web, this book aimed to address this broader dynamic by examining a particular legal phenomenon, constitution-making, in a particular setting, democratic transitions. This study challenged the adage attributed to Otto von Bismarck, 'if you like laws and sausages, you should never watch either one being made'.[1] At its heart, this work contributed to the literature by providing an empirical analysis of how constitutions are made while shedding light on external actor involvement in constitution-making.

The central motivation of this project was to contribute to a better understanding of the transnational dimension of constitution-making. While scholars have addressed this topic, few have actually examined the on-the-ground involvement of external actors during constitution-making processes. One of the reasons for this lacuna in the literature is the inadequacy of the concept that grounds comparative constitutional scholarship: the constituent power theory. The concept of constituent power fails to grasp the presence of external actors in constitution-making as it presupposes a certain political and legal understanding that obfuscates their involvement. Because scholars are trapped in the wrong theory, they are unable to capture the wide array of external actors that are indeed involved in constitution-making processes. This book provided an alternative theory to analyse transnational involvement in constitution-making: the development enterprise. Throughout this book, the development enterprise has proven to be a useful lens to understand the transnational dimension of constitution-making; revealing the continuity of the rationale of liberal legalism, as well as the centrality of the figure of the expert. The development enterprise framework further demonstrates the inadequacy of the concept of constituent power, which remains the dominant theoretical approach of constitutional scholarship. Studies that rely on constituent power fail to capture the full range of external actors involved, thus providing an incomplete picture of how constitution-making happens on the ground.

DOI: 10.4324/9781003386186-9

Law and society approach to constitution-making and the value of descriptive work

To answer this project's research questions, a law and society approach, grounded in New Legal Realism, was adopted. At the core of this approach lies the simple idea that grasping the empirical dimension is necessary to understand legal phenomena. This necessitates approaching constitution-making from an 'external' point of view, as opposed to the 'internal' perspective of doctrinal studies of law. The development enterprise was introduced as an analytical framework to provide an external perspective, informed by social science scholarship that addresses legal reforms in Third World territories. To adopt an external perspective on constitution-making, this work relied on research in other disciplines – such as development studies, history, political science, and sociology. Thus, a peripheral contribution of this book is demonstrating the utility of interdisciplinarity, especially when examining the multifaceted social, political, and legal phenomenon that is constitution-making. Indeed, interdisciplinarity has resulted in a stronger analysis, which is not a novel insight for New Legal Realism scholars but still remains a rarity in legal positivist scholarship.

Before proceeding, it is valuable to reflect on a comment from Thomas Carothers regarding the rule of law movement, which also rings true for transnational constitution-making:

> Even if we leave aside the problem of where the essence of the rule of law resides and accept the institutionalist approach that has become the norm, we see that rule-of-law aid providers face a *problem of knowledge* with regard to the very basic question of how change in systems actually occurs.[2]

Thus, at the very least, more empirical research on constitution-making processes is needed to understand the effects that certain institutional choices can produce.[3] This is a difficult endeavour as, methodologically, it is challenging to isolate the effect that a particular institutional framework has on a desired social goal. Data availability to study constitution-making processes is another challenge and will depend on the archival work available. Also, this work will always be context-dependent, which limits the potential for comparability.

Future avenues of research include evaluating the impact of external actors on particular constitution-making processes. This book is an invitation to examine constitution-making more holistically and re-examine certain tropes that are taken for granted, particularly regarding process. Ginsburg, Elkins and Blount, for instance, have examined the causal link between participatory process and outcome, pointing out that 'many of the assumptions of proponents of participation remain untested, and the precise relationships between participation and desirable outcomes of interest remain underspecified'.[4] It is therefore important to undertake more in-depth empirical analysis that centres on the process itself. Fruitful potential research questions include: what kind of participatory process took place? Was the participation substantively meaningful or more like an afterthought to varnish the constitution with democratic legitimacy ex-post? How was the process of constitution-making conceived within broader questions of the democratic transition?[5] Similarly, further research is needed to describe external elements to the constitution-making process, such as the impact of media discourse. The findings of this book also call for further empirical research on the outcome of transnational involvement in constitution-making; however, this involves significant methodological challenges (i.e., isolating a causal relationship beyond mere correlation). Finally, this study's law and society approach to constitution-making provides a model on how to undertake this type of research to examine other areas of constitutional studies. For instance, it could be used to examine other stages of law-making, such as the adoption of legislative norms or their implementation.

Constitutions within regulatory webs: governing by objectives

This book has shown that constitutions, as an object of research, cannot be understood in a silo; indeed, this fact gains particular salience given the set of transnational norms that are developing with regard to constitution-making. The observation that constitution-making occurs within a transnational web of soft law norms was the starting point of this inquiry. Throughout this analysis of external actor involvement in constitution-making, several references have been made to soft law instruments such as the two UN Guidance Notes or to 'international standards' more broadly. While scholars have addressed the role of the Venice Commission in developing these standards, further research should focus on other external actors, such as UNDP, International IDEA, or INGOs.[6] Transnational norms on constitution-making are at an embryonic stage of standardisation, and focusing on the transnational dimension of constitution-making reveals the urgent need for more research into how constitutions operate within a broader web of soft law norms.

This book indicates the value of empirically grounded research to approach the topic of constitutional law. In particular, examination of the provision of constitutional expertise during post-Cold War constitution-making suggests a shift towards public policy governance, which has been recognised in the wider literature on legal reform. Scholars studying public governance have pointed to a move towards 'governing by objectives' at both the international and domestic level.[7] Alexandre Flückiger has noted a shift from 'law as planning' to a conception of law as embedded within governance by public policy objectives.[8] While legislation was the sole legal vessel used to achieve legal reform, it is now one of many legal tools available to achieve a set of objectives. As Flückiger puts it, 'We have moved from a 'nomocracy' to an era of 'teleocracy', with the emergence of *targeted legislation*'.[9] In the 'governing by objectives' paradigm, a public policy approach is followed, where the law is evaluated according to the particular objectives stated, and the legislation becomes part of a broader scheme of non-legal norms.[10] This shift is evident in other fields, such as transitional justice or peace-building. Briony Jones notes that 'transitional justice is framed as a set of *policy choices* aimed at certain outcomes: reconciliation, peace, stability, democracy'.[11]

Translated to constitution-making, the 'governing by objectives' framework highlights the fact that the constitution, in practice, does not possess an exceptional, untouchable status that political theorists and constitutional scholars have often ascribed to it. Contrary to the idea of constitutions as isolated higher norms, the lens of the development enterprise serves to demystify constitutions, showing how external actors treat them as one of many legal vessels used to achieve their diverse policy objectives.

The development enterprise: an antifoundationalist vision of constitution-making

The most significant theoretical contribution of this book is its repudiation of the constituent power theory, which continues to animate most comparative constitutional scholarship. Constitutional scholars are grounded in foundationalism when theorising the making of constitutions; this has resulted in an understanding of constitution-making centred on the constituent power, which, at a specific point in time – in a single, authoritative, superlative movement – creates the constitution that will govern the new democratic polity.[12] Instead, this book proposed a new analytical lens, the development enterprise, informed by Angelica Bernal's conception of 'antifoundationalist founding'. This shift from the singular figure of the founder (in this case the constituent power) to a more multifaceted dynamic effectively broadens the scope of actors involved.[13] This framework allows for a more comprehensive understanding of the transnational dimension of constitution-making, exposing the full range of external actor involvement. The development enterprise shows that such involvement is a significant feature of constitution-making that ought to be taken into account to develop an explanatory and empirically grounded model of the legal phenomenon and not an idealised theory.

Chapter 1 explained why the concept of constituent power is inadequate to examine the transnational dimension of constitution-making as it serves two different functions: defending a particular political theory (liberal constitutionalism) and a particular philosophy of law (legal positivism). This results in a theoretical dilemma, since legal positivists separate the analysis of law from the political realm. As the majority of comparative constitutional scholars are legal positivists, the study of transnational constitution-making tends to be limited to those external actors that are *legally framed*. This arbitrarily restricts the scope to a handful of cases where external actor involvement is framed by international law (i.e. Bosnia and Herzegovina, Afghanistan, South Sudan). However, this misses other cases of constitution-making where external actor involvement occurs in the absence of a specific international legal framework, as is often the case in the context of democratic transition. The chapter also addressed and refuted various reinterpretations of the concept of constituent power, which do not integrate the transnational dimension.

Following this conceptual groundwork, Chapters 2 and 3 developed an alternative analytical framework, the development enterprise, to examine the transnational dimension of constitution-making more comprehensively. In order to adopt an antifoundationalist approach, this analytical lens took cues from ongoing scholarly discussions in the field of legal reform in the context of development. The development enterprise adopts an antifoundationalist view of founding by taking seriously the stage before the adoption of the constitution: *constitutional drafting*. This fills a gap in the literature as most comparative constitutional scholarship on constitution-making focuses on the later stages of *adoption* and *implementation*. This is the first in-depth examination of constitutional drafting, and further research is needed in order to fully understand this specific stage of constitution-making; future studies could focus on the dialectical relationship between the transnational and national dimensions, locating points of friction and resistance.

An antifoundationalist approach better captures the diverse legal actors involved in constitution-making. The lens of the development enterprise serves to expand the scope of actors involved in the stage of constitutional drafting, beyond the constitution-making body adopting the constitution (i.e. a National Constituent Assembly). External actors, such as International IDEA and UNDP, are rarely acknowledged by constitutional scholars as relevant to the making of constitutions. It is only by moving away from the lens of constituent power – and a foundationalist approach to constitution-making – that the significant roles of these external actors can be understood.

Further research is needed to expand on the mosaic of legal actors involved in constitution-making and to increase our understanding of how fundamental norms are created. For instance, future projects could explore how external actors interact with civil society organisations; how social movements (local and transnational) interact with constitution-makers; the interrelation between constitution-making concerns and the broader concerns of democratic transitions; disagreements within national constitution-makers; and, perhaps most importantly for understanding the transnational dynamic, how local constitution-makers interact with external actors.[14]

This book's focus on constitutional drafting – and its examination of a wider set of legal actors involved in the process – is relevant for other areas of constitutional studies interested in how legal rules are made. Foundationalism also translates into the area of law-making. Showing that the making of legal norms comes from contested visions of what the law is or ought to be, challenges many of the core concepts used in the discipline. The antifoundationalist approach paired with an empirical examination of how the law gets made calls for theory building that is not developed in abstracto. It is a wider acknowledgement that work in this field must reflect the realities unfolding on the ground. As such, attention must be paid to the transnational dimension that pervades law-making at any stage. As an example: in the general imaginary, the main legal actor involved in making laws is the parliament, as it is where they are adopted. An antifoundationalist view of law-making would include different actors involved in making laws at various stages, paying particular attention to the phases that go beyond adoption.

The politics of constitutional expertise

The development enterprise exposes the continuity between decolonisation and post-Cold War constitution-making; while the paradigm of liberal legalism unites different cases of legal reform in Third World territories through time. This book explored transnational constitution-making during an era that is generally ignored by constitutional scholars: decolonisation. It identified the colonial lineage of the development enterprise, as well as its explicit and implicit rebranding. The development enterprise challenges a foundationalist conception of democratic founding – which can be directly translated to constitutional founding – in that it 'obscures the multiplicity of founding action and actors across time',[15] ultimately erasing certain actors that do not fit the narrative of an 'authoritative founding moment', distorting the process by casting it in an 'apolitical' light. As Bernal notes:

> it is also a distorting picture. Most troubling, it renders flat contingency and power struggle in the making of political orders, and masks the disagreements, conflicts, injustices, violences, and exclusions present in the original founding events of constitutional democracies.[16]

An antifoundationalist perspective warns against an 'apolitical' understanding of the process. Chapter 4 applied the lens of the development enterprise to the history of constitution-making, highlighting its colonial roots and the '*mission civilisatrice*' by examining the involvement of the British, Belgian, and United States Empires, as well as the UN, in constitution-making processes undertaken in the context of decolonisation. It also countered an idea prevalent in the literature, that post-Cold War constitution-making is fundamentally different from constitution-making in the context of decolonisation, by indicating the continuity of the rationale of liberal legalism. In addition to discussion of the Venice Commission, the chapter examined the role of UNDP, International IDEA, and the Max Planck Foundation, drawing on a variety of institutional documentation. The lens of the development emphasised the political dimension of constitutional expertise.

This chapter also explored the colonial lineage of the use of comparative law in legal reforms, looking at the roots of the discipline that is today mobilised by external actors. While a critical strand of comparative law has addressed this topic for more than 30 years, the critique has yet to translate into the field of constitution-making.[17] What this scholarship has shown is that the political dimension of comparative constitutional law first affects the explanatory function of comparative law, where there is a complete exclusion of the ideological factor in constructing explanatory schemes.[18] This book has aimed to uncover the ideological component of external actor involvement, through the rationale of liberal legalism.

Liberal legalism is grounded in a Western understanding of the role of law, which dictates the kind of law that should be used to achieve desired social goals. Upendra Baxi explains how 'global epistemic hegemonic practices which consolidate the view that the masters and makers of the modern law have nothing worthy to learn from the discursive traditions of the Euro-American tradition's Other'.[19] He highlights how different legal traditions that could be fruitful are dismissed:

> strategic comparatists guiding the legal/juridical reconstruction of the so-called 'transitional' post-communist societies resolutely forfeit any possibility of learning from the juristic and juridical traditions of the decolonized worlds (for instance, from India in the middle of the last Christian century and from southern Africa at the end of it).[20]

Critical comparative scholars point the way to further avenues of research. For instance, Ran Hirsch has identified the problem of case selection in comparative constitutional law, where there is a

> presumption that insights based on the constitutional experience of a small set of 'usual suspect' settings – all prosperous, stable constitutional democracies of the 'global north' – are truly representative of the wide variety of constitutional experiences worldwide, and constitute a 'gold standard' for its understanding and assessment.[21]

Critical comparative scholars have also pointed out the political dimension of comparative constitutional law itself. As Maxim Bönnemann and Laura Jung explain, 'the comparison of constitutions is driven by implicit or explicit normative preferences and might even be part of specific hegemonic projects'.[22] In the same way that the authors describe the 'global community of comparative constitutional lawyers push[ing] forward a very specific ideology of human rights',[23] David Kennedy has illustrated that in the human rights movement, this has led to the dismissal of 'other experiences of emancipation and non-western conceptions of human rights'.[24] Significant work is needed to develop alternatives to Western liberal constitutionalism, as Zoran Oklopcic notes, 'at the moment, such constitutionalism exists only on Mars, whose constitutional system, unshackled from Western constitutional imagination exhibits a "whole polyarchic array" of institutions'.[25] These scholars show that it is a deplorable waste of experience and knowledge to ignore non-Western legal traditions.[26]

Further empirical description of the actual content of the constitutional expertise provided by external actors is needed in order to better assess the methods used to make certain recommendations; this would bring the field of constitution-making in line with broader discussions taking place in comparative law. Lorianne Updike Toler described, for instance, an instance of transnational expertise provided in the Libyan process:

> On 4 June 2014, the United Nations Support Mission in Libya (UNSMIL) provided the Constitution Drafting Assembly (CDA) with USB drives for each of its members containing a handful of documents for use in making decisions about Libya's new constitution and writing process [. . .] One of the documents was a comparison chart of eighteen different post-conflict constitution-writing processes from historical and contemporary comparative practice.[27]

It is important not to take the expertise for granted and to challenge the methods used to reach particular 'technical' opinions. As discussed, empirical examinations of constitution-making by legal scholars is relatively recent if we compare the literature to the actual history of writing constitutions.

Inspiration for the way forward can be found in the field of transitional justice. Scholars have investigated the 'politics of knowledge' related to legal reform, and further work is required to translate these findings to constitution-making. Critiques have been forwarded regarding the Western-centric conception of the legalistic state-led institutional approach set forth by international actors, as well as the concrete political impact of their involvement.[28] Patricia Lundy and Mark McGovern have criticised the purported apolitical nature of international actors, pointing out that international assistance always involves political implications.[29] This kind of scholarship is much needed in the field of constitution-making, which to date lacks critical engagement with the politics of transnational constitutional expertise.

Additionally, the blurriness between policy and research points to the necessity of addressing the ethical implications of constitutional expertise. Further research should interrogate the construction of knowledge in comparative constitutional law, as the expertise mobilised by external actors is not produced in a void; experts are embedded within material and ideological conditions.[30] The relationship among power, knowledge, and expertise is even more acute in the context of democratic transition, where an indistinct line separates policy and research. Jones observes that this 'blurriness' stems from the fact that in the case of transitional justice, scholarship was 'not born of a distinct intellectual tradition but rather a bricolage of activism and practice'.[31] Scholars in the fields of transitional justice and constitution-making are often encouraged to provide policy advice, which further blurs the line between research and advising. Zinaida Miller argues that this dynamic hinders the critical potential for scholarship, 'rather than offering a critical exploration of the influence of one area on another or of resulting patterns of invisibility, the literature tends to discuss the possible "toolbox" or the "lessons learned" in a particular area'.[32]

This blurriness between research and advising also characterises constitution-making, which, as a relatively young scientific field, would benefit from clear boundaries between policy and academic research.[33] Indeed, the genesis of the field was the *practical* need to address democratic transitions in the post-Cold War context.[34] Until 1989, constitution-making had been understood as an object of study belonging to topics related to democratisation in general. Thus, the ambiguity between scholarship and practical policy work makes sense, yet establishing clear boundaries is required in order to improve both the explanatory potential of academic research and the quality of constitutional advice. On one side, this book calls for further research on empirically driven comparative constitutional law, and on the other, it calls for caution and humility from external actors and constitution-makers alike. This study has shown that despite their own discursive understanding, external actors carry on their own politics in the expertise they provide to constitution-makers; this is not per se a problem, so long as actors – both external and local – are aware of this dynamic. We have seen that the constitutional architecture proposed by constitutional experts in a sensitive constitution-making process has a political component, and ultimately it is up to the local constitution-makers to decide how to frame this involvement and how to restrain, if necessary, such political elements.

Finally, the political dimension of expertise emphasises another normative implication: relying on 'best practices' and comparative knowledge prioritises *replication* over *innovation* in constitution-making. As such, it ignores the vast literature and practical manifestations of democratic innovation that have emerged recently, such as deliberative democracy and sortition.[35] The development enterprise highlights the importance of understanding the figure of the expert in order to better grasp the transnational dynamics of constitution-making. From the drafting of constitutions of future independent territories, to contemporary drafting in the context of democratic transition, the provision of expertise has been a key element of the development enterprise throughout history; indeed it could be said that this is a defining feature of the transnational dimension of constitution-making.

Grounding constitution-making within broader development endeavours has allowed this work to highlight the same pitfalls that have been pointed out by international relations scholars. Jan Eijking notes that 'the assumption persists that technical international cooperation successfully escapes politics: a complex, globalized world, this intuition goes, needs specialists to tackle transnational challenges'.[36] This book has shown that similar discursive practices exist when it comes to constitution-making – conceived as a technical issue that can be tacked by legal experts.

Chapter 5 argued that the involvement of experts is not an anomalous part of constitution-making, as often treated by the literature but in fact a central, even defining, dimension. The chapter argued that the core activity of external actors is the provision of expertise, and that the expert has played a crucial role throughout the history of constitution-making: from decolonisation through to the institutionalisation of expertise in the post-Cold War period. Constitutional experts are characterised by two elements: the possession of specialised knowledge and an understanding of their involvement as outside the realm of politics. The chapter showed that experts justify their involvement in constitution-making processes by framing their expertise as technical, neutral, and, most importantly, apolitical.

Framing and knowing *who* the experts are in this context is crucial. Drafting a constitution is a political battlefield, and behind the 'technical' aspects of drafting lie huge political consequences. While constitution-makers are often aware of the politics of *national* expertise, the same caution ought to be heeded with the provision of *international* expertise.[37] Building a new state architecture and deciding which fundamental rights should be guaranteed are inherently political activities. Choosing a constitution is choosing the social contract that will govern a territory. This is especially the case in the context of democratic transition, where two models of the state tend to be in dispute: one grounded on emancipatory rights, one nostalgic for the dictatorial past.

The empirical analysis of the transnational dimension of constitution-making could also inform future constitution-makers. By drawing attention to the political dimension of expertise and the informal pathways of involvement, future constitution-making processes could account for these aspects *procedurally* or at least be aware of the discursive practices of external actors (i.e. conceiving of their involvement in purely technical, apolitical terms), for example, in the context of the recent Chilean constitutional process, when it was revealed that international organisations offered constitutional expertise to local constitution-makers.[38] The response from constitutional scholars at the time, in the press and on social media, was to reassure the public that the legitimacy and popular sovereignty of the constitution-making process would not be undermined by foreign experts, as the actual process would take place within the National Constituent Assembly. The findings of this book could inform domestic actors about the dynamics of external actor involvement, the modes of action for the provision of foreign expertise, and the fact that constitutions have always had a transnational dimension.

At a more practical level, difficult questions remain to future constitution-makers and scholars alike. How should the political dimension of expertise be addressed and how should external actor involvement be framed – legally or not – in the constitution-making process? Indeed, the transnational dimension of constitution-making is particularly relevant for the strand of scholarship that emphasises the role that *public participation* in constitution-making plays in strengthening the legitimacy and longevity of new constitutions. If a participatory process is desired, then the role of external actors and experts must be better understood. The normative principles of transparency, accountability, and democratic legitimacy are all at stake.[39] If the democratisation of the constitution-making process is to be taken seriously, a normative theory should integrate participation at the drafting stage and not merely as a consultation at the end of the process.

En route to a new normative theory

This study points to normative and practical implications for domestic actors in the constitution-making process, especially at the constitutional drafting stage. This could manifest through the development of a Rules of Procedure for a constitution-making body. Demystifying constitution-making reveals blind spots that are outside the common imaginary of how the process unfolds on the ground. The new analytical lens proposed by this book, grounded in an antifoundationalist understanding of constitution-making, is not only theoretically and empirically valuable but also has normative implications. Before assessing whether constitutions achieve particular social, political, and legal goals, it is first necessary to understand the process through which they are made. This is especially true in the context of democratic transition, where securing the legitimacy of new institutions is essential in order to guarantee their longevity.

A central message of this book is that constitutional scholars are trapped in the wrong theory; constituent power is not only insufficient to address the complex nature of transnational constitution-making, but its restricted scope means that it obfuscates significant actors involved in the process. The goal of this project was to develop an alternative theory of constitution-making and to approach the legal phenomenon through a new analytical lens. This has been accomplished in largely *descriptive* terms. What is needed in parallel is the development of a *normative* theory that takes external actor involvement seriously. Recent proposals for theories that challenge constituent power have emerged; however, they too fail to capture the transnational dimension of constitution-making.[40]

Scholars in the TWAIL tradition have pointed out the ambivalent nature of the law. Law is a double-edged sword that can reproduce old dynamics based on existing hierarchies *and* be a tool for emancipation. Issa Shivy rightly points out that 'a radical lawyer must disabuse herself or himself of the notion that law is neutral and apolitical'.[41] This book has argued that the emancipatory power of constitutional law is unlocked only when all of its complex, blurry, and colonial dimensions are acknowledged. It serves neither scholars nor constitution-makers to put blind faith in the law as an instrument of social and political change and to ignore aspects that do not fit within traditional theoretical boundaries, such as transnational involvement and the politics of expertise.

What all studies of constitution-making reveal is how much remains unknown about the legal phenomenon. To progress towards a better understanding of this process, the presence of external actors must be widely acknowledged, and the construction and provision of constitutional expertise must be investigated further. Despite the methodological and empirical advances in the discipline, constitution-making continues to be shrouded in the same quasi-mythical cloak as it was in the time of Sieyès, where the very analytical foundation that many constitutional scholars still follow creates arbitrary blinders that hinder a comprehensive and concrete understanding. This book provides a possible path forward to better grasp the transnational dimension of constitution-making, while acknowledging that more work is needed to answer the deceptively simple question: how are constitutions made?

Notes

1 Cited in Alexandre Flückiger, *(Re)faire la loi: Traité de légistique à l'ère du droit souple* (Stämpfli Verlag 2019) 2.
2 Thomas Carothers, 'The Problem of Knowledge' in Thomas Carothers (ed), *Promoting the Rule of Law Abroad: In Search of Knowledge* (Carnegie Endowment for International Peace 2006) 21. [Emphasis added].
3 See Adam Chilton and Mila Versteeg, *How Constitutional Rights Matter* (OUP 2020).
4 Tom Ginsburg, Zachary Elkins and Justin Blount, 'Does the Process of Constitution-Making Matter?' (2009) 5 Annual Review of Law and Social Science 201, 219.
5 See Alexander Hudson, *The Veil of Participation: Citizens and Political Parties in Constitution-Making Processes* (CUP 2021); Abrak Saati, 'Participation: To Unveil a Myth' in Tania Abbiate, Markus Böckenförde and Veronica Federico (eds), *Public Participation in African Constitutionalism* (Routledge 2018).
6 See Wolfgang Hoffmann-Riem, 'The Venice Commission of the Council of Europe – Standards and Impact' (2014) 25 European Journal of International Law 579, 582.
7 See Alain Supiot, *La Gouvernance par les nombres* (Fayard 2015); Sally Engle Merry and John Conley, 'Measuring the World: Indicators, Human Rights, and Global Governance' (2011) 52 Current Anthropology 83.
8 Flückiger (n 1) 41.
9 ibid 259. [My own translation. Emphasis in original].
10 See Patricia Popelier and Victoria Verlinden, 'The Context of the Rise of Ex Ante Evaluation' in *The Impact of Legislation* (Brill Nijhoff 2009); Andreas Ladner and others, *Swiss Public Administration: Making the State Work Successfully* (Springer 2019).

11 Briony Jones, 'The Performance and Persistence of Transitional Justice and Its Ways of Knowing Atrocity' [2020] Cooperation and Conflict 1, 3.
12 Angelica Maria Bernal, *Beyond Origins: Rethinking Founding in a Time of Constitutional Democracy* (OUP 2017) 10.
13 ibid.
14 See Amelia Odida, 'Making Policy, Problems, and Constitutions: Decolonising the UN Policy of Constitutional Assistance' (UCL (University College London) 2022).
15 Bernal (n 12) 2.
16 ibid.
17 For a great summary see Maxim Bönnemann and Laura Jung, 'Critical Legal Studies and Comparative Constitutional Law' in Rainer Grote, Frauke Lachenmann and Rüdiger Wolfrum (eds), *Max Planck Encyclopedia of Comparative Constitutional Law* (Max Planck Foundation for International Peace and the Rule of Law 2017). See also Gunter Frankenberg, *Comparative Constitutional Studies: Between Magic and Deceit* (Edward Elgar Publishing 2018).
18 Duncan Kennedy, 'Political Ideology and Comparative Law' in Ugo Mattei and Mauro Bussani (eds), *The Cambridge Companion to Comparative Law* (CUP 2012) 37.
19 Upendra Baxi, 'The Colonialist Heritage' in Pierre Legrand and Roderick Munday (eds), *Comparative Legal Studies: Traditions and Transitions* (CUP 2003) 50.
20 ibid.
21 Ran Hirschl, *Comparative Matters: The Renaissance of Comparative Constitutional Law* (OUP 2014) 16.
22 Bönnemann and Jung (n 22) §35.
23 ibid §36.
24 David Kennedy, 'International Human Rights Movement: Part of the Problem?' (2002) 15 Harvard Human Rights Journal 101, 114.
25 Zoran Oklopcic, 'The South of Western Constitutionalism: A Map Ahead of a Journey' in Usha Natarajan and others (eds), *Third World Appraoches to International Law on Praxis and the Intellectual* (Routledge 2016) 139.
26 See Sara Araújo, 'Modern Constitutionalism, Legal Pluralism and the Waste of Experience' in Sara Araújo, Orlando Aragón Andrade and Boaventura de Sousa Santos (eds), *Decolonizing Constitutionalism: Beyond False or Impossible Promises* (Routledge 2023).
27 See Lorianne Updike Toler, 'Mapping the Constitutional Process: Lessons from 18 Constitution-Writing Procedures' (2014) 3 Cambridge Journal of Comparative and International Law 1–2.
28 Rosemary Nagy, 'Transitional Justice as Global Project: Critical Reflections' (2008) 29 Third World Quarterly 275.
29 Patricia Lundy and Mark McGovern, 'Whose Justice? Rethinking Transitional Justice from the Bottom Up' (2008) 35 Journal of Law and Society 265.
30 Jones (n 11) 9.
31 ibid 5.
32 Zinaida Miller, 'Effects of Invisibility: In Search of the "Economic" in Transitional Justice' (2008) 2 The International Journal of Transitional Justice 266, 290.
33 Mark Tushnet, 'Comparative Constitutional Law' in Mathias Reimann and Reinhard Zimmermann (eds), *The Oxford Handbook of Comparative Law* (OUP 2017) 1228.
34 Michel Rosenfeld and András Sajó, *The Oxford Handbook of Comparative Constitutional Law* (OUP 2012) 2.
35 See Hélène Landemore, *Open Democracy: Reinventing Popular Rule for the Twenty-First Century* (Princeton UP 2020).

36 Jan Eijking, 'Historical Claims to the International: The Case of the Suez Canal Experts' (2023) 67 International Studies Quarterly 1–2.
37 See Alicia Pastor y Camarasa, 'Demystifying How Constitutions Are Made: External Actors' Modes of Actions in the 2014 Tunisian Constitution' [2022] Michigan Journal of Law & Society 51.
38 For more on this see Camilla Vergara, *Burying Pinochet* (New Left Review 12 January 2021).
39 See Sheila Jasanoff, '(No?) Accounting for Expertise' (2003) 30 Science and Public Policy 157–62.
40 Amal Sethi, 'Looking Beyond the Constituent Power Theory: The Theory of Equitable Elite Bargaining' [2023] Global Constitutionalism 1.
41 Issa Gulamhussein Shivji, 'Do Constitutions Matter? The Dilemma of a Radical Lawyer' (2020) 5 Strathmore Law Review 157, 159.

References

Abat i Ninet A and Tushnet M, *The Arab Spring: An Essay on Revolution and Constitutionalism* (Edward Elgar Publishing 2015).
Adams W, *The First American Constitutions: Republican Ideology and the Making of the State Constitutions in the Revolutionary Era* (Rowman & Littlefield Publishers 2001).
Aguilera-Barchet B, *A History of Western Public Law* (Springer 2015).
Ailincai MA, 'La soft law est-elle l'avenir des droits fondamentaux?' [2017] Revue des droits et libertés fondamentaux Chron n° 20.
Al-Ali Z, 'Constitutional Drafting and External Influence' in Ginsburg T and Dixon R (eds), *Comparative Constitutional Law* (Edward Elgar Publishing 2011).
Al-Dabbagh H, 'Le droit comparé comme instrument de modernisation: l'exemple des codifications civiles des Etats arabes du Moyen-Orient' (2013) 43 Revue de Droit: Université de Sherbrooke 388–441.
Allorant P and Badier W, 'La société de législation comparée: boîte à idées du parlementarisme libéral de l'Empire libéral à la République opportuniste' (2017) 13 Revue électronique d'histoire du droit 1–11.
Andzoka-Atsimou S, *L'ingénierie constitutionnelle, solution de sortie de crise en Afrique? les exemples de l'Afrique du Sud, de la République démocratique du Congo, du Burundi et du Congo-Brazzaville* (L'Harmattan 2016).
Anghie A, 'Finding the Peripheries: Sovereignty and Colonialism in Nineteenth-Century International Law' (1999) 40 Harvard International Law Journal 1–80.
——, 'The Evolution of International Law: Colonial and Postcolonial Realities' (2006) 27 Third World Quarterly 739–53.
Arato A, 'Forms of Constitution Making and Theories of Democracy' (1995) 17 Cardozo Law Review 191–232.
——, *Constitution Making Under Occupation: The Politics of Imposed Revolution in Iraq* (Columbia UP 2009).
——, 'Conventions, Constituent Assemblies, and Round Tables: Models, Principles and Elements of Democratic Constitution-Making' (2012) 1 Global Constitutionalism 173–200.
——, *Post Sovereign Constitution Making: Learning and Legitimacy* (OUP 2016).
——, 'Constitution-Making' in Lang A and Wiener A (eds), *Handbook on Global Constitutionalism* (Edward Elgar Publishing 2017).
Araújo S, 'Modern Constitutionalism, Legal Pluralism and the Waste of Experience' in Araújo S, Andrade OA and de Sousa Santos B (eds), *Decolonizing Constitutionalism: Beyond False or Impossible Promises* (Routledge 2023).
Armitage D and David A, *The Ideological Origins of the British Empire* (CUP 2000).
Arneil B, *John Locke and America: The Defence of English Colonialism* (OUP 1996).

Assemblée nationale, 'Jules Ferry (1885): Les fondements de la politique coloniale (28 juillet 1885)' (Undated) <http://www2.assemblee-nationale.fr/decouvrir-l-assemblee/histoire/grands-discours-parlementaires/jules-ferry-28-juillet-1885> accessed February 2020.

Aucoin L, 'The Role of International Experts in Constitution-Making: Myth and Reality' (2004) 5 Georgetown Journal of International Affairs 89–95.

Autesserre S, *Peaceland: Conflict Resolution and the Everyday Politics of International Intervention* (CUP 2014).

The Avalon Project, 'Inaugural Address of Harry S. Truman' (20 January 1949) <https://avalon.Law.yale.edu/20th_century/truman.asp> accessed July 2020.

Barnett M, *The International Humanitarian Order* (Routledge 2009).

——, 'International Paternalism and Humanitarian Governance' (2012) 1 Global Constitutionalism 485–521.

Bastien F, *Le régime politique de la Ve République* (La Découverte 1999).

Bates R, 'Political Development' in Lancaster C and Van de Walle N (eds), *The Oxford Handbook of the Politics of Development* (OUP 2018).

Baxi U, 'Constitutionalism as a Site of State Formative Practices' (1999) 21 Cardozo Law Review 1183–210.

——, 'Postcolonial Legality' in Schwarz H and Ray S (eds), *A Companion to Postcolonial Studies* (Blackwell Publishing 2000).

——, 'The Colonialist Heritage' in Legrand P and Munday R (eds), *Comparative Legal Studies: Traditions and Transitions* (CUP 2003).

Bdira M, *Relations internationales et sous-développement. La Tunisie 1857–1864* (Acta Universitatis Upsaliensis 1978).

Beaud O, *La puissance de l'Etat* (Presses Universitaires de France 1994).

Belgium, Chambre des représentants, *Rapport du groupe de travail pour l'étude du problème politique au Congo du 20 janvier 1959* (Chambre des représentants 1958–1959).

——, Loi fondamentale du 19 mai 1960 relative aux structures du Congo (19 May 1960), Moniteur belge.

Belissa M, 'Rousseau, la Corse et la Pologne' [2009] Annales historiques de la Révolution française 238–39.

Bell C, 'Peace Agreements: Their Nature and Legal Status' (2006) 100 American Journal of International Law 373–412.

Ben Achour R and Ben Achour S, 'La transition démocratique en Tunisie: entre légalité constitutionnelle et légitimité révolutionnaire' [2012] Revue française de droit constitutionnel 715–32.

Benomar J, *Constitution-Making and Peace Building: Lessons Learned from the Constitution-Making Processes of Postconflict Countries* (United Nations Development Programme 2003).

Berger M-S, 'La Commission de Venise et l'élaboration de la Constitution tunisienne du 27 janvier 2014' in *Mouvances du droit: Études en l'honneur du Professeur Rafâa Ben Achour Tome I* (Konrad Adenauer Stiftung 2015).

Bernal AM, *Beyond Origins: Rethinking Founding in a Time of Constitutional Democracy* (OUP 2017).

Bertrand R, 'Les organisations de "promotion de la démocratie" et la construction des bureaucraties électorales indonésiennes' [2008] Critique Internationale 51–72.

Billias GA, *American Constitutionalism Heard Round the World, 1776–1989: A Global Perspective* (New York UP 2009).

Bisarya S, 'No Strings Attached? Constraints on External Advice in internationalized Constitution-Making' in De Groof E and Wiebusch M (eds), *International Law and Transitional Governance* (Routledge 2020).

——, *Protecting Ethnic Minorities Within Minorities* (International IDEA 2020).
——, *Advice on Applying Mediation Fundamentals in UN Constitutional Assistance* (UNDPPA November 2022).
Blaustein A, 'Constitution Drafting: The Good, the Bad, and the Beautiful' (1991) 2 Scibes Journal of Legal Writing 49–61.
Blouët A, 'Le pouvoir pré-constituant: contribution à l'étude de l'exercice du pouvoir constituant originaire à partir du cas de l'Egypte après la révolution du 25 janvier (février 2011-juillet 2013)' (PhD dissertation, Université Paris 1. Panthéon Sorbonne 2018).
Böckenförde M, Hedling N and Wahiu W, *A Practical Guide to Constitution Building* (International IDEA 2011).
Bonnard R, *Les actes constitutionnels de 1940* (Librairie générale de droit et de juriprudence 1942).
Bönnemann M and Jung L, 'Critical Legal Studies and Comparative Constitutional Law' in Grote R, Lachenmann F and Wolfrum R (eds), *Max Planck Encyclopedia of Comparative Constitutional Law* (Max Planck Foundation for International Peace and the Rule of Law 2017).
Borgeaud C, *Établissement et révision des constitutions en Amérique et en Europe* (Thorin et fils 1893).
Boutros-Ghali B, *An Agenda for Democratization* (UN Department of Public Information 20 December 1996).
Brandt M, *Constitutional Assistance in Post-Conflict Countries. The UN Experience: Cambodia, East Timor & Afghanistan* (UNDP June 2005).
Brandt M and others, *Constitution-Making and Reform: Options for the Process* (Interpeace 2011).
Brown N, *Constitutions in a Nonconstitutional World: Arab Basic Laws and the Prospects for Accountable Government* (State University of New York Press 2012).
Bryde B-O, 'North and South in Comparative Constitutional Law – from Colonial Imposition Towards a Transnational Constitutionalist Dialogue' in Benedek W, Isak H and Kicker R (eds), *Development and Developing International and European Law Essays in Honour of Konrad Ginther on the Occasion of his 65th Birthday* (Peter Lang 1999).
——, 'Constitutional Law in "Old" and "New" Law and Development' (2008) 41 Verfassung und Recht in Übersee/Law and Politics in Africa, Asia and Latin America 10–15.
Bui NS, 'Contextualizing the Global Constitution-Making Process: The Case of Vietnam' (2016) 64 The American Journal of Comparative Law 931–79.
——, 'Globalization of Constitutional Identity' (2017) 23 Washington International Law Journal 463–533.
——, *Constitutional Change in the Contemporary Socialist World* (OUP 2020).
Buquicchio G and Granata-Menghini S, 'The Venice Commission Twenty Years On, Challenges Met, but Challenges Ahead' in Roosmalen M and others (eds), *Fundamental Rights and Principles Liber Amicorum Pieter Van Dijk* (Intersentia 2013).
Buratti A, *Western Constitutionalism: History, Institutions, Comparative Law* (Springer 2019).
Burg E, 'Law and Development: A Review of the Literature and a Critique of "Scholars in Self-Estrangement"' [1977] The American Journal of Comparative Law 492–530.
Burundi, Arusha Peace and Reconciliation Agreement for Burundi (28 August 2000), UN Peacemaker
——, Constitution of Burundi (2005), Constitute Project.

Cain B, 'Symposium: What, if Anything, Do We Know About Constitutional Design?' [2009] Texas Law Review Symposium 1265–693.

Carothers T, 'The Problem of Knowledge' in Carothers T (ed), *Promoting the Rule of Law Abroad: In Search of Knowledge* (Carnegie Endowment for International Peace 2006).

——, *Aiding Democracy Abroad: The Learning Curve* (Carnegie Endowment 2011).

Carré de Malberg R, *Contribution à la théorie générale de l'Etat spécialement d'après les données fournies par le droit constitutionnel français. Tome Premier* (Sirey 1922).

Cassese S, *A World Government?* (Global Law Press 2018).

Chalev D, Shaquoura M and Abass A, 'Rôle des Nations Unies dans le processus constitutionnel tunisien et résultat en termes de garanties relatives aux droits de l'homme' in *La Constitution de la Tunisie – Processus, principes et perspectives* (United Nations Development Programme 2016).

Champeil-Desplats V, *Méthodologies du droit et des sciences du droit* (Dalloz 2016).

Chandra B, 'Colonialism, Stages of Colonialism and the Colonial State' (1980) 10 Journal of Contemporary Asia 272–85.

Charte de la Francophonie [23 November 2005].

Chesterman S, *You, the People: The United Nations, Transitional Administration, and State-Building* (OUP 2005).

Chilton A and Versteeg M, *How Constitutional Rights Matter* (OUP 2020).

Cohen A, 'Legal Professionals or Political Entrepreneurs? Constitution making as a Process of Social Construction and Political Mobilization' (2010) 4 International Political Sociology 107–23.

Collins H and Evans R, 'A Sociological/Philosophical Perspective on Expertise: The Acquisition of Expertise Through Socialization' in Ericsson A and others (eds), *The Cambridge Handbook of Expertise and Expert Performance* (CUP 2018).

Colonial Office, *Ceylon. Report of the Commission on Constitutional Reform* (Colonial Office 1945).

Colonial Office, *Kenya. Proposals for New Constitutional Arrangements* (Colonial Office November 1957).

Colón-Ríos J, *Constituent Power and the Law* (OUP 2020).

Conklin A, *A Mission to Civilize: The Republican Idea of Empire in France and West Africa, 1895–1930* (UP Stanford 1997).

Convention relative à l'agence de coopération culturelle et technique (ACCT) [20 March 1970] OIF.

Cooper F, 'Modernizing Bureaucrats, Backward Africans, and the Development Concept' in Cooper F and Packard R (eds), *International Development the Social Sciences: Essays on the History Politics of Knowledge* (University of California Press 1997).

——, *Colonialism in Question: Theory, Knowledge, History* (University of California Press 2005).

——, 'Decolonization in Tropical Africa' in Thomas M and Thompson A (eds), *The Oxford Handbook of the Ends of Empire* (OUP 2018).

Cope K, 'The Intermestic Constitution: Lessons from the World's Newest Nation' (2012) 53 Virginia Journal of International Law 667–724.

Corten O, *Méthodologie du droit international public* (Éditions de l'Université de Bruxelles 2009).

Cotterrell R, 'What is Transnational Law?' (2012) 37 Law & Social Inquiry 500–24.

Council of Europe, *Resolution (90) 6 on a Partial Agreement Establishing the European Commission for Democracy through Law* (Venice Commission [CM]/Res(90)6E 10 May 1990).

Covenant of the League of Nations [28 June 1919] League of Nations.
Cowen M and Shenton R, *Doctrines of Development* (Routledge 1996).
Craggs R, 'Development in a Gobal-Historical Context' in Desai V and Potter R (eds), *The Companion to Development Studies* (Routledge 2014).
Craig P, 'Transnational Constitution-Making: The Contribution of the Venice Commission on Law and Democracy' (2017) 2 UC Irvine Journal of International, Transnational, and Comparative Law 57–86.
Crawford J, *The Creation of States in International Law* (OUP 2006).
Crouch M, 'Pre-emptive Constitution-Making: Authoritarian Constitutionalism and the Military in Myanmar' (2020) 54 Law & Society Review 487–515.
Dale W, 'The Making and Remaking of Commonwealth Constitutions' (1993) 42 International & Comparative Law Quarterly 67–83.
Dann P and Al-Ali Z, 'The Internationalized Pouvoir Constituant – Constitution-Making Under External Influence in Iraq, Sudan and East Timor' (2006) 10 Max Planck Yearbook of United Nations Law 423–63.
David R, 'Civil Code for Ethiopia: Considerations on the Codification of the Civil Law in African Countries' (1962) 37 Tulane Law Review 187–204.
——, 'Sources of the Ethiopian Civil Code' (1967) 4 Journal of Ethiopian Law 341–67.
Davis K and Trebilcock M, 'The Relationship Between Law and Development: Optimists Versus Skeptics' (2008) 56 The American Journal of Comparative Law 895–946.
De Brabandere E, *Post-Conflict Administrations in International Law: International Territorial Administration, Transitional Authority and Foreign Occupation in Theory and Practice* (Martinus Nijhoff Publishers 2009).
De Groof E, *State Renaissance for Peace: Transitional Governance Under International Law* (CUP 2020).
de La Buissière JB and Dumont G-H, 'Les autorités belges et la décolonisation du Congo' [2010] Courrier hebdomadaire du CRISP 9–117.
de Poorter J and others, 'Introduction: Mapping the Emerging Field of Constitutional Advice' [2022] European Yearbook of Constitutional Law 1–11.
Declaration, International Institute for Democracy and Electoral Assistance [27–28 February 1995] International IDEA.
Deforge Q, 'La fabrique transnationale du politique. Une sociologie historique du champ réformateur de la "gouvernance" (1961–2019)' (PhD dissertation, Université Paris-Dauphine 2019).
——, 'Une expertise internationale sans "bonnes pratiques": Soutenir la professionnalisation du travail parlementaire dans la Tunisie d'après 2011' [2019] Critique Internationale 127–45.
Dezalay Y, Bigo D and Cohen A, 'Enquêter sur l'internationalisation des noblesses d'Etat. Retour réflexif sur des stratégies de double jeu. Entretien avec Yves Dezalay' [2015] Cultures & Conflits 15–52.
Dezalay Y and Garth B, *The Internationalization of Palace Wars: Lawyer, Economists, and the Contest to Transform Latin American States* (The University of Chicago Press 2002).
Dicey A, *Introduction to the Study of the Law of the Constitution* (Macmillan and Co 1965).
Diehl K and others, *Max Planck Manuals on Constitution Building: Structures and Principles of a Constitution* (Max Planck Institute 2009).
Dixon R, 'Constitutions Inside Out: Outsider Interventions in Domestic Constitutional Contexts' (2013) 48 Wake Forest Law Review 149–210.

——, 'Constitutional Drafting and Distrust' (2015) 13 International Journal of Constitutional Law 819–46.
Dobbins J, 'Europe's Role in Nation Building' (2008) 50 Survival 83–110.
Douglas W, 'Lawyers of the Peace Corps' (1962) 48 American Bar Association Journal 909–13.
DRI, 'DRI. Constitutions' (Undated) <https://Democracy-reporting.org/constitutions/> accessed August 2019.
——, 'DRI. Who We Are' (Undated) <https://Democracy-reporting.org/who-we-are/> accessed August 2019.
——, 'What We Do' (Undated) <https://Democracy-reporting.org/what-we-do/> accessed August 2019.
——, 'Where We Work' (Undated) <https://Democracy-reporting.org/where-we-Work/> accessed August 2019.
——, *Annual Report 2011* (DRI December 2012).
——, *Annual Report 2012* (DRI December 2013).
——, *Annual Report 2013* (DRI December 2014).
——, *Annual Report 2014* (DRI December 2015).
——, *Annual Report 2015* (DRI December 2016).
——, *Annual Report 2017* (DRI December 2018).
Drinoczi T and Bien-Kacala A, 'Illiberal Constitutionalism: The Case of Hungary and Poland' (2019) 20 German Law Journal 1140–66.
Droubi S and d'Aspremont J, *International Organisations, Non-State Actors, and the Formation of Customary International Law* (Manchester UP 2020).
Du Bois de Gaudusson J, 'Le rôle de l'expertise constitutionnelle dans la transition constitutionnelle' in Philippe X and Danelciuc-Colodrovschi N (eds), *Transitions constitutionnelles et constitutions transitionnelles* (Institut Universitaire Varenne 2014).
Duchacek I, *Power Maps: Comparative Politics of Constitutions* (American Bibliographical Center-Clio Press 1973).
Dudziak M, 'Working Toward Democracy: Thurgood Marshall and the Constitution of Kenya' (2006) 56 Duke Law Journal 721–80.
Dufournet H, 'Quand techniciser c'est faire de la politique "sans le dire". Récit d'une "technicisation réussie" au ministère de la Défense' (2014) 3 Gouvernement et action publique 29–49.
Duguit L, *L'Etat, le droit objectif et la loi positive* (Fontemoing 1901).
Dujardin V, 'Les droits constitutionnels originaires' in Verdussen M and Bonbled N (eds), *Les droits constitutionnels en Belgique* (Bruylant 2011).
Duranti F, 'Constitution of Tunisia, Venice Commission and International Constitutionalism' in Dell'Aguzzo L and Diodato E (eds), *The 'State' of Pivot States in South-Eastern Mediterranean: Turkey, Egypt, Israel, and Tunisia After the Arab Spring* (Stranieri UP 2016).
Dyzenhaus D, 'Constitutionalism in an Old Key: Legality and Constituent Power' (2012) 1 Global Constitutionalism 229–60.
Eidgenössische Technische Hochschule Zürich (Recknagel C), 'Iraq Oil Scandal Threatens Former Diplomat' (Undated) <https://ethz.ch/content/specialinterest/gess/cis/center-for-securities-studies/en/services/digital-library/articles/article.html/108606> accessed October 2023.
Eijking J, 'Historical Claims to the International: The Case of the Suez Canal Experts' (2023) 67 International Studies Quarterly 1–12.
Eisenberg T, 'Why Do Empirical Legal Scholarship' (2004) 41 San Diego Law Review 1741–46.

El Khoury T, 'Pouvoir constituant' in Grote R (ed), *Max Planck Encyclopedia of Comparative Constitutional Law* (OUP 2017).
El Mechat S and Renucci F, *Les décolonisations au XXe siècle. Les hommes de la transition. Itinéraires, actions et traces* (L'Harmattan 2014).
Elster J, 'Forces and Mechanisms in the Constitution-Making Process' (1995) 45 Duke Law Journal 364–96.
Emerson R, 'Colonialism, Political Development, and the UN' (1965) 19 International Organization 484–503.
Fatin-Rouge Stéfanini M (ed), *Internationalisation des constitutions et constitutionnalisation du droit international: Réflexions sur quelques interactions entre droit constitutionnel et droit international* (Les cahiers de l'institut Louis-Favoreu, Presses Universitaires d'Aix-Marseille 2015).
Fauvarque-Cosson B, 'Deux siècles d'évolution du droit comparé' (2011) 63 Revue internationale de droit comparé 527–40.
FDR Presidential Library, 'March 1935' (Undated) <www.fdrlibrary.marist.edu/daybyday/resource/march-1935–15/> accessed July 2020.
Feldman N, 'Imposed Constitutionalism' (2004) 37 Conn Law Review 857–90.
Ferguson J, *The Anti-Politics Machine: 'Development', Depoliticization and Bureaucratic Power in Lesotho* (Routledge 1990).
Fiji, Decree No 57 on Fiji Constitutional Process (Constitution Commission) (18 July 2012), Government of Fiji Gazette 1589.
Fischer F, *Technocracy and the Politics of Expertise* (Sage 1990).
——, *Democracy and Expertise: Reorienting Policy Inquiry* (OUP 2009).
——, *Climate Crisis and the Democratic Prospect: Participatory Governance in Sustainable Communities* (OUP 2017).
Fischer G, 'La décolonisation et le rôle des traités et des constitutions' (1962) 8 Annuaire français de droit international 805–36.
Fitoussi E and Bénszet A, *L'Etat tunisien et le protectorat français: Histoire et organisation (1525 à 1881)(1881 à 1931)* (Rousseau & Cie 1931).
Fitzmaurice A, 'The Justification of King Leopold II's Congo Enterprise by Sir Travers Twiss' in Dorsett S and Hunter I (eds), *Law and Politics in British Colonial Thought* (Palgrave MacMillan 2011).
Flückiger A, *(Re)faire la loi: Traité de légistique à l'ère du droit souple* (Stämpfli Verlag 2019).
Fombad CM, 'Constitutional Reforms and Constitutionalism in Africa: Reflections on Some Current Challenges and Future Prospects' (2011) 59 Buffalo Law Review 1007–108.
Fontana D, 'The Rise and Fall of Comparative Constitutional Law in the Postwar Era' (2011) 36 Yale Journal of International Law 1–54.
France, Loi relative aux mesures propres à assurer l'évolution des territoires relevant du ministère de la France d'outre-mer (23 June 1956), Journal officiel de la République française 5781.
Franck T, 'The Emerging Right to Democratic Governance' (1992) 86 American Journal of International Law 46–91.
—— and Thiruvengadam A, 'International Law and Constitution-Making' (2003) 2 Chinese Journal of International Law 467–518.
Frankema E and Buelens F, *Colonial Exploitation and Economic Development: The Belgian Congo and the Netherlands Indies Compared* (Routledge 2013).
Frankenberg G, 'Stranger Than Paradise: Identity & Politics in Comparative Law' [1997] Utah Law Review 259–75.
——, 'Constitutional Transfer: The IKEA Theory Revisited' (2010) 8 International Journal of Constitutional Law 563–79.

——, *Comparative Constitutional Studies: Between Magic and Deceit* (Edward Elgar Publishing 2018).
Fresia M, 'La fabrique des normes internationales sur la protection des réfugiés au sein du comité exécutif du hcr' [2012] Critique Internationale 39–60.
Friedrich C, 'Rebuilding the German Constitution' (1949) 43 The American Political Science Review 461–82.
Frydman B, 'Les défis du droit global' in Bricteux C and Benoît Frydman B (eds), *Les défis du droit global* (Bruylant 2018).
Galanter M, 'The Modernization of Law' in Weiner M (ed), *Modernization: The Dynamics of Growth* (Basic Books 1966).
Gardner J, *Legal Imperialism: American Lawyers and Foreign Aid in Latin America* (University of Wisconsin Press 1980).
Gargarella R, *Latin American Constitutionalism, 1810–2010: The Engine Room of the Constitution* (OUP 2013).
General Framework Agreement for Peace in Bosnia and Herzegovina [Initiated in Dayton on 21 November 1995 and signed in Paris on 14 December 1995] OSCE.
Gérard-Libois J and Verhaegen B, *Congo 1960* (Centre de Recherche et d'Information Socio-Politiques 1961).
Ghai Y, 'A Journey Around Constitutions: Reflections on Contemporary Constitutions' (2005) 122 South African Law Journal 804–31.
—— and Cottrell J, 'The State and Constitutionalism in Postcolonial Societies in Africa' in Paliwala A, McCrudden C and Baxi U (eds), *Law's Ethical, Global and Theoretical Contexts: Essays in Honour of William Twining* (CUP 2015).
Gilissen J, 'Le caractère collégial des premières formes de gouvernement et d'admnistration de l'Etat belge (1830–1831)' (1981) 3 Belgisch Tijdschrift voor Nieuwste Geschiedenis 609–39.
Gilmartin M, 'Colonialism/Imperialism' in Gallaher C and others (eds), *Key Concepts in Political Geography* (Sage 2009).
Ginsburg T, *Constitutional Design for Territorially Divided Societies* (International IDEA August 2018).
——, 'Constitutional Advice and Transnational Legal Order' in Shaffer G, Halliday TC and Ginsburg T (eds), *Constitution-Making and Transnational Legal Order* (CUP 2019).
——, 'Some Advice on Constitutional Advice' in *European Yearbook of Constitutional Law 2021: Constitutional Advice* (Springer 2022).
——, Elkins Z and Blount J, 'Does the Process of Constitution-Making Matter?' (2009) 5 Annual Review of Law and Social Science 201–23.
——, Huq A and Versteeg M, 'The Coming Demise of Liberal Constitutionalism?' (2018) 85 The University of Chicago Law Review 239–56.
—— and Versteeg M, 'Why Do Countries Adopt Constitutional Review?' (2014) 30 The Journal of Law, Economics, & Organization 587–622.
Giovalucchi F and De Sardan J-P, 'Planification, gestion et politique dans l'aide au développement: le cadre logique, outil et miroir des développeurs' [2009] Revue Tiers Monde 383–406.
Glanz J and Gibbs W, 'U.S. Adviser to Kurds Stands to Reap Oil Profits' *The New York Times* <www.nytimes.com/2009/11/12/world/middleeast/12galbraith.html>.
Glenn P, *The Cosmopolitan State* (OUP 2013).
Go J, 'Modeling the State: Postcolonial Constituitions in Asia and Africa' (2002) 39 Southeast Asian Studies 558–83.
——, 'American Colonial Empire: The Limit of Power's Reach' [2005] Lessons of Empire 201–16.

——, 'The Provinciality of American Empire: "Liberal Exceptionalism" and US Colonial Rule, 1898–1912' (2007) 49 Comparative Studies in Society and History 74–108.

Gonidec P-F, *Droit d'outre-mer. Tome I. De l'empire Colonial de la France à la Communauté* (Editions Montchrestien 1959).

Gopal S and Prior K, 'Rau, Sir Benegal Narsinga' (2004) Oxford Dictionary of National Biography <https://doi.org/10.1093/ref:odnb/35681> accessed 13 November 2023.

Gouvêa CB, *As intervenções da ONU no processo de constitution-making nos estados em transição política: O papel das Nações Unidas no resgate da ordem democrática* (Juruá 2016).

—— and Benvenuto J, 'United Nations Assistance to Constitution-Making Processes: Pre-Constituent and Constituent phases' (2019) 75 Revista da Faculdade de Direito da Universidade Federal de Minas Gerais 65–90.

Granata-Menghini S, 'La Commission de Venise du Conseil de l'Europe: méthodes et perspectives de l'assistance constitutionnelle en Europe' [2017] Les Nouveaux Cahiers du Conseil constitutionnel 69–85.

Greenberg D, 'Law and Development in Light of Dependency Theory' (1980) 3 Research in Law and Sociology 129–59.

Grimm D, *Constitutionalism: Past, Present, and Future* (OUP 2016).

Grote R, 'Definition of Constitutions' in Grote R (ed), *Max Planck Encyclopedia of Comparative Constitutional Law* (OUP 2017).

Grundmann R, 'The Rightful Place of Expertise' (2018) 32 Social Epistemology 372–86.

Guilluy T, *Du 'self-government' des Dominions à la dévolution: Recherches sur l'apparition et l'évolution de la Constitution britannique* (Editions Panthéon-Assas 2014).

——, 'Visions of Constitutionalism. The Implementation of Representative Institutions in the British Colonies' in Grotke K and Prutsch M (eds), *Constitutionalism, Legitimacy, and Power: Nineteenth-Century Experiences* (OUP 2014).

Guimezanes M, 'Les transitions constitutionnelles "internationalisées": Étude de droit interne' [2015] Revue française de droit constitutionnel 801–22.

Guzman A and Meyer T, 'International Soft Law' (2010) 2 Journal of Legal Analysis 171–225.

Haas P, 'Introduction: Epistemic Communities and International Policy Coordination' (1992) 46 International organization 1–35.

Hahm C and Kim SH, 'To Make "We the People": Constitutional Founding in Postwar Japan and South Korea' (2010) 8 International Journal of Constitutional Law 800–48.

——, *Making We the People: Democratic Constitutional Founding in Postwar Japan and South Korea* (CUP 2015).

Hall RB and Biersteker TJ, *The Emergence of Private Authority in Global Governance* (CUP 2002).

Hall S, 'The West and the Rest: Discourse an Power' in Hall S and others (eds), *Modernity: An Introduction to Modern Societies* (Blackwell Publishers 1996).

Halliday T and Karpik L, 'Political Liberalism in the British Post-Colony' in Halliday T, Karpik L and Feeley M (eds), *Fates of Political Liberalism in the British Post-Colony: The Politics of the Legal Complex* (CUP 2012).

Halliday T and Shaffer G, 'Transnational Legal Orders' in Halliday TC and Shaffer G (eds), *Transnational Legal Orders* (CUP 2015).

Halpérin J-L, *Profils des mondialisations du droit* (Dalloz 2009).

Harding A, 'The "Westminster Model" Constitution Overseas: Transplantation, Adaptation and Development in Commonwealth States' (2004) 4 Oxford University Commonwealth Law Journal 143–66.

Hartz MR, 'Constitutional Provisions in the Occupier's Interest: Lessons from Article 9 of the Japanese Constitution' (2012) 45 New York University Journal of International Law and Politics 861–900.
Hauriou M, *Précis de droit constitutionnel* (Librarie du Recueil Sirey 1929).
Havinden M and Meredith D, *Colonialism and Development: Britain and its Tropical Colonies, 1850–1960* (Routledge 1996).
Hawaii Nation, 'Draft Constitution of January 14, 1893' (Unknown) <www.hawaiination.org/constitution-1893.html> accessed October 2023.
Hayek F, 'The Counter-Revolution of Science' (1941) 8 Economica 119–50.
——, *The Counter-Revolution of Science: Studies on the Use and Abuse of Reason* (Liberty Fund Inc. 1952).
Hely-Hutchinson WJ, *Ceylon: Report of the Special Commission on the Constitution* (H. M. Stationery Office 1928).
Hertig Randall M, 'L'internationalisation de la juridiction constitutionnelle: défis et perspectives' (2010) 129 Revue de droit suisse 221–380.
Hirschl R, *Comparative Matters: The Renaissance of Comparative Constitutional Law* (OUP 2014).
Hodge J, *Triumph of the Expert: Agrarian Doctrines of Development and the Legacies of British Colonialism* (Ohio UP 2007).
Hoffmann-Riem W, 'The Venice Commission of the Council of Europe – Standards and Impact' (2014) 25 European Journal of International Law 579–97.
Hoogvelt A, *Globalization and the Postcolonial World: The New Political Economy of Development* (Palgrave Macmillan 2007).
Horowitz D, 'Constitution-Making: A Process Filled with Constraint' (2006) 12 Review of Constitutional Studies 1–17.
——, 'Conciliatory Institutions and Constitutional Processes in Post-Conflict States' (2007–2008) 49 William & Mary Law Review 1213–48.
Hudson A, *The Veil of Participation: Citizens and Political Parties in Constitution-Making Processes* (CUP 2021).
Huntington S, 'Democracy's Third Wave' (1991) 2 Journal of Democracy 12–34.
Husa J, 'Classification of Legal Families Today – Is It Time for Memorial Hymn?' (2004) 56 Revue internationale de droit comparé 11–38.
Indian Statutory Commission, *Report of the Indian Statutory Commission. Volume II – Recommendations* (Indian Statutory Commission 1930).
International Court of Justice, *Nicaragua vs United States of America, Merits* (International Court of Justice 27 June 1986).
International IDEA, 'Board of Advisers' (Undated) <www.idea.int/about-us/board_of_advisers> accessed February 2021.
——, 'Tunisia: Constituent Assembly's Rules of Procedure' (Unknown) <https://constitutionnet.org/vl/item/tunisia-constituent-assemblys-rules-procedure> accessed 13 November 2023.
——, 'What We Do – Constitution-Building' (Undated) <www.idea.int/our-Work/what-we-do/Constitution-building> accessed October 2021.
——, *Annual Results Report 1999* (International IDEA 2000).
——, *Annual Results Report 2003* (International IDEA 2004).
——, *Ten Years of Supporting Democracy Worldwide* (International IDEA 2005).
——, *Annual Results Report 2005* (International IDEA 2006).
——, *Annual Results Report 2007* (International IDEA 2008).
—— Statutes [21 November 2008] International IDEA.
——, *Annual Results Report 2008* (International IDEA 2009).
——, *A Record of Actions 2012* (International IDEA 2013).
——, *A Record of Actions 2013* (International IDEA 2014).
——, *A Record of Actions 2014* (International IDEA 2015).

——, *A Record of Actions 2015* (International IDEA 2016).
——, *A Record of Actions 2016* (International IDEA 2017).
——, *International IDEA. Supporting Democracy Worldwide a Retrospective Report on our Work 2012–17* (International IDEA 2018).
——, *A Record of Actions 2018* (International IDEA 2019).
——, *Annual Results Report 2019* (International IDEA 2020).
——, *Annual Results Report 2021* (International IDEA 2022).
——, *Annual Results Report 2022* (International IDEA 2023).
International Peace Conference, The Hague, Official Record, 'Hague Convention (IV) Respecting the Laws and Customs of War on Land and its Annex: Regulations Concerning the Laws and Customs of War on Land' (18 October 1907) <https://ihl-databases.icrc.org/applic/ihl/ihl.nsf/0/1d1726425f6955aec125641e0038bfd6>.
Ip EC, 'Globalization and the Future of the Law of the Sovereign State' (2010) 8 International Journal of Constitutional Law 636–55.
Jakab A, Dyevre A and Itzcovich G, *Comparative Constitutional Reasoning* (CUP 2017).
James CLR, *The Life of Captain Cipriani: An Account of British Government in the West Indies* (Duke UP 2014).
Jasanoff S, '(No?) Accounting for Expertise' (2003) 30 Science and Public Policy 157–62.
Jellinek G, *L'Etat moderne et son droit. Deuxième partie. [Allgemeine Staatslehre]* (V. Giard & E. Brière 1913).
——, *Allgemeine Staatslehre* (Verlag von Haring 1914).
Jessup P, *Transnational Law* (Yale UP 1956).
Jones B, 'The Performance and Persistence of Transitional Justice and its Ways of Knowing Atrocity' [2020] Cooperation and Conflict 1–18.
Kabwe Sabwa H, *Droit minier en République Démocratique du Congo* (Bruylant 2019).
Kadelbach S, 'Constitution-Making in Occupied Countries' in Frankenberg G (ed), *Order from Transfer Comparative Constitutional Design and Legal Culture* (Edward Elgar Publishing Limited 2013).
Kalyvas A, 'Popular Sovereignty, Democracy, and the Constituent Power' (2005) 12 Constellations 223–44.
Kelsen H, *Pure Theory of Law* (The Lawbook Exchange 2005).
Kendall S, '"Constitutional Technicity": Displacing Politics Through Expert Knowledge' (2015) 11 Law, Culture and the Humanities 363–77.
Kennedy D, 'International Human Rights Movement: Part of the Problem?' (2002) 15 Harvard Human Rights Journal 101–26.
——, 'The "Rule of Law", Political Choices, and Development Common Sense' in Trubek DM and Santos A (eds), *The New Law and Economic Development: A Critical Appraisal* (CUP 2006).
——, 'Political Ideology and Comparative Law' in Mattei U and Bussani M (eds), *The Cambridge Companion to Comparative Law* (CUP 2012).
——, *A World of Struggle: How Power, Law, and Expertise Shape Global Political Economy* (Princeton UP 2018).
Kenya, Committee of Experts on Constitutional Review, The Constitution of Kenya Review Act (2009), National Council for Law Reporting.
——, *Report of the Committee of Experts on Constitutional Review Issued on the Submission of the Reviewed Harmonized Draft Constitution to the Parliamentary Select Committee* (Committee of Experts on Constitutional Review 8 January 2010).

Kirkby C, 'A Cure for Coups: The South African Influence on Fijian Constitutionalism' in Dixon R and Theunis R (eds), *Constitutional Triumphs, Constitutional Disappointments: A Critical Assessment of the 1996 South African Constitution's Local and International Influence* (CUP 2018).

—— and Murray C, 'Constitution-Making in Anglophone Africa: We the People?' in Ndulo M and Gazibo M (eds), *Growing Democracy in Africa: Elections, Accountable Governance, and Political Economy* (Cambridge Publishers 2016).

Klein C, *Théorie et pratique du pouvoir constituant* (Presses Universitaires de France 1996).

—— and Sajó A, *Constitution-Making: Process and Substance* (OUP 2012).

Klug H, *Constituting Democracy: Law, Globalism, and South Africa's Political Reconstruction* (CUP 2000).

——, 'Postcolonial Collages: Distributions of Power and Constitutional Models: With Special Reference to South Africa' (2003) 18 International Sociology 114–31.

Koh HH, 'The Globalization of Freedom' (2001) 26 Yale Journal of International Law 305–12.

Kothari U, 'From Colonialism to Development: Reflections of Former Colonial Officers' (2006) 44 Commonwealth & Comparative Politics 118–36.

Krisch N, 'Pouvoir Constituant and Pouvoir Irritant in the Postnational Order' (2016) 14 International Journal of Constitutional Law 657–79.

Kritzer H, 'The (Nearly) Forgotten Early Empirical Legal Research' in Cane P and Kritzer H (eds), *Oxford Handbook of Empirical Legal Research* (OUP 2010).

Kroncke J, 'Law and Development as Anti-Comparative Law' (2012) 45 Vanderbilt Journal of Transnational Law 477–555.

Kumarasingham H (ed), *Constitution-Maker: Selected Writings of Sir Ivor Jennings* (CUP 2015).

—— (ed), *The Road to Temple Trees: Sir Ivor Jennings and the Constitutional Development of Ceylon: Selected Writings* (Center for Policy Alternatives 2015).

——, *Constitution-Making in Asia: Decolonisation and State-Building in the Aftermath of the British Empire* (Routledge 2016).

——, 'Eastminster – Decolonisation and State-Building in British Asia' in Kumarasingham H (ed), *Constitution-Making in Asia Decolonisation and State-Building in the Aftermath of the British Empire* (Routledge 2016).

——, 'Liberal Ideals and the Politics of Decolonisation' (2018) 46 The Journal of Imperial and Commonwealth History 815–20.

——, 'Written Differently: A Survey of Commonwealth Constitutional History in the Age of Decolonisation' (2018) 46 The Journal of Imperial and Commonwealth History 874–908.

——, 'A Transnational Actor on a Dramatic Stage – Sir Ivor Jennings and the Manipulation of Westminster Style Democracy in Pakistan' in Shaffer G, Halliday T and Ginsburg T (eds), *Constitution-Making and Transnational Legal Order* (CUP 2019).

Kumm M, 'Constituent Power, Cosmopolitan Constitutionalism, and Post-Positivist Law' (2016) 14 International Journal of Constitutional Law 697–711.

Ladner A and others, *Swiss Public Administration: Making the State Work Successfully* (Springer 2019).

Lainé J, 'Empirisme et conceptualisme en droit constitutionnel' (PhD dissertation, Université Lille II 2011).

Lambert E, *Etude de droit commun législatif ou de droit civil comparé. Première série* (T. Giord et E. Brière 1903).

Landau D, 'Constitution-Making Gone Wrong' (2012) 64 Alabama Law Review 923–80.

—— and Lerner H, *Comparative Constitution Making* (Edward Elgar Publishing 2019).

—— and Lerner H, 'Introduction to Comparative Constitution Making: The State of the Field' in Landau D and Lerner H (eds), *Comparative Constitution Making* (Edward Elgar Publishing 2019).

Landemore H, *Open Democracy: Reinventing Popular Rule for the Twenty-First Century* (Princeton UP 2020).

Lane J-E, *New Public Management* (Routledge 2000).

Lang A and Wiener A, 'A Constitutionalising Global Order: An Introduction' in Lang A and Wiener A (eds), *Handbook on Global Constitutionalism* (Edward Elgar 2017).

Lanni A and Vermeule A, 'Constitutional Design in the Ancient World' (2012) 64 Stanford Law Review 907–49.

Law D, 'Globalization and the Future of Constitutional Rights' (2008) 102 Northwestern University Law Review 1277–350.

——, 'Constitutions' in Cane P and Kritzer H (eds), *The Oxford Handbook of Empirical Legal Research* (OUP 2010).

——, 'Constitutional Archetypes' (2016) 95 Texas Law Review 153–243.

Law J, *A Dictionary of Law* (OUP 2015).

Le Divellec A, 'Le style des Constitutions écrites dans l'histoire moderne. Une esquisse sur les trois types de l'écriture constitutionnelle (XVIIe – XXe siècles)' (2013) 9 Jus Politicum 1–28.

Lee JM, *Colonial Development and Good Government: A Study of the Ideas Expressed by the British Official Classes in Planning Decolonization 1939–1964* (Clarendon Press 1967).

Lee Y-S, 'General Theory of Law and Development' (2017) 50 Cornell International Law Journal 415–71.

Lefranc S, 'Convertir le grand nombre à la paix. Une ingénierie internationale de pacification' (2007) 80 Politix 7–29.

Lenowitz J, 'Why Ratification? Questioning the Unexamined Constitution-Making Procedure' (PhD dissertation, Columbia University 2013).

Letter to John Trumbull from T. Jefferson written on 15 February 1789 (Undated) <https://www.loc.gov/exhibits/jefferson/18.html> accessed February 2024.

Littoz-Monnet A, *Governing Through Expertise: The Politics of Bioethics* (CUP 2020).

Locke J, *Second Treatise of Government and a Letter Concerning Toleration* (OUP 2016).

Loughlin M, *The Idea of Public Law* (OUP 2003).

——, 'Constituent Power Subverted: From English Constitutional Argument to British Constitutional Practice' in Loughlin M and Walker N (eds), *The Paradox of Constitutionalism Constituent Power and Constitutional Form* (OUP 2007).

——, 'The Concept of Constituent Power' (2014) 13 European Journal of Political Theory 218–37.

—— and Walker N, *The Paradox of Constitutionalism. Constituent Power and Constitutional Form* (OUP 2007).

Louis M and Maertens L, *Why International Organizations Hate Politics: Depoliticizing the World* (Routledge 2021).

Ludsin H, 'Peacemaking and Constitution-Drafting: A Dysfunctional Marriage' (2011) 33 University of Pennsylvania Journal of International Law 239–311.

Lundy P and McGovern M, 'Whose Justice? Rethinking Transitional Justice from the Bottom up' (2008) 35 Journal of Law and Society 265–92.

Madden A, 'Constitution-Making and Nationhood: The British Experience – An Overview' (1988) 26 Journal of Commonwealth & Comparative Politics 123–34.

Madsen M, 'The International Judiciary as Transnational Power Elite' (2014) 8 International Political Sociology 332–34.

——, 'Sociological Approaches to Constitutional Law' (2020) iCourts Working Paper Series, No 212, 1–30.

Maertens L and Parizet R, '"On ne fait pas de politique!" Les pratiques de dépolitisation au PNUD et au PNUE' [2017] Critique Internationale 41–60.

Mahon P and Weerts S, 'La procédure d'adoption et de révision de la Constitution fédérale' (2020) 3 Verfassungsrecht der Schweiz/Droit constitutionnel suisse 1883–911.

Malagodi M, 'Constitution Drafting as Cold War Realpolitik: Sir Ivor Jennings and Nepal's 1959 Constitution' in Kumarasingham H (ed), *Constitution-making in Asia Decolonisation and State-Building in the Aftermath of the British Empire* (Routledge 2016).

Massoud MF, 'Work Rules: How International NGOs Build Law in War-Torn Societies' (2015) 49 Law & Society Review 333–64.

Mather L, 'Law and Society' in Whittington K, Kelemen D and Caldeira G (eds), *The Oxford Handbook of Political Science* (OUP 2011).

Mattei U, 'Three Patterns of Law: Taxonomy and Change in the World's Legal Systems' (1997) 45 The American journal of Comparative Law 5–44.

Max Planck Foundation, 'Staff' (Undated) <www.mpfpr.de/foundation/staff/> accessed August 2019.

——, *Annual Report 2013* (Max Planck Foundation 2014).

——, *Annual Report 2021* (Max Planck Foundation 2022).

——, *Annual Report 2022* (Max Planck Foundation 2023).

Mayer-Schonberger V, 'Into the Heart of the State: Intervention Through Constitution-Making' (1994) 8 Temple International and Comparative Law Journal 315–34.

M'Barek M, 'Makers of Our Own History' in Ginsburg T and Bisarya S (eds), *Constitution Makers on Constitution Making: New Cases* (CUP 2022).

McEvoy K and McGregor L, *Transitional Justice from Below: Grassroots Activism and the Struggle for Change* (Hart Publishing 2008).

McLaren J, 'The Uses of the Rule of Law in British Colonial Societies in the Nineteenth Century' in Dorsett S and Hunter I (eds), *Law and Politics in British Colonial Thought* (Palgrave Macmillan 2010).

McPetrie J, 'Survey of Constitutions Drafted at the Colonial Office since 1944' in Anderson J (ed), *Changing Law in Developing Countries* (George Allen & Unwin LTD 1963).

Mednicoff D, 'A Tale of Three Constitutions: Common Drives and Diverse Outcomes in Post-2010 Arab Legal Politics' (2014) 28 Temple International & Comparative Law Journal 215–51.

—— and Springer J, 'The Rule of Law and Political Liberalization in the Arab Gulf' in Hudson M and Kirk M (eds), *Gulf Politics and Economics in a Changing World* (World Scientific 2014).

Mendez F and Triga V, 'Constitution-Making, Constitutional Conventions and Conflict Resolution: Lesson Drawing for Cyprus' (2009) 11 Journal of Balkan and Near Eastern Studies 363–80.

Merillat H, 'Law and Developing Countries' (1966) 60 American Journal of International Law 71–79.

Merry SE, 'Colonial and Postcolonial Law' in Sarat A (ed), *The Blackwell Companion to Law and Society* (Blackwell Publishing 2004).

—— and Conley J, 'Measuring the World: Indicators, Human Rights, and Global Governance' (2011) 52 Current Anthropology 83–95.

Merryman JH, 'Comparative Law and Social Change: On the Origins, Style, Decline & Revival of the Law and Development Movement' [1977] The American Journal of Comparative Law 457–91.

Mertz E, Macaulay S and Mitchell T, *The New Legal Realism: Volume 1: Translating Law-and-Society for Today's Legal Practice* (CUP 2016).

Michaels R, 'The Functional Method of Comparative Law' in Reinmann M and Zimmermann R (eds), *Oxford Handbook of Comparative Law* (OUP 2006).

Michel N and Del Mar K, 'Transitional Justice' in Clapham A and others (eds), *The Oxford Handbook of International Law in Armed Conflict* (OUP 2014).

Mieg H and Evetts J, 'Professionalism, Science, and Expert Roles: A Social Perspective' in Ericsson A and others (eds), *The Cambridge Handbook of Expertise and Expert Performance* (CUP 2018).

Miller L and Aucoin L, *Framing the State in Times of Transition: Case Studies in Constitution Making* (US Institute of Peace 2010).

Miller Z, 'Effects of Invisibility: In Search of the "Economic" in Transitional Justice' (2008) 2 The International Journal of Transitional Justice 266–91.

Mitchell T, *Rule of Experts: Egypt, Techno-Politics, Modernity* (University of California Press 2002).

——, 'The Work of Economics: How a Discipline Makes its World' (2005) 46 European Journal of Sociology/Archives Européennes de sociologie 297–320.

Moreau F, *Régime parlementaire et principe représentatif. Procès-verbaux des séances et documents. Congrès International de droit comparé tenu à Paris du 31 juillet au 4 août 1900* (Librairie générale de droit et de jurisprudence 1905).

Morgan DJ, *The Official History of Colonial Development: Developing British Colonial Resources, 1945–1951* (Macmillan 1980).

Morgan E, *Inventing the People: The Rise of Popular Sovereignty in England and America* (WW Norton 1988).

Mukherjee G, 'Shaping Sovereignties: The Role of International Financial Institutions in Constitution-Making' (2023) 117 American Journal of International Law Unbound 251–56.

Munck R and O'Hearn D, *Critical Development Theory: Contributions to a New Paradigm* (Zed Books 1999).

Muritala M, 'Modern Political Experience: Constitutional Development in Nigeria, 1960–2020' in Suleiman Ajala A and Oluwole Ogundele S (eds), *Nigerian Cultural History and Challenges of Postcolonial Development* (Cambridge Scholars Publishing 2023).

Murray C, 'Making and Remaking Kenya's Constitution' in Ginsburg T and Bisarya S (eds), *Constitution Makers on Constitution Making: New Cases* (CUP 2022).

—— and Wittke C, 'International Institutions, Constitution-Making and Gender' in Irving H (ed), *Constitutions and Gender* (Edward Elgar Publishing 2017).

—— and others, *Constitutions and Peace Processes a Primer* (United Nations DPPA – Berghof Foundation 2020).

Muschik E-M, 'Managing the World: The United Nations, Decolonization, and the Strange Triumph of State Sovereignty in the 1950s and 1960s' (2018) 13 Journal of Global History 121–44.

Nader L, 'Promise or Plunder? A Past and Future Look at Law and Development' (2007) 7 Global Jurist [i]-24.

Nagy R, 'Transitional Justice as Global Project: Critical Reflections' (2008) 29 Third World Quarterly 275–89.

National Archives, 'Declaration of Independence: A Transcription' (4 July 1776) <www.archives.gov/founding-docs/declaration-transcript> accessed July 2018.

Ndulo MB, 'Constitution Making: The Role of External Actors' (2014) 1 Southern African Journal of Policy and Development 4.
Negretto G, *Redrafting Constitutions in Democratic Regimes: Theoretical and Comparative Perspectives* (CUP 2020).
Nepal, Comprehensive Peace Accord Signed between Nepal Government and the Communist Party of Nepal (Maoist) [22 November 2006].
——, Interim Constitution of Nepal (2007), Constitute Project.
Nigeria, Nigeria (Constitution) Order in Council (30 September 1960), Federation of Nigeria Official Gazette 221–393.
Nootens G, 'Constituent Power and People-as-the-Governed: About the "Invisible" People of Political and Legal Theory' (2015) 4 Global Constitutionalism 137–56.
O'Connell J, 'Common Interests, Closer Allies: How Democracy in Arab States Can Benefit the West' (2012) 48 Stanford Journal of International Law 341–404.
Odida A, *Making Policy, Problems, and Constitutions: Decolonising the UN Policy of Constitutional Assistance* (UCL University College London 2022).
OHCHR, *Human Rights and Constitution-Making* (OHCHR 2018).
OIF, 'L'Organisation internationale de la Francophonie' (Undated) <www.francophonie.org/lorganisation-internationale-de-la-francophonie-81> accessed April 2019.
——, Déclaration de Bamako [3 November 2000] OIF.
——, *Rapport du Secrétaire Général de la Francophonie 2008–2010* (OIF 2010).
——, *Rapport sur l'état des pratiques de la démocratie, des droits et des libertés dans l'espace francophone. 2000–2010* (OIF 2010).
——, *Rapport sur l'état des pratiques de la démocratie, des droits et des libertés dans l'espace francophone – 2012* (OIF 2012).
——, *Rapport du Secrétaire Général de la Francophonie 2012–2014* (OIF 2014).
——, *Rapport sur l'état des pratiques de la démocratie, des droits et des libertés dans l'espace francophone – 2014* (OIF 2014).
——, *Rapport du Secrétaire Général de la Francophonie 2014–2016* (OIF 2016).
——, *Rapport sur l'état des pratiques de la démocratie, des droits et des libertés dans l'espace francophone – 2018* (OIF 2018).
——, *Rapport sur l'état des pratiques de la démocratie, des droits et des libertés dans l'espace – – 2022* (OIF 2023).
Oklopcic Z, 'The South of Western Constitutionalism: A Map Ahead of a Journey' in Natarajan U and others (eds), *Third World Approaches to International Law on Praxis and the Intellectual* (Routledge 2016).
——, *Beyond the People: Social Imaginary and Constituent Imagination* (OUP 2018).
Oliver D and Fusaro C, *How Constitutions Change: A Comparative Study* (Hart Publishing 2011).
Olivier M, 'The Emergence of a Right to Democracy – An African Perspective' in Panara C and Wilson G (eds), *The Arab Spring New Patters for Democracy and International Law* (Martinus Nijhoff Publishers 2013).
Orford A, *International Authority and the Responsibility to Protect* (CUP 2011).
Overseas Development Institute, *Colonial Development: A Factual Survey of the Origins and History of British Aid to Developing Countries* (Overseas Development Institute 1964).
Parkinson C, *Bills of Rights and Decolonization: The Emergence of Domestic Human Rights Instruments in Britain's Overseas Territories* (OUP 2007).
Pastor y Camarasa A, 'Demystifying How Constitutions Are Made: External Actors' Modes of Actions in the 2014 Tunisian Constitution' [2022] Michigan Journal of Law & Society 51–112.
——, 'Constitution-Making and Transnational Expertise: Lessons from the 2014 Tunisian Constitution' in Howard R, Randazzo K and Reid R (eds), *Research Handbook on Law and Political Systems* (Edward Elgar 2023).

Pastorella G, 'Technocratic Governments: Power, Expertise and Crisis Politics in European Democracies' (PhD dissertation, The London School of Economics and Political Science (LSE) 2016).
Pelt A, *Libyan Independence and the United Nations: A Case of Planned Decolonization* (Yale UP 1970).
Perju V, 'Constitutional Transplants, Borrowing, and Migrations' in Rosenfeld M and Sajó A (eds), *The Oxford Handbook of Comparative Constitutional Law* (OUP 2012).
Perry B, 'Constitutional Johnny Appleseeds: American Consultants and the Drafting of Foreign Constitutions' (1992) 55 Albany Law Review 767–91.
Peters A and Schwenke H, 'Comparative Law Beyond Post-Modernism' (2000) 49 International & Comparative Law Quarterly 800–34.
Petric B, *Where Are All Our Sheep? Kyrgyzstan, a Global Political Arena* (Berghahn Books 2015).
—— and Blundo G, 'Good Governance and Democracy Promotion: Empirical Perspectives on Transnational Powers' in Petric B (ed), *Democracy at Large: NGOs, Political Foundations, Think Tanks and International Organizations* (Springer 2012).
Pfister T and Horvath A, 'Reassessing Expert Knowledge and the Politics of Expertise' (2014) 27 Innovation: The European Journal of Social Science Research 311–16.
Philippe X, 'Le rôle des organisations non gouvernementales dans les processus constituants postconflictuels: expertise ou plaidoyer' in Philippe X and Danelciuc-Colodrovschi N (eds), *Transitions constitutionnelles et constitutions transitionnelles* (Institut Universitaire Varenne 2014).
Philippines, Constitution of the Philippines (1935) <https://www.officialgazette.gov.ph/constitutions/the-1935-constitution/> accessed February 2024.
Picard MH, 'Le constitutionnalisme d'occupation en Iraq' (PhD dissertation, Université du Québec à Montréal 2017).
Pimentel CM, 'Du contrat social à la norme suprême: L'invention du pouvoir consituant' [2009] Jus Politicum 1–17.
Poland, Constitution of Poland (1791), Constitute Project.
Popelier P and Verlinden V, 'The Context of the Rise of Ex Ante Evaluation' in *The Impact of Legislation* (Brill Nijhoff 2009).
Powles G, 'Constitution Making in Western Samoa' (1961) 22 The Indian Journal of Political Science 179–94.
Preuss UK, 'Constitutional Powermaking for the New Polity: Some Deliberations on the Relations Between Constituent Power and the Constitution' (1992) 14 Cardozo Law Review 639–60.
——, 'Constitutionalism' in Craig E (ed), *Routledge Encyclopedia of Philosophy* (Routledge 1998).
——, 'Perspectives on Post-Conflict Constitutionalism: Reflections on Regime Change Through External Constitutionalization' (2007) 51 New York Law School Law Review 466–94.
Pugh AT, *Records of the Colonial Office, Dominions Office, Commonwealth Relations Office, and Commonwealth Office* (Her Majesty's Stationery Office 1995).
Qazbir H, *L'internationalisation du droit constitutionnel* (Dalloz 2015).
Quast C, 'Towards a Balanced Account of Expertise' (2018) 32 Social Epistemology 397–419.
Quentin-Baxter A, 'Making Constitutions, From the Perspective of Constitutional Adviser' (2002) 33 Victoria University Wellington Law Review 239–75.
Rajagopal B, *International Law from Below: Development, Social Movements and Third World Resistance* (CUP 2003).

Raymond A, 'British Policy towards Tunis (1830–1881)' (PhD dissertation, University of Oxford October 1953).

Renucci F, 'La "décolonisation doctrinale" ou la naissance du droit d'Outre-mer (1946-début des années 1960)' [2011] Revue d'Histoire des Sciences Humaines 61–76.

Richardson III H and Proehl P, 'Crossroads for Law in Africa' (1970) 18 UCLA Law Review 219–51.

Riegner M and Stacey R, *Democracy Without Political Parties: Constitutional Options* (Center for Constitutional Transitions June 2014).

Rigaux M-F, *La théorie des limites matérielles à l'exercice de la fonction constituante* (Larcier 1987).

Rist G, *Développement: histoire d'une croyance occidentale* (Les Presses de Sciences Po 1996).

Roberts-Wray K, 'The Legal Machinery for the Transition from Dependence to Independence' in Anderson J (ed), *Changing Law in Developing Countries* (Allen & Unwin 1963).

Roger C, *The Origins of Informality: Why the Legal Foundations of Global Governance are Shifting, and Why it Matters* (OUP 2020).

Rosenfeld M and Sajó A, *The Oxford Handbook of Comparative Constitutional Law* (OUP 2012).

Rothermund D, 'Constitution Making and Decolonization' (2006) 53 Diogenes 9–17.

Rothkopf I, *Constituting Peace: Foreign Actors, Constitution-Making, and Armed Conflict* (University of Notre Dame 2022).

Rowen JR, *Searching for Truth in the Transitional Justice Movement* (CUP 2017).

——, '"We Don't Believe in Transitional Justice": Peace and the Politics of Legal Ideas in Colombia' (2017) 42 Law & Social Inquiry 622–47.

Roznai Y, '"We the People", "Oui, the People" and the Collective Body: Perceptions of Constituent Power' in Jacobsohn GJ and Schor M (eds), *Comparative Constitutional Theory* (Edward Elgar Publishing 2018).

Rubinelli L, *Constituent Power: A History* (CUP 2020).

Saada E, 'France: The Longue Durée of French Decolonization' in Thomas M and Thompson A (eds), *The Oxford Handbook of the Ends of Empire* (OUP 2019).

Saati A, 'The Participation Myth: Outcomes of Participatory Constitution Building Processes on Democracy' (PhD dissertation, Umeå universitet 2015).

——, 'Participatory Constitution-Making as a Transnational Legal Norm: Why Does it Stick in Some Contexts and Not in Others' (2017) 2 UC Irvine Journal of International Transnational & Comparative Law 113–36.

——, 'Participation: To Unveil a Myth' in Abbiate T, Böckenförde M and Federico V (eds), *Public Participation in African Constitutionalism* (Routledge 2018).

Samuels K, 'Post-Conflict Peace-Building and Constitution-Making' (2005) 6 Chicago Journal of International Law 663–82.

Saunders A, 'Constitution-Making as a Technique of International Law: Reconsidering the Post-War Inheritance' (2023) 117 American Journal of International Law 251–308.

Saunders C, 'Constitution-Making in the 21st Century' [2012] International Review of Law 1–10.

——, *Courts in Federal Countries* (International IDEA April 2019).

——, 'International Involvement in Constitution Making' in Landau D and Lerner H (eds), *Comparative Constitution Making* (Edward Elgar Publishing 2019).

——, *Constitutions and International Law* (International IDEA February 2020).

Schauer F, 'On the Migration of Constitutional Ideas' (2004) 37 Connecticut Law Review 907–20.

Scheppele KL, 'Constitutional Ethnography: An Introduction' (2004) 38 Law & Society Review 389–406.
Schmahl S and Breuer M, *The Council of Europe: Its Law and Policies* (OUP 2017).
Schmidt GW, 'The New Constitutional Developments in the Republic of Liberia' [1981] Verfassung und Recht in Übersee/Law and Politics in Africa, Asia and Latin America 243–68.
Schnably S, 'Emerging International Law Constraints on Constitutional Structure and Revision: A Preliminary Appraisal' (2007) 62 University of Miami Law Review 417–90.
Scholte JA, 'Defining Globalisation' (2008) 31 World Economy 1471–502.
Scott C, '"Transnational Law" as Proto-Concept: Three Conceptions' (2009) 10 German Law Journal 859–76.
Seidel K, *Involvement and Impact of External Actors on Constitution Making in South Sudan and Somaliland: A Comparative Study* (Global Cooperation Research Papers 2017).
Senior P, Crowther-Dowey C and Long M, *Understanding Modernisation in Criminal Justice* (Open UP 2007).
Sethi A, 'Looking Beyond the Constituent Power Theory: The Theory of Equitable Elite Bargaining' [2023] Global Constitutionalism 1–28.
Shaffer G, *Transnational Legal Ordering and State Change* (CUP 2012).
——, Ginsburg T and Halliday T (eds), *Constitution-Making and Transnational Legal Order* (CUP 2019).
—— and Pollack MA, 'Hard Versus Soft Law in International Security' (2011) 52 Boston College Law Review 1147–241.
Sharp D, 'Addressing Dilemmas of the Global and the Local in Transitional Justice' (2014) 29 Emory International Law Review 71–117.
Shivji IG, 'Law in Independent Africa: Some Reflections on the Role of Legal Ideology' (1985) 46 Ohio State Law Journal 689–95.
——, 'Do Constitutions Matter? The Dilemma of a Radical Lawyer' (2020) 5 Strathmore Law Review 157–61.
Sieyès EJ, *Observations sur le rapport du comité de Constitution concernant la nouvelle organisation de la France* (Chez Baudouin 1789).
——, *Préliminaire de la Constitution. Reconnoissance et exposition raisonnée des droits de l'homme et du citoyen* (Chez Baudouin 1789).
——, *Qu'est-ce que le Tiers-Etat?* (Librairie Droz 1970).
——, *Emmanuel Joseph Sieyès: The Essential Political Writings* (Brill 2014).
Singh P, 'The Scandal of Enlightenment and the Birth of Disciplines: Is International Law a science?' (2010) 12 International Community Law Review 5–34.
Somek A, 'Constituent Power in National and Transnational Contexts' (2012) 3 Transnational Legal Theory 31–60.
South Africa, Constitution of South Africa (1996), Constitute Project.
Spevack E, *Allied Control and German Freedom. American Political and Ideological Influences on the Framing of the West German Basic Law (Grundgesetz)* (LIT Verlag 2001).
Sripati V, 'The United Nation's Role in Post-Conflict Constitution-Making Processes: TWAIL Insights' (2008) 10 International Community Law Review 411–20.
——, 'UN Constitutional Assistance Projects in Comprehensive Peace Missions: An Inventory 1989–2011' (2012) 19 International Peacekeeping 93–113.
——, 'Hammarskjöld and International Executive Rule: A Third World Perspective on International Law' in Melber H and Stahn C (eds), *Peace Diplomacy, Global Justice and International Agency: Rethinking Human Security and Ethics in the Spirit of Dag Hammarskjöld* (CUP 2013).

——, 'United Nations Constitutional Assistance in State-Building' in *Routledge Handbook of International State-Building* (Routledge 2013).

——, *Constitution-Making Under UN Auspices: Fostering Dependency in Sovereign Lands* (OUP 2020).

Sriram CL, 'Justice as Peace? Liberal Peacebuilding and Strategies of Transitional Justice' (2007) 21 Global Society 579–91.

Stampnitzky L and Ettinger D, 'Experts, états et théorie des champs. Sociologie de l'expertise en matière de terrorisme' [2013] Critique Internationale 89–104.

Steinberger H, 'Venice Commission' in *Max Planck Encyclopedia of Public International Law* (OUP May 2007).

Stockwell S, 'Imperial Liberalism and Institution Building at the End of Empire in Africa' (2018) 46 The Journal of Imperial and Commonwealth History 1009–33.

Stovall T, 'Empires of Democracy' in Huggan G (ed), *The Oxford Handbook of Postcolonial Studies* (OUP 2013).

Suchman M and Mertz E, 'Toward a New Legal Empiricism: Empirical Legal Studies and New Legal Realism' (2010) 6 Annual Review of Law and Social Science 555–79.

Sultany N, *Law and Revolution: Legitimacy and Constitutionalism After the Arab Spring* (OUP 2017).

Sung Ho K, 'Max Weber' in Edward Z and Nodelman U (eds), *The Stanford Encyclopedia of Philosophy* (Metaphysics Research Lab 2019).

Supiot A, *La Gouvernance par les nombres* (Fayard 2015).

Suteu S, 'The Populist Turn in Central and Eastern Europe: Is Deliberative Democracy Part of the Solution?' (2019) 15 European Constitutional Law Review 488–518.

——, *Eternity Clauses in Democratic Constitutionalism* (OUP 2021).

Swedberg R and Agevall O, *The Max Weber Dictionary: Key Words and Central Concepts* (Stanford UP 2016).

Tamanaha B, 'The Primacy of Society and the Failures of Law and Development' (2011) 44 Cornell International Law Journal 209–47.

Théry I, 'Expertises de service, de consensus, d'engagement: Essai de typologie de la mission d'expertise en sciences sociales' [2005] Droit et société 311–27.

Thompson Z, *History of Vermont, Natural, Civil, and Statistical, in Three Parts* (Chauncey Goodrich 1842).

Thornhill C, *A Sociology of Constitutions: Constitutions and State Legitimacy in Historical-Sociological Perspective* (CUP 2011).

——, 'Contemporary Constitutionalism and the Dialectic of Constituent Power' (2012) 1 Global Constitutionalism 369–404.

Thürer D, 'Soft Law' in Peters A and Rüdiger W (eds), *Max Planck Encyclopedia of Public International Law* (OUP 2000).

Tietje C and Nowrot K, 'Laying Conceptual Ghosts of the Past to Rest: The Rise of Philip Jessup's Transnational Law Regulatory Governance of the International Economic System' in Tietje C, Nowrot K and Brouder A (eds), *The Regulatory Governance of the International Economic System* (Institute for Economic Law 2006).

Töpperwien N, *From Armed Intra-State Conflict to a Functioning Constitutional Order Reconciling Principles of Third-Party Support – A Reflection* (Berghof Foundation 2019).

Tourard H, 'L'internationalisation des constitutions nationales' (PhD dissertation, Université Robert Schuman 1998).

Trubek D, 'Toward a Social Theory of Law: An Essay on the Study of Law and Development' (1972) 82 The Yale Law Journal 1–50.

——, 'Law and Development: 40 Years After Scholars in Self Estrangement – A Preliminary Review' (2014) 66 University of Toronto Law Journal 301–29.

—— and Galanter M, 'Scholars in Self-Estrangement: Some Reflections on the Crisis in Law and Development Studies in the United States' [1974] Wisconsin Law Review 1062–102.

Tully J, *Strange Multiplicity: Constitutionalism in an Age of Diversity* (CUP 1995).

——, 'The Imperialism of Modern Constitutional Democracy' in Loughlin M and Walker N (eds), *The Paradox of Constitutionalism: Constituent Power and Constitutional Form* (OUP 2007).

Tunisia, Rules of Procedure (20 January 2012), Official Gazette of the Republic of Tunisia 0354.

Turner C and Houghton R, 'Constitution Making and Post-Conflict Reconstruction' in *International Law and Post-Conflict Reconstruction Policy* (Routledge 2015).

Tushnet M, 'Some Skepticism about Normative Constitutional Advice' (2007) 49 William and Mary Law Review 1473–96.

——, 'The Inevitable Globalization of Constitutional Law' (2008) 49 Virginia Journal of International Law 985–1006.

——, 'Comparative Constitutional Law' in Reimann M and Zimmermann R (eds), *The Oxford Handbook of Comparative Law* (OUP 2017).

——, 'The Politics of Constitution-Making' in Tushnet M and Kochenov D (eds), *Elgar Handbook on the Politics of Constitutional Law* (Edward Elgar 2023).

Tzouvala N, *Capitalism as Civilisation: A History of International Law* (CUP 2020).

UN, *UN Charter* (26 June 1945) United Nations 1 UNTS XVI.

——, *Yearbook of the United Nations, 1963* (UN 1965).

UN Human Rights Committee, *CCPR General Comment No. 25: Article 25 (Participation in Public Affairs and the Right to Vote), The Right to Participate in Public Affairs, Voting Rights and the Right of Equal Access to Public Service* (UN Human Rights Committee 12 July 1996) CCPR/C/21/Rev.1/Add.7.

UNDP, 'Goal 16: Peace, Justice and Strong Institutions' (Undated) <www.UNDP.org/content/UNDP/en/home/sustainable-Development-goals/goal-16-peace-justice-and-strong-institutions.html> accessed August 2019.

——, *Annual Report of the Administrator for 2000* (UNDP 16 May 2001).

——, *Annual Report of the Administrator for 2001* (UNDP 6 May 2002).

——, *2003 Annual Report* (UNDP June 2003).

——, *Annual Report of the Administrator for 2002* (UNDP 17 April 2003).

——, *2004 Annual Report* (UNDP June 2004).

——, *Annual Report of the Administrator 2003* (UNDP 12 May 2004).

——, *2005 Annual Report* (UNDP June 2005).

——, *Multi-Year Funding Framework Report on UNDP Performance and Results for 2004: Executive Board of UNDP and UNFPA* (UNDP 12 May 2005).

——, *2006 Annual Report* (UNDP June 2006).

——, *2007 Annual Report* (UNDP June 2007).

——, *Annual Progress Report Nepal – 2007* (UNDP 2007).

——, *2008 Annual Report* (UNDP June 2008).

——, *Annual Progress Report Nepal – 2008* (UNDP 2008).

——, *Evaluation of the Democratic Governance Trust Fund. Consolidated Report* (UNDP May 2008).

——, *UNDP Strategic Plan, 2008–2011 – Accelerating Global Progress on Human Development* (UNDP 2008).

——, *2009 Annual Report* (UNDP June 2009).

——, *2010 Annual Report. Global Programme on Strengthening the Rule of Law in Conflict and Post-Conflict Situations* (UNDP 2011).

——, *Annual Report 2010/2011* (UNDP May 2011).

——, *Annual Report 2011/2012* (UNDP June 2012).

——, *Annual Report 2013/2014* (UNDP June 2013).
——, *UNDP Strategic Plan: 2014–2017. Changing the World* (UNDP 2013).
——, *Democratic Governance and Diverging Pathways to More Inclusive Societies* (UNDP 2014).
——, *UNDP Guidance Note on Constitution-Making Support* (UNDP 2014).
——, *UNDP Thematic Trust Funds Annual Report 2015* (UNDP 2015).
——, *Annual Report 2016. UNDP Thematic Trust Funds 2016. Crisis Prevention and Recovery, Democratic Governance, Environment* (UNDP June 2016).
——, *UNDP Strategic Plan 2018–2021* (UNDP 2017).
UNDP-DPA, *Joint UNDP-DPA Annual Report 2015* (UNDP-DPA 2016).
——, *Joint UNDP-DPA Programme on Building National Capacities for Conflict Prevention Annual Report 2016* (UNDP-DPA 2017).
——, *Joint UNDP-DPA Programme on Building National Capacities for Conflict Prevention Annual Report 2017* (UNDP-DPA 2018).
UNGA, *Resolution No 289. Question of the Disposal of the Former Italian Colonies* (21 November 1949) GAOR, 4th sess A/RES/289.
——, *Declaration on the Granting of Independence to Colonial Countries and Peoples* (14 December 1960) GAOR, 15th sess, Suppl no 16 A/RES/1514(XV).
——, *Declaration on Principles of International Law Concerning Friendly Relations and Co-Operation among States in Accordance with the Charter of the United Nations* (24 October 1970) GAOR, 25th sess, Suppl no 28 Res 2625.
——, *Basic Principles of the Legal Status of the Combatants Struggling Against Colonial and Alien Domination and Racist Regimes* (12 December 1973) GAOR, 28th sess, Suppl no 30 Res 3103.
——, *Report of the OHCHR on the Human Rights Situation and the Activities of her Office, Including Technical Cooperation, in Nepal* (5 February 2010) UNGA UN Doc A/HRC/13/73.
United Kingdom, India Independence Act (8 July 1947), H.M. Stationery Office.
——, Ceylon Independence Act (10 December 1947), H.M. Stationery Office.
——, Ghana Independence Act (7 February 1957), H.M. Stationery Office.
——, Malaya Independence Act (31 July 1957), H.M. Stationery Office.
——, Nigeria Independence Act (29 July 1960), H.M. Stationery Office.
——, Sierra Leone Independence Act (28 March 1961), H.M. Stationery Office.
——, Tanganyika Independence Act (22 November 1961), H.M. Stationery Office.
——, Jamaica Independence Act (19 July 1962), H.M. Stationery Office.
——, Uganda Independence Act (1 August 1962), H.M. Stationery Office.
——, Trinidad Independence Act (11 August 1962), H.M. Stationery Office.
——, Kenya Independence Act (3 December 1963), H.M. Stationery Office.
——, Malawi Independence Act (10 June 1964), H.M. Stationery Office.
——, Malta Independence Act (31 July 1964), H.M. Stationery Office.
——, Zambia Independence Act (31 July 1964), H.M. Stationery Office.
——, Gambia Independence Act (17 December 1964), H.M. Stationery Office.
——, Guyana Independence Act (12 May 1966), H.M. Stationery Office.
——, Botswana Independence Act (3 August 1966), H.M. Stationery Office.
——, Lesotho Independence Act (3 August 1966), H.M. Stationery Office.
——, Barbados Independence Act (17 November 1966), H.M. Stationery Office.
——, Mauritius Independence Act (29 February 1968), H.M. Stationery Office.
——, Swaziland Independence Act (26 July 1968), H.M. Stationery Office.
United States Institute for Peace, 'Louis Aucoin' (Undated) <https://bookstore.usip.org/browse/author/7d597673-e9c0–490d-83cf-f9e5a1a04f5d/Aucoin-Louis?page=1> accessed August 2019.
United States of America, The Fundamental Constitutions of Carolina (1 March 1669), The Avalon Project Yale University.

——, The Philippines Independence Act. Tydings McDuffie Act (24 March 1934), United States Statutes at Large 48 Stat. 456.
United States of America Senate, *Hearings before the Committee on the Philippines* (Government Printing Office 1915).
University of Virginia, 'Howard Named among Greatest 20th-Century Virginians' (2008) <www.Law.virginia.edu/html/news/2007_fall/howard.htm> accessed July 2020.
UNSC, Resolution 1740 [23 January 2007].
UNSG, *Report of the Secretary-General on the Prevention of Armed Conflict* (UNSG 7 June 2001) A/55/985-S/2001/574.
——, *Report of the Secretary-General on the Work of the Organization* (UNSG 2005) GAOR, 60th sess, Suppl no 1 A/60/1.
——, *Guidance Note of the Secretary-General Regarding United Nations Assistance to Constitution-Making Processes* (UNSG 2009).
——, *Ten-year Appraisal and Review of the Implementation of the Brussels Programme of Action for the Least Developed Countries for the Decade 2001–2010* (UNSG 7 February 2011).
——, *Guidance Note of the Secretary-General on United Nations Constitutional Assistance* (UNSG 2020).
Updike Toler L, 'Mapping the Constitutional Process: Lessons from 18 Constitution-Writing Procedures' (2014) 3 Cambridge Journal of Comparative and International Law 1–27.
Van Reybrouck D, *Congo. Une histoire* (Actes Sud 2012).
Vandenhole W, 'Law and Development Revisited: From Self-Estrangement to Revival – Review of M.J. Trebilcock and M.M. Prado, Advanced Introduction to Law and Development' (2015) 9 Human Rights & International Legal Discourse 112–18.
Vattel Ed, *Le droits des gens ou principes de la loi naturelle appliqués à la conduite et aux affaires des nations et des souverains* (Imprimerie de la Société Typographique 1773).
Vauchez A, *Brokering Europe: Euro-Lawyers and the Making of a Transnational Polity* (CUP 2015).
Venice Commission, 'For Democracy through Law' (Undated) <www.venice.coe.int/WebForms/pages/?p=01_Presentation&lang=EN> accessed April 2020.
——, *Annual Report of Activities 1990* (Venice Commission 22 February 1991).
——, *Annual Report of Activities 1991* (Venice Commission 14 February 1992).
——, *Annual Report of Activities 1992* (Venice Commission 10 February 1993).
——, *Annual Report of Activities 1993* (Venice Commission 24 February 1994).
——, *Annual Report of Activities 1999* (Venice Commission 1 April 2000).
——, *Annual Report of Activities 2000* (Venice Commission 10 March 2001).
——, Resolution Adopting the Revised Statute of the European Commission for Democracy through Law (27 February 2002), Venice Commission CDL (2002).
——, *Annual Report of Activities 2001* (Venice Commission 9 March 2002).
——, *Annual Report of Activities 2002* (Venice Commission 15 March 2003).
——, *Annual Report of Activities 2003* (Venice Commission 13 March 2004).
——, *Annual Report of Activities 2004* (Venice Commission 12 March 2005).
——, *Annual Report of Activities 2005* (Venice Commission 2006).
——, *Annual Report of Activities 2006* (Venice Commission 2007).
——, *Annual Report of Activities 2007* (Venice Commission 2008).
——, *Annual Report of Activities 2008* (Venice Commission 2009).
——, *Annual Report of Activities 2011* (Venice Commission August 2012).
——, *Annual Report of Activities 2012* (Venice Commission August 2013).
——, *Annual Report of Activities 2013* (Venice Commission September 2014).

——, *Annual Report of Activities 2017* (Venice Commission August 2018).

——, Rules of Procedure (22 October 2018), Venice Commission CDL-AD(2018)2018.

——, *Annual Report of Activities 2021* (Venice Commission August 2022).

——, *Annual Report of Activities 2022* (Venice Commission August 2023).

Vergara C, *Burying Pinochet* (New Left Review 12 January 2021).

Visser MD, 'A Critical Assessment of the Role of the Venice Commission in Processes of Domestic Constitutional Reform' (2015) 63 The American Journal of Comparative Law 963–1008.

Voorhoeve M, 'Judicial Discretion in Tunisian Personal Status Law' in Voorhoeve M (ed), *Family Law in Islam Divorce, Marriage and Women in the Muslim World* (I.B. Tauris 2012).

Weber M, *Economy and Society: An Outline of Interpretive Sociology* (University of California Press 1978).

——, *From Max Weber: Essays in Sociology* (Routledge 1991).

——, *The Protestant Ethic and the Spirit of Capitalism* (Routledge 2005).

Webley L, 'Qualitative Approaches to Empirical Legal Research' in Cane P and Kritzer H (eds), *The Oxford Handbook of Empirical Legal Research* (OUP 2010).

Webster D, 'Development Advisors in a Time of Cold War and Decolonization: The United Nations Technical Assistance Administration, 1950–59' (2011) 6 Journal of Global History 249–72.

Weerts S, 'Droit' in Soguel N and others (eds), *Comprendre et concevoir l'administration publique, le modèle IDHEAP* (EPFL Press 2023).

Widner J, 'Constitution Writing in Post-Conflict Settings: An Overview' (2007) 49 William & Mary Law Review 1513–41.

Wilde R, *International Territorial Administration: How Trusteeship and the Civilizing Mission Never Went Away* (OUP 2010).

Williams D, 'Smith, Stanley Alexander De' in *Oxford Dictionary of National Biography* (OUP 23 September 2004).

Williams P and others, *Post-Conflict Constitution Drafter's Handbook* (The Public International Law & Policy Group 2007).

Winton MG, 'Decolonisation and the Westminster Model' in Kirk-Greene A (ed), *Africa in the Colonial Period III the Transfer of Power: The Colonial Administrators in the Age of Decolonization* (OUP 1979).

Wolf-Phillips L, 'Why "Third World"? Origin, Definition and Usage' (1987) 9 Third World Quarterly 1311–27.

Wolfrum R, Gruss D and Röder T, *Ten Years of Global Knowledge Transfer 2002–2012* (Max Planck Institute 2012).

——, *Global Knowledge Transfer Working Group – Ten Years of Global Knowledge Transfer Projects and Research 2002–2012* (Max Planck Foundation 2013).

Womble TL, 'Early Constitutionalism in Tunisia, 1857–1864: Reform and Revolt' (PhD dissertation, Princeton University 1997).

Wood G, *The Creation of the American Republic, 1776–1787* (Norton 1993).

World Bank, *Legal and Judicial Reform: Strategic Directions* (World Bank 2003).

——, *Interim Strategy for Nepal for the period FY 2010–2011* (World Bank 2009).

Yale D, 'Professor S. A. De Smith' [1974] Cambridge Law Journal 177–78.

Young C, *Politics in Congo: Decolonization and Independence* (Princeton UP 1965).

Zumbansen P, 'Comparative, Global and Transnational Constitutionalism: The Emergence of a Transnational Legal-Pluralist Order' (2012) 1 Global Constitutionalism 16–52.

Index

West as standard 57–8, 63–7, 91, 115–6; definition 21n22; legal reform 59

Made in the USA
Las Vegas, NV
28 March 2026

a604e6b3-f26f-468a-b256-b535467cd1b9R01